NEHRU AND HIS WORLD ORDER
A GLOBAL SURVEY

Nehru and His World Order

A GLOBAL SURVEY

ATTAR CHAND

Forewords

R. Venkataraman
President of India
Rajiv Gandhi
Prime Minister of India
Jagmohan
Governor, J & K
Rene Maheu
UNESCO
Vijaylakshmi Pandit
P.D. Tandon
K.K. Birla
Dr. R.P. Dua
S.N. Yadav
Dr. R. Voitlaender, GDR
Romesh Bhandari
M.P. Singh
Prof. Rasheeduddin Khan

SHARADA

SHARADA PRAKASHAN
DELHI

Nehru and his world order : a global survey / compiled and edited with an introd. by Attar Chand. — Delhi : Sharada Prakashan, 1989.

xliv, 303 p. : 23 cm.

Includes bibliogr[...]lex.

ISBN : 81-85320[...]

1. Nehru, Jawal[...] and social views. 2. India—Economic policy. I. Attar Chand.

First Published 1989

ISBN 81-85320-01-2

Published by
SHARADA PRAKASHAN
707/43, Tri Nagar
DELHI-110035 (India)

Printed by
AMAR PRINTERS
at Mohan Printing Corpn. Padam Nagar, Delhi-110007.

Foreword

NEHRU—A CHARISMATIC PERSONALITY

Pandit Jawaharlal Nehru was the symbol of hope and aspirations of the people of the country. He was the most lovable, friendly, affable, compassionate and forgiving person who respected human dignity.

In Nehru, people saw a leader who understood them and in whose hand their future was safe.

Nehru was one of the precious possessions of India whose personality was charismatic.

I am sure the new generation can draw inspiration from Nehru, who guided the country to the path of modernization.

Nehru was a Bharat Ratna in the true sense of the term who set up the Planning Commission for bringing about economic democracy, encouraged balanced regional development and developed scientific temper by setting up a large number of national laboratories and got the country engaged in exploitation of atomic energy and oil wealth. He tried to bring about world peace by organizing Non-Aligned Movement.

R. VENKATARAMAN
President of India

Foreword

NEHRU—THE GREAT TECHNOCRAT

On this day (Nehru's birth anniversary) our minds go back to the focus and thrust Nehru had given to India's development through technological progress. While Nehru had looked into every aspect of modern science he did not lose sight involving the poor in the path of modernism. Nehru immensely loved children as he knew they were the country's future.

Today there is the need to take modern technology to the villages to fully realise Nehru's dreams. It is wrong to suggest that science and technology are meant only for the poor.

People who once criticized Nehru for introducing science and technology for development later took the position that he was deviating from science.

We shall continue to pursue the path envisaged by Nehru in scientific and technical fields.

RAJIV GANDHI
Prime Minister of India
New Delhi

Foreword

NEHRU—THE GREAT VISIONARY

Twenty-four years (May, 1964-1988) have passed since Jawaharlal Nehru passed away—a period offering greater clarity in looking at the path of his life, helping assess objectively the significance and outcome of his many-sided activities. These 24 years were crowded with dramatic political events which did not leave unaffected many state and party figures. This has not been the case with Nehru. His image remains unfaded as the outstanding leader of India and as one of the best exponents of the idea of liberation and economic progress which, in the latter half of our century, has become the driving force of the peoples of the developing world.

The interest in this prominent personality is everlasting. To a certain extent, it is sustained by the personal charm Nehru had which captivated not only those who were fortunate to meet him but also those who are familiar with his rich literary legacy, with the numerous scholarly publications and monographs devoted to him. The main factor explaining the attention paid by researchers and readers to Nehru and to his enormous historical role is that as a thinker, he touched upon a number of problems relevant to mankind to this day.

As India awoke to freedom and Indians became masters of their own destiny and architects of their own future, Nehru warned the people that freedom and power bring responsibility and that "that responsibility rests on the Parliament, a sovereign body representing the sovereign people of India". The future was "not one of ease or resting but one of incessant striving". It was, therefore, only proper that Nehru reminded the nation and the framers of the Constitution of future India, which the Father of the Nation, Mahatma Gandhi had envisaged :

> "The ambition of the greatest man of our generation has been to wipe every tear from every eye. That may be beyond us but as long as there are tears and suffering so long our work will not be over."

It is needless to stress that Nehru as the man is to be seen throughout the Constitution of India.

Jawaharlal Nehru had a great faith in the viability of democratic traditions and institutions. It was his conviction that freedom is best secured and maintained under the rule of law and by democratic methods. Nehru writes that "I would say that democracy is not only political, not only economic but something of the mind. . . it involves a certain inquisitive search for truth. . . and for, let us say the right thing". His approach to the economic development was scientific and rational and he located the answer to manifold problems of development in scientific planning. As chairman of the Planning Commission, Nehru laid the firm foundations of industrial development and consequently India has emerged as the 8th biggest industrial power with the third largest scientific and technological manpower poll in the world.

Like Nehru, our Prime Minister Rajiv Gandhi has laid great stress on technological innovation and up-gradation as this alone would ensure accelerated growth and social justice. He wants the country to forge ahead so that it does not lag behind in the race for reaching the ever widening frontiers of knowledge and achievement. Only the best is enough for our great nation.

Mr. Attar Chand has examined in the light of Nehru's own statements, and writings what he stood for and what were his accomplishments in the concrete application of his policies and principles.

JAGMOHAN
Governor
Jammu & Kashmir, Srinagar

Foreword

NEHRU—THE PUREST FLAME OF OUR HUMAN CONSCIENCE

A great light has gone out. After burning and shining for thirty years as the unquenchable flame of the campaign of non-violence waged for his country's independence, Jawaharlal Nehru, since that independence was won seventeen years ago, has radiated over the world like a beacon of tolerance and understanding among the peoples. This is because, all his life long, he never ceased to believe in the supremacy of the spirit in history and because never, not even while in prison and not even while holding power, which is also a prison in many respects, did he allow the call of human brotherhood and the demands of individual and national freedom to become separate spiritual aspirations. That is why he was so great, why he was so rich and complex a personality, while remaining so easy to approach and so gracious in his way of life. To come into contact with him as was my privilege on several occasions, was not only a valuable political experience—as was natural, since he was one of the most important heads of government in the world; it was also an unforgettable spiritual experience.

It was because of this deep and abiding belief in the supremacy of the spirit, because of the faith it enabled him to have in a future for the whole world of peace and progress founded upon the only kind of human solidarity which transcends differences and antagonisms between castes and races, between ideologies and nations, that is to say, intellectual and moral solidarity; it was undoubtedly for these reasons that he had special diliection for UNESCO. He often liked to recall as he did in October 1960 at the General Assembly of the United Nations and during his visit to UNESCO Headquarters on 21 September, 1962, the well-known phrase contained in the preamble to the Constitution of our Organization : "Since wars begin in the minds of men, it is in the minds of men that the defences of peace must be constructed." Few statesmen have placed so much faith in this humanistic maxim, whose underlying meaning is that man is master of his destiny and that man is his own continuing handiwork.

UNESCO largely enjoyed the benefit of his solicitude and his conviction. For instance, it can pride itself on having been, at his invitation, the first organization of the United Nations family to hold a session of its General Conference in Asia, at New Delhi, in 1956.

Others will speak of the great void he has left in the affairs of the world. We will lay stress on the unique place that he occupied in the hearts of men. Others will speak of his glory and his remarkable destiny as party leader and head of government. We will recall his tireless quest for truth and love. Others will calculate the effects of his death on the balance and future of the forces in his own country, in the vast expanse of Asia, and indeed, in the whole world. We, for our part, wonder how, deprived of this guide and this example, we shall be able to choose and follow our path amid the raging confusion of this world in upheaval, now that the kindliness of that smile, often so gay then suddenly so tired, the warmth of those brown eyes, the charm of that red rose, have disappeared from our view, now that great light which shone in the East has gone out forever—that light from whose radiance millions, nay tens and hundreds of million, of us had become accustomed to nurture and rekindle the purest flame of our human conscience.

RENE MAHEU
Director-General
UNESCO

Foreword

REMEMBERING MY DEAR BROTHER

As I write these words, the India of 40 years ago comes back to me and there are pictures in mind of those we looked up to respected, loved and trusted. There were Rajendra Prasad, Sardar Patel, Maulana Azad, Rajagopalachari, Govind Ballabh Pant—towering figures in their own right with the added lustre that came from their association with Gandhiji. There were others of the highest integrity and capability, like Rafi Ahmed Kidwai and B.C. Roy. The country was safe in their hands and men and women in the country were able to put in their best efforts for the great fight for freedom.

My thoughts go back to historic event when Congress decided to contest elections to the provincial Assemblies under the Government of India Act of 1935. After more than a decade of non-cooperation and going to jail, the idea of co-operating with the British was unacceptable, but finally an agreement was reached and the election campaigns began. Thinking of it now is like the memory of a fairy tale read long ago. Congress faced the heavy opposition of rajas, zamindars and other vested interests who were openly being supported by the British. We had nothing but our ideals, our determination and conviction that came through them. They had all the material advantages.

I remember canvassing in my own rural constituency of Bilhaur, Kanpur in a rickety old car which kept breaking down while Opposition members whizzed past us in smart new cars. Then, as election day approached, my supporters were full of anxiety. How would Congress get its voters to the polling booths ? At this moment Jawaharlal Nehru gave his famous slogan to the electorate: On Foot to the Polling Booth. In his speeches he reminded the people that the casting of a vote was not only a political act but a sacred duty and the distance between their homes and the polling booth should be regarded as a pilgrimage.

VIJAYLAKSHMI PANDIT

Formerly President of the United Nations General Assembly
A Distinguish Diplomat and Politician
Sister of Jawaharlal Nehru

Foreword

NEHRU—THE NOBLE SOUL

What is the difference between Nehru and other leaders ? Nehru used to lead and no leader or party was big enough to lead him when the lead was in doubt. He could stand successfully the onslaught of unpopularity and was big enough to face calmly the big gusts of opposition. He knew how to lead, because he was a born leader of men. His image is safely enshrined in the hearts of his countrymen. He needs no monuments and memorials to keep him alive. He will live as long as people yearn for peace and love peaceful co-existence. He will live as long as mankind values the noble urges of the human heart. He will live as long as there is place for greatness in the world.

P.D. TANDON
Veteran Freedom Fighter

Foreword

NEHRU'S FAITH IN SECULARISM

The fullness of Jawaharlal Nehru's multifaceted personality must be projected. His abiding faith in secularism and national integration, his love for children and youth, his commitment to science and technology should all be adequately taken care of in the presentations to coincide with the birth centenary.

K.K. BIRLA
Industrialist & Member of Parliament
New Delhi

Foreword

NEHRU AND ECONOMIC PROGRESS

Every year on November 14 the nation gratefully celebrates the birth anniversary of one of her greatest sons, the architect of modern India and the first Prime Minister of independent India, Jawaharlal Nehru. Volumes have been written and will be written in future also on his contribution to laying the foundation of economic, scientific and industrial resurgence of our country which was impoverished by the colonial rulers of Britain. It was an enormous task and Nehru realised the daunting responsibility which fell on him. With foresight he planned the country's path towards development and laid great emphasis on building giant infrastructure industries even in the face of stiff opposition from his trusted colleagues. He was firm in his conviction that it was the huge steel plants, power-houses and dams the modern temples of India which would be of utmost importance if India were to achieve self-sufficiency. In his quest for socio-economic reconstruction, he enthused the people to actively participate in the gigantic task and he gave for this purpose a slogan '*Aram Haram Hai*' which continued to inspire people for years.

I am sure that the present valuable study by India's well-read writer Mr. Attar Chand whom I have known since his college days, will stimulate rightful thinking among the intellectuals and leaders in public life and help in preserving the best of Indian traditions and values as Nehru so ardently desired.

DR. R.P. DUA
Department of History
Dr. Zakir Hussain College
University of Delhi

Foreword

NEHRU—THE CHAMPION OF WORLD PEACE

It is now nearly 25 years since Jawaharlal Nehru passed away and, much as the idea was pooh-poohed at the time, socialism, as interpreted by him, has been developing. Nehru himself would have frowned upon such a development, for he was an iconoclast and modernist who refused to accept any dogma *in toto*. Specially, he was allergic to deifying even the most valuable of ideas, contending that to confer finality on anything was unscientific. Even though Nehru founded no ism, his ardent striving for socialism developed into a set of attitudes or a frame of mind; it is because the man was so far ahead of his times that his ideas are still valid in most contexts 25 years after his death.

Nehru's contribution to world peace is remembered with reverence the world over. For the Third World he was the dynamic force fighting for their cause at various world forums. It was he, along with other world leaders, who put a new lease of life in the United Nations Organisation and made others to realise the vital importance of the world body in keeping world peace. The two super-powers and many other warring nations were taught to use the UN as a forum where international disputes could be settled and not on the battle field. It was because of this belief in peaceful negotiations and cordial neighbourly relations between nations that Nehru opposed building armies. It is tragic that after his demise the global atmosphere should have vitiated to such menacing proportions. Now the world is faced with the prospect of a nuclear holocaust. It is in this surcharged international situation that Nehru's absence is felt.

The present indispensable volume by Mr. Attar Chand whom I have known for more than a decade, has presented Nehru in his correct perspective with an intermingling of domestic and foreign happenings.

S.N. YADAV
Deputy Secretary
FICCI
New Delhi

Foreword

NEHRU AND THE NON-ALIGNED MOVEMENT

The idea of non-alignment in connection with Panchashila had its origin in Asia, and surely it is no overstatement to say that its "cradle" stood in India. The first one who used the term non-alignment was Jawaharlal Nehru. Later on the general principle of non-alignment had been formulated and its anti-imperialist, particularly anti-colonial content widely determined.

For the establishment of the movement of non-aligned countries forthcoming successes of the national liberation movements and the formation of new independent nations were of great importance. Late in the fifties and during the early sixties the process of decay of the imperialist colonial system spread also to the African scene. Only in 1960 seventeen African countries gained their independence, emerging from the anti-colonial struggle, also inclined towards non-alignment and peaceful co-existence.

DR. ROSWITHA VOITLAENDER
Institute of Internationol Relations
The German Democratic Republic
(GDR)

Foreword

NEHRU IN FRIENDLY LANDS

Freedom 40 and Nehru 100 activities are taking place in all countries with whom India has links. Freedom 40 clubs are being started by NRIs and Friends of India societies in different countries. The effort is to foster greater awareness of India abroad and remove traditional misconceptions about our country. The major work is being supervised by the External Affairs Ministry and the Indian missions abroad. Exhibitions, seminars, cultural programmes, naming street squares after Nehru, are some of the ideas already finalised. The response has been very encouraging in the international arena.

ROMESH BHANDARI
Lt. Governor
Delhi.

Foreword

NEHRU THE ARCHITECT OF MODERN INDIA

Nehru's mind, unusually convoluted and sophisticated, symbolised the thinking of a large number of his educated countrymen at a time when, because of circumstance, their thinking mattered more than was normal.

Individuals do matter in History, not in the old fashionable sense, as Carlyle would make us believe, of changing the course of history, for history is not epitomized in an individual; it is not the game of personalities, but the interplay of social forces, economic factors, and new or hegemonic ideas. However, individual counts in the sense of recognizing and making a significant contribution in the process of change. The question then is, was Nehru such a significant and representative figure ? The answer is an unqualified 'yes'!

The cross currents and reactions in Nehru's mind were shared, to a lesser or greater degree, by the many Indians who found in him their spokesman and leader both before and after 1947.

For the next seventeen years Nehru guided the destiny of India. India is what it is among a handful of countries in the Third World where democratic system of government, periodic election, rule of law, freedom of expression and secularism still prevail. India today is the 8th among the industrialized countries of the world and represents the third largest reservoir of technical man power. It is largely because of the emphasis Nehru laid in the early 1950s, on heavy industry and development of science and technology. Indeed, every face of India's life bears the indelible imprint of the vision and leadership that Nehru provided during independent India's formative years and beyond. Nehru as an individual, then mattered and for the good. Mr. Attar Chand has in this pioneering work made an intensive study of Jawaharlal Nehru's ideology and mind. The architect of modern India, Nehru had different shades of ideas applicable to different disciplines, and it requires a deep insight and careful understanding to pick out and interpret his ideas in a systematic and concise manner.

I am sure this excellent work of Mr. Attar Chand is a valuable addition to the growing literature on the life and works of our national personalities one like Jawaharlal Nehru.

DR. M.P. SINGH
Professor of Criminal Justice
Grambling State University
(USA)

Foreword

NEHRU AND ASIAN IDENTITY

Jawaharlal Nehru emerges in the perspective of History, as one of the most sensitive and perceptive Asian leaders, whose innovative mind and dynamic qualities of leadership could not only comprehend the many complexities of the evolving situation at the national and international level but also evolve appropriate responses to newer challenges. He was probably the first leader of the emerging Asian polity who addressed himself to the necessity of evolving a collective Asian perspective and responses to the problems of security and development. Today, when problems of Asian security have acquired primacy in global strategy, it is useful to assess Nehru's pioneering role as the first powerful articulator of the concept of collective Asian security, as an input into the maintenance of world peace.

Jawaharlal Nehru's most conspicuous impact on the course of history—Indian, Asian and global—is probably as a powerful and consistent protagonist of the historic urges and suppressed impulses of the people in the struggle against imperialism and inequity and as a system-builder for a democratic secular polity. He was not only an architect of resurgent

India, but also of an awakened and emancipated Asia, and the emerging decolonised world.

Nehru's thinking and understanding is imprinted on the many resolutions on international affairs adopted by the Indian National Congress, twenty years preceding national independence, that is, 1927 to 1947. In fact, he was the conscience-keeper of the Congress on world affairs and on foreign policy matters. In 1942, Gandhiji said that in international affairs "Pandit Nehru is my Guru". After 1927, he took keen interest not only in larger global concerns, but also in extending support and succour to other national and liberation movements, with the result that by the time India became independent, the major thrust and objectives of his foreign policy were already articulated in the resolutions and statements of the Indian National Congress.

RASHEEDUDDIN KHAN
Professor,
Jawaharlal Nehru University
New Delhi

Acknowledgement

The present study of "Nehru and His World Order" could not have reached fruition without the encouragement of my well-wishers: Jagmohan (Governor, Jammu & Kashmir), Dr. V.P. Dutt (Professor, Delhi University), Lalit Bhasin (Advocate, Supreme Court of India), S.N. Yadav, Y.P. Srivastava, G.K. Kwatra and H.S. Wadhwa (FICCI), Chanderjit Yadav (Chairman, Centre for Social Justice), Dr. S.M.L. Mathur (Principal, Shardanand College), Dr. J.S. Yadav (Director, IIMC), Dr. Peter Pritam T. Merani (Towson State University), K. Subrahmanyam (Formerly Director, IDSA), Raju G.C. Thomas (Marquette University), Nandrajog (PHDCCI), M.K. Dhar (Hindustan Times), Dr. M.K. Saini, Dr. R.P. Singh (Delhi University), Vinay Rai (Industrialist), Mehmoud Hussein (Films Director), V.D. Chopra (Patriot), B.K. Batra (Advocate), Manohar Lal (Librarian) Rajinder Singh (Public Prosecutor), O.P. Sethi (Research Fellow, Delhi University), Krishan Gopal (JNU), Dr. M.P. Singh (Professor, Gramblin State University, USA), H.C. Joshi (President, Indian Council of World Affairs), Dr. Niranjan M. Khilani (Former Director, Ministry of External Affairs), Prof. Z.M. Khan (Jamia Millia Islamia) Dr. K.L. Sharma (Dr. Zakir Hussain College), Navin Chandra Joshi (Freelance Writer), Hari Sharan Chhabra (Editor, World Focus), Dr. J.K. Chopra, Prof. B.R. Grover (Historian), Dr. S.C. Mehta (Dayal Singh College), Dr. A. Naik (Vishva Bharati University, Shantiniketan), Dr. B. S. Narang (Educationist), Dr. Rajendra Prasad (Ramjas College), Dr. Dharmpal (Secretary, Indian Society for Afro-Asian Studies), Dr. Hari Singh (P.G. Government College, Faridabad), Jagdish Nandan Singh (National

Herald), Dr. S.C. Saxena (India-Africa Society), Dr. S.N. Srivastava (IINS), M.L. Dhawan (ICWA), and my sons Dr. Harish Kumar and Gulshan, who suggested sundry improvements and provided nourishing guidance and inspiration. I am also much obliged to my fellow writers, journalists and academicians whose writings I have consulted, and taken notes in writing this book.

ATTAR CHAND

Contents

Abbreviations

EFNIG : *Economic Failures of Nehru and Indira Gandhi*, M.L. Gujral, Vikas, 1979, 255 pp.

FON : *Facets of Nehru*, B.K. Ahluwalia (*ed.*), Delhi, SES, 1967, 97 pp.

LON : *Legacy of Nehru : A Memorial Tribute*, K. Natwar Singh (*ed.*), New York, John Day, 1965, 128 pp.

MDN : *My Days with Nehru*, M.O. Mathai, New Delhi, Vikas, 1979, 272 pp.

NAG : *Nehru Abhinandan Granth : A Birthday Book*, New Delhi, 1949, 709 pp.

NCV : *Nehru Commemoration Volume*, Trichur, Working Journalists' Association, 1964, 239 pp.

NFC : *Nehru Flings a Challenge*, Bombay, Hamara Hindustan, 1947, 135 pp.

NP : *Nehru and Parliament*, Subhash C. Kashyap (*ed.*), New Delhi, Lok Sabha Secretariat, 1986, 218 pp.

QON : *Quintessence of Nehru*, K.T. Narasimhachar (*ed.*), London, 1961, 271 pp.

REW : *Recent Essays and Writings*, Jawaharlal Nehru, Allahabad, Kitabistan, 1934, 148 pp.

SON : *Studies on Nehru*, V.T. Patil, New Delhi, Sterling, 1987, 412 pp.

UMG : *Understanding Minority Groups*, J.B. Gitter (*ed.*), New York, John Wiley, 1956, 139 pp.

Introduction

HUNDRED YEARS OF NEHRU

On November 14, 1989 the world will celebrate the birth centenary of one of its greatest sons. The very name evokes sublime sentiments in people of all walks of life throughout India, to whom he bequeathed noble ideals and legacy of service. He is a legendary figure whom the international community held in high esteem for his contributions in bringing the countries together.

Jawaharlal Nehru did lay firm foundations of the independent India, and it was he who gave a new direction and dimension to rebuilding India on planned and scientific lines. A man of immense sacrifices and love for the country and the people, Nehru correctly comprehended the needs of modern India and laid, with great vision, a base for national development and international amity. He was a nationalist to the core with an international understanding.

Once Nehru said: "To serve India in the battle of freedom is honour enough. To serve her under a leader like Mahatma Gandhi is doubly fortunate. But to suffer for the dear country; what greater good fortune could befall an Indian unless it be death for the cause or the full realisation of our glorious dream."

In India mass movements for freedom began in 1919. Jawaharlal Nehru is one of those who spent the longest terms in Jail—3,262 days. Sixty years ago, in the twenties, Nehru declared that "free India may be worthy of a place in the coming order of things". These were prophetic words.

Emperor Ashoka has been described as the greatest king in the world. He proclaimed that the only true conquests were those of peace. Nehru, conditioned by the stress which Gandhi laid on truth and non-violence, and by his own study of history, had a repugnance for militarism, and he spoke with his whole being when he endorsed UNESCO's declaration that the defences of peace are to be created in the minds of men, or when he quoted Euripides to disapprove of "the hand uplifted in hate".

India to me is many things. It is a large country, but I sometimes think that people are not clear about its size. It is often described as a "vast land". I do not think it is vast. It is large in the sense that it is not small or negligible. And it cannot be said that what happens to India is not of much consequence. But purely geographically it is the smallest of the large countries. It is a third, or much less than a third, the size of any of the really large countries of the world—USSR, China, USA, Brazil, Australia. India's size and resources-base cannot, at any time, be of no account. Whether captive or free, these factors, combined with India's location, have made a big impact on history. Apart from the size, India's population can truly be described as vast somewhere in the region of 800 million or more now. Even at independence it was far from small—about 350 million, a population whose human and material resources have spelt the difference between the making and the breaking of an empire.[1]

India is also a great civilisation with a long history of high achievements in many fields: a civilisation which over the centuries has shown an astonishing ability to absorb almost any influence that came along, and to transmute it into a continuous living process, into a total entity of versatility, of great depth and breadth. It highlights, on the one hand, the intellectual capacity and the social coherence to face challenges, and, on the other hand, national self-assurance to take initiative when the situation so demands. India, more than any country that can be named, has a colossal diversity on every plane—racial, linguistic, religious, cultural, social, economic and ideological. This is something fundamental to the nature, ethos, and very existence of this country. It has implications at every level—philosophical, abstract and ideological, or practical and political. India, more than any other country, has believed that diversity, not uniformity, is normal. Diversity is not an inconvenient fact to be lived with, but a positive asset to be understood and valued. India has never been xenophobic; or hated or rejected foreigners under glorified tribal labels like God, king and country. Armed invaders apart, any people who came to our shores, from ancient time to the present, have been accepted—

Central Asians, Arabs, Parsis, Europeans, Africans, Tibetans, Bahai's—or anybody else. Even our freedom movement was clear in its objective: it was anti-colonial, not anti-British.

Whereas before Independence, India's prime objective was freedom and equality of nations and peoples, the record since Independence has been less clear. From its stated aim of independence and broad-based progress, India went on to enunciate non-alignment as the principal plank of its foreign policy. Three things automatically followed. First, whereas independence was a concept based on recognition of the world system of domination of some nations by others, non-alignment focused on the conflict between the two power blocs, one fighting for the maintenance of its traditional position of dominance and the second trying to end its own so-called containment by the first. A continued pursuit of independence of people would have aimed at ending the hegemony of one side and the threat perception of the other. But a change in emphasis from independence to non-alignment resulted distorting our policy making from formulating a strategy for evolving a more democratic world system to merely reacting to developments in the East-West conflict. The situation demands ending the vulnerability of the dominated nations so that they are no longer passive objects of the scheme of the strong powers. We have repeatedly had to take part in many wars because these were forced on us. To that extent, we have no control over our policies. Third world resources are still controlled, whether it be oil or mineral wealth or agricultural produce. We are just as much victims of the policies of the great powers as any of the other exploited nations.[2]

Secondly, non-alignment as a foreign policy ideology implied acceptance of a hyper-nationalistic entity for India, which was a departure from the earlier identification with the interests of other subjugated peoples. In pursuit of this nationalistic view of self-interest, India switched to the cultivation of the goodwill of the rich—another name for the dominant nations—with a view to securing trade and aid. Inevitably, this placed India in active rivalry with fellow third world countries for the favour of the developed countries, a policy detrimental to the interests of the developing countries including India. In the early years of the global independence struggles, the Bandung conference had enunciated the objective of cooperation among subject nations. India merely paid lip service to cooperation. In fact, it set its face against cooperation with these nations, and firmly hitched its policies to the cultivation of relations with what it perceived as the great powers. India's basic preoccupation with the great powers, especially in the early years of independence, meant that there were minimal contacts with Asian neighbours, even those which were English-speaking former British colonies. The question of friendly relations with former French colonies was even more remote. Combined with this was a wholly unrealistic attitude of patronising superiority towards the smaller Asian countries, almost any of whom was more prosperous, stable, and less problem-ridden than India. This was so in spite of the immense goodwill for India in the fifties and sixties among former subject nations which had high faith in India's goodwill and friendliness and in its commitment to the causes of freedom.[3]

Thirdly, the enunciation of non-alignment as our policy left us without a policy. It was a brand new word, a shining new addition to the political dictionary. But what did it mean in actual practice? Simply that you would not take sides in quarrels between the two power blocs. It was a statement of what would not do. The negative and empty nature of the slogan must have struck its makers at some point, as the clarification was offered that it would be positive non-alignment. A further clarification was found to be necessary about what this "positive" element was, and this was given as judging issues on merits. That still leaves the question; if there are no so-called issues will there be no policy ?[4]

Jawaharlal, with the blessings of Mahatma Gandhi, and amidst the acclaim of the nation, became the Indian head of the Interim Government, and on 15 August, 1947, the Prime Minister of the Indian Union. The best and most human qualities of the Nehru leadership were amply demonstrated in those anxious days when he successfully ensured that Indian independence was not drowned in blood, and fratricidal conflict was brought to an end, despite the deliberately provoked communal riots all over the land and Pakistani armed invasion of Kashmir. As the situation settled down under his conscience-stirring leadership he gave his first thought to the welfare of the Indian peasant and the just solution of the agrarian problem. He saw to it that one of the first acts of the Congress after achievement of independence was the appointment of the J.C. Kumarappa Committee to study and make recommendations on the subject. The anti-feudal national tradition and solemn pledges to the Indian peasantry were a living reality in those early independence yeais. The Kumarappa Committee Report was very just and true to past pledges, pro-peasant and anti-feudal, which would have transformed the face of rural India, unleashed mass peasant initiative and carried the Indian revolution forward. The state governments were asked to implement its recommendations. At the state-level they were first diluted and later all progress halted. Bihar was the first to introduce zamindari abolition legislation which did help to abolish the old feudal type of influence in the countryside. Bihar leaders like Dr. Rajendra Prasad who soon after became the first Rashtrapati, Shree Krishna Sinha who became the Chief Minister, and Anugraha Narayan Sinha, next important Bihar Minister, were all middle class landlords. But with the advent of freedom and to garner its fruits all the big zamindars, who had not only remained out of the Congress in the past but had supported the British, came trooping into the Congress. The inevitable happened. The anti-feudal legislation got diluted, distorted and ultimately halted. The successful negotiation and consolidation of independence and the abolition of zamindari, despite the weaknesses and limitations, gave the Congress a big majority in Parliament and in all the states. Jawaharlal came to Bihar for the 1952 election campaign. Lakhs came to listen to him. He frankly admitted that nothing much had been done for the people and the peasants in particular and his forthright honest self-criticism endeared Nehru still more to the peasants.

Jawaharlal Nehru had three great founts of strength, and three great causes to serve—India, the Indian people and the Indian National Congress. In his address to the Lucknow session he described how the Congress had grown from small beginnings into a powerful democratic organization, deeply rooted in the Indian soil and the Indian masses. Nehru's contribution towards this conversion and the evolution of the Congress tenets of democracy, secularism and socialism were significant. He worked indefatigably among peasants, artisans and the rural masses. Through his extraordinary hold on the minds of the young and his appeal for the working class, he lined the younger generation and the radicals behind Mahatma Gandhi's strategy of non-violent struggle. The building up of the central office of the Congress was again largely Jawaharlal Nehru's work. Further, it was he who made the rank and file of the Congress realize that "our struggle was but a part of a far wider struggle for freedom". The credit for India taking its stand with the progressive forces of the world goes to Nehru.

The Indian National Congress led India to freedom. Its ideals shaped the spirit of the Constitution, guaranteeing personal freedom and social and economic justice. Through its advocacy of planning, the Congress helped the country to modernise its agriculture, industry and science and to move securely towards self-reliance. The Congress commitment to pluralism enabled the minorities to enjoy equality in all its forms and India's regional cultures to flower. The exertions of the Congress enabled the Scheduled Castes and Tribes to break through the old barriers which blocked the road to opportunity. Again, due to the Congress insistence on independence in judgement and decision-making in foreign policy, India came to be considered a pillar of the Non-Aligned Movement and a consistent voice for peace.

Jawaharlal Nehru was first elected President of the Congress in 1929 and had the privilege of holding that high office thrice more. Earlier Nehru had also twice been General Secretary of the party. To him work and service were more important than prestige or position.

No matter how one looks at the ideals of the two men (Mahatma Gandhi and Jawaharlal Nehru), they have practically nothing in common as regard economic models and policies, political systems and above all in values and norms. It is in respect of the last mentioned area that the nation feels cheated. In the late thirties Gandhi had hoped that Nehru, claiming to be radical, would take up the long postponed task of radicalising the Congress on economic policies and social justice. It is precisely at that time that Nehru moved to the middle and used this position to manoeuvre out Subhas Chandra Bose through an unsuspecting Gandhi. By a remarkable quirk of history which pitchforked Nehru to the top, we have come to be ruled by an elite which, irrespective of its ideologies, is corrupt to the core and is becoming more and more valueless. The triple elite—the politicians, the bureaucrats and business—supported by non-governing elites, the intellectual, the religious men, the media, etc. have all joined in this conspiracy. Nehru himself may have been more respectful to governmental laws and norms, although there is enough evidence to show that he was not always so. But his models were a curious combination of modernism, liberalism, Fabianism and the static Indian social order that were to sustain the new imperial-bureaucratic order. Gandhi not only made men out of clay but set up people's institutions as a countervailing force against the imperialist structure and then put the right people in the right jobs. Gandhi combined elements both of a creator and a destroyer through a strict adherence to values. Nehru was an institution builder but, like most liberals, was careless and even indulgent towards second-rate men and women, including those of his own family. Over the centuries the Indian character has been shaped by capacity and willingness to sacrifice values, norms and offer respect to the State. Gandhi gave to people the courage to revolt against an unjust State. The main focus of Hindu religious philosophies and traditions has been on freedom and not on morality. That is why Indian civilisation degenerated but never disappeared. Gandhi tried to weave the two and won national approval despite the harsh criticism of the Hindu orthodoxy. Nehru, unwillingly perhaps, brought India back to the old situation, strangely through the ideology of modernisation. His first step of insisting on setting up an imperial bureaucratic state with the help of the ICS and through the new Constitution was a monumental betrayal of both India and Gandhi. What India needed most of all was a value institution and for that a temporary dose of austerity and strict adherent laws were absolutely necessary. Nehru's own life was not terribly relevant. What is important is that he let values erode so much that we have now reached a position where crime is the highest freedom and corruption the most successful politics.[5]

Jawaharlal Nehru's most conspicuous impact on the course of history—Indian, Asian and global—is probably as a system-builder. He was not only an architect of resurgent India, but also of an awakened and emancipated Asia, and the de-colonised world. Again, no one more than him in the national movement had such clarity of understanding about the linkage and the organic ties between India's struggle for freedom, and the mass upsurge in many parts of Asia and Africa, and the new forces of the world scene—the Arab awakening, Egyptian nationalism, modernisation of Turkey and Iran, the Palestinian struggle for identity, the mass anti-colonial strivings in what was then called French Indo-China and in the Dutch colonies of Indonesia, the emergence of Japan and the turns and twists in the fortunes of republican China, Italian fascist aggression on Ethiopia, the barricades of Barcelona and the fall of the Spanish republic, the rise and threat of fascism in Europe, the crises of capitalism and the impoverishment of the colonies, the relevance of the United States in world affairs and the new dawn in Russia and the meaning and implication of Soviet power to the struggling people everywhere. Nehru's thinking and understanding is imprinted on the many resolutions on international affairs adopted by the Indian National Congress. In fact he was the conscience-keeper of the Congress on world affairs and on foreign policy matters. After 1927, he took keen interest not only in larger global concerns, but also in extending support and succour to other national and liberation movements, with the result, that by the time India became independent, the major thrust and objectives of his foreign policy were already articulated in the resolutions and statements of the Indian National Congress. The anti-imperialist, anti-colonial, anti-fascist and anti-racist underpinnings were clear and forthright. So were the imperatives of solidarity with liberation struggles and friendship with socialist countries, particularly the Soviet Union, and of fraternal ties with Asian and African countries. What subsequently evolved as the principles of co-existence and postures of Non-Alignment, in a more specific international setting of the post-war bi-polar world, were already in evidence in an embryonic form in the policy resolutions of the Congress, drafted with political acumen and foresight by Nehru. There is now a greater realization of India's early contribution in providing initial stability and direction to NAM, especially the creative role that the architect of its foreign policy, Jawaharlal Nehru, had played as the precursor (1947-55), progenitor (1955-61) and pioneer (1961-64) of the Non-Aligned Movement, thereby committing the largest newly liberated developing country, with an active democratic policy and expanding industrial base, to the global task of building a de-colonised world of equals with shared goals for a common future. Non-alignment, in the sense of independence from alignment, has been the dominant ethos of India's foreign policy. As a term signifying a 'value' and a 'norm', non-alignment is an integral part of India's political culture in international affairs, even as the terms 'secular nationalism', 'participatory democracy', 'composite culture', 'egalitarian society', remain the guiding objectives of new India's emerging federal polity. For a country that had launched the biggest mass movement against the world's most widespread and organised imperialism, even as *nationalism* in the pre-independence phase represented the symbol of its assertive independence in the domestic realm, so also *non-alingment* in the post-independence phase represents its affirmation of independence in external affairs, in an inter-dependent world dominated by power-blocs.[6]

Examined more carefully, both 'nationalism' and 'non-alignment' as two distinct but mutually reinforcing processes determining India's collective action, one in domestic realm and the other in external sphere, reveal a sort of historical inevitability. Existence of imperialism determined nationalism, and existence of bi-polar alignments determines non-alignment. This is implied in Jawaharlal Nehru's assertion: "I have not originated the policy of non-alignment. It is a policy inherent in the circumstances of India, . . . inherent in the *conditioning of the Indian mind during our struggle for freedom*, and inherent in the very circumstances of the world today." (Emphasis added). To this Krishna Menon added, almost as a conclusion: "Non-alignment is more or less a residue of historical circumstances, . . . we cannot align ourselves with the West with its colonialism, and there is no question of course of joining the Soviet bloc".

To trace the indegenous roots of non-alignment in India and comprehend what Nehru meant by the "conditioning of the Indian mind during our struggle for freedom", let us briefly recapitulate the traditions of the national movement. The Indian National Congress, as Leo Mates in a comprehensive study of Non-alignment rightly notes, "Is the oldest and the most articulate anti-colonial movement, not only in Asia, but in the world as a whole. It very early formulated both the policies of internal evolution, . . . and those for external relations." In *Discovery of India*, Nehru noted that "the Congress gradually developed a foreign policy, which was based on the elimination of political and economic imperialism everywhere and on the cooperation of free nations . . . As early as 1920, a resolution on foreign policy was passed by the Congress, in which our desire to cooperate with other nations, and especially to develop friendly relations with all our neighbouring countries was emphasized."

In 1927, a Foreign Affairs Department of the AICC was established under Jawaharlal Nehru. In the three successive sessions of the Congress at Gauhati (1926), Madras (1927) and Calcutta (1928), series of resolutions were adopted against imperialism, in support of liberation struggle and for strengthening bonds of solidarity with the peoples of Asia and Africa. The Congress pledged India's support to the republican secular struggle in Turkey and congratulated Mustafa Kamal on his victorious leadership, which it recognised as a presage of the freedom of all the nations of the East. The Congress sent fraternal greetings to the Wafd Party of Egypt and supported the struggles of Zaghlul Pasha and Nahas Pasha for freedom and reform. It also supported the struggle of the people of Palestine, Iraq and Syria, and China in their "fight for the emancipation of their people" from imperialist designs, and declared that the Chinese people were the "comrades of the Indian people in their joint struggle against imperialism". A Congress medical mission was sent to China in 1938, to show India's solidarity and concern. The Congress demanded, in 1927, the withdrawal of all Indian troops, police and consulate guards from Mesopotamia (Iraq) and Persia (Iran) and from all British colonies and foreign countries. The Congress also developed an interest in nationalist movements in the Dutch East Indies and Indo-China, as well as in Ceylon.

It was at this moment that a catalytic event took place that played a crucial role in the development of a coherent foreign policy of the Indian National Congress. This was the convening of the Second International Congress of the League against Imperialism at Brussels in February, 1927, in which representative delegates from Asia, Africa, the Arab world and Latin America (most of whom later played key role in the liberation of their respective countries) participated, and built not only valuable personal contacts at the top leadership level, but also exchanged notes on the problems facing the many countries and regions under European colonial rule. At the Gauhati session of the Congress (1926), Jawaharlal Nehru was deputed as the Congress representative to attend the Brussels meeting. Nehru called it "the outward symbol of the intense desire for mutual co-operation which had taken possession of the oppressed and the exploited all over the world".

From there, together with his father Motilal Nehru, he went to Moscow to participate in the tenth anniversary session of the October Revolution, which gave him an opportunity to see the new Soviet state and society at close quarters. Nehru's visit to Brussels and Moscow and to other cities in Europe, together with his talks and deliberations with leaders of liberation movements in many parts of the world, provided him with a world perspective. A meeting of the Pan-Asiatic Federation of racist European imperialism was sought to be convened in India during 1930.

Jawaharlal Nehru's historic presidential address to the Congress session in Lucknow (1936), was a clarion call for forging a world-wide anti-imperialist front. In *Discovery of India*, Jawaharlal Nehru wrote: ". . . our struggle was but a part of a far wider struggle for freedom; the forces that moved us were moving millions of people all over the world and driving them into action. All Asia stirs from the Mediterranean to the Far East, from the Islamic West to the Buddhist East, Africa responds to the new spirit; Europe, broken by the war, was struggling to find a new equilibrium ... and in the Soviet territories, a new conception of human freedom and social equality fought desperately against a host of enemies .. . . If once we understand this organic bond, the world situation becomes easier to understand and our national problems take their proper place in a wider picture .... We realize that we cannot isolate India or the Indian problem from the rest of the world."[7]

In fact it was immediately after the end of World War II, in the wake of the crystallization of bipolarity, that Jawaharlal Nehru (even before he became the Prime Minister and Foreign Minister of the Republic of India) soon after assuming charge of the foreign affairs portfolio in the Interim Government of India made a statement on September 7, 1946, which is probably the first more or less clear enunciation of the policy that has since developed into the concept of non-alignment. This statement needs to be quoted rather extensively. Nehru said: "We will take full part in international conferences as a free nation with our own policy and not merely as a satellite of another nation. We hope to develop close direct contacts with other nations and to cooperate with them in the furtherance of world peace and freedom. We propose, as far as possible, to keep away from the power politics of groups, aligned against one another, which have led in the past two world wars and which may again lead to disasters on an even vaster scale. We believe that peace and freedom are indivisible and the denial of freedom anywhere must endanger freedom elsewhere and lead to conflict and war. We are particularly interested in the emancipation of colonial and dependent countries and peoples, and in the recognition in theory and practice of equal opportunities for all races. We repudiate utterly the Nazi doctrine of racialism, wheresoever and in whatever form it may be practised. We seek no domination over others and we claim no privileged position over other peoples. But we do claim equal and honourable treatment for our people wherever they may go, and we cannot accept any discrimination against them. The world, in spite of its rivalries and hatred and inner conflicts, moves inevitably towards closer cooperation and building up of a world commonwealth. It is for this one world that free India will work, a world in which there is the free cooperation of free peoples, and no class or group exploits another."

It is, therefore, not surprising to learn that Winston Churchill admitted that "the majority of politically active Indians had decided in favour of non-alignment as early as during the war. But these policies could not be put into practice at that time. The Congress Party and the majority of leaders were interned or confined. The intensification of political life could only come after the war..." Nehru and the Congress were clear that "if the war is to defend the *status quo*, imperialist possessions, colonies, vested interests and privileges, then India can have nothing to do with it. If, however, the issue is democracy and a world order based on democracy, then India is intensely interested in it." This is an explicit articulation of the basic premises of independent India's future foreign policy. Indeed this was enunciated with greater political and juridical authority in a historic statement made by Jawaharlal Nehru on September 24, 1946, when he was Vice-Premier and foreign minister in the last British Government in India. He said: "In the sphere of foreign affairs, India will follow an independent policy, keeping away from the power politics of groups aligned one against another. She will uphold the principle of freedom for dependent peoples and will oppose racial discrimination wheresoever it may occur. She will work with other peace-loving nations for international cooperation and goodwill without the exploitation of one nation by another ... (she) should establish contact with all the great nations of the world and that her relations with her neighbouring countries in Asia should become still closer."

It was this basic commitment that prompted Nehru to convene the Asian Relations Conference in New Delhi in March, 1947—five months before independence. Nehru said: "For too long have we of Asia been petitioners in the western courts and chancelleries. That story must now belong to the past." He declared that after her independence, "it would be India's task .... to chart a new course in world politics for all states which wished to join in breaking with political alignments centring on the established great powers."

India is recognised as a country of "special distinction" in any study of non-alignment, "....not only because it is the largest of the non-aligned countries or because it was first in the post-war wave of decolonization to acquire independence, but also because a continued liberation struggle in India lasted from the First World War until its independence in 1947 and inspired anti-colonial movements in many other countries. During the decades of struggle for independence, in peace and in war, India experienced all the basic problems of a liberation movement. In other words, India is undoubtedly the best example on which we can study in detail the ideological, political and economic problems of the struggle for independence and the gradual maturing of the conception of non-alignment."

Within four months of India's independence, on December 4, 1947, Nehru reiterated the basic premises of India's evolving policy of non-alignment when he said in the Constituent Assembly that what India has "proclaimed during this past year (that is, from the pre-independence preparatory phase called the 'Interim Government' formed in September, 1946) .....is that *we will not attach ourselves to any particular group*", which he added "*has nothing to do with neutrality or passivity*" and later affirmed that "we propose, therefore, to *look after India's interest in the context of world cooperation and world peace* ...... We propose to keep on terms of friendship with other countries unless they themselves create difficulties.... We intend cooperating with the United States of America. We intend cooperating fully with the Soviet Union."

The century-long path travelled by the Indian National Congress (INC) also marks a definite historical stage in the movement of the Indian people itself from colonial enslavement to national liberation, from backwardness and poverty to a cultural revival and social progress.

The second half of this path is directly connected with the activity of the two most outstanding INC leaders—Mahatma Gandhi and Jawaharlal Nehru, who exerted an enormous, perhaps even the decisive influence on the political character, the ideological credo and the organisational principles of this party. Their ideological legacy is diverse, complex and contradictory. Nor everything in it is of equal value. Moreover, it is known that Jawaharlal Nehru seriously disagreed with Mahatma Gandhi already when the latter was still alive on a number of basic questions of the tactics, ways and tools of national liberation struggle. Nehru even openly subjected a number of propositions of Gandhi's teaching to a fairly sharp criticism, such as the obscurantist tendencies, the glorification of the "simple life" and poverty, the concept of wardship, the moralisation of politics and the doctrine of a unity of politics and religion. On the other hand, Nehru, far from ever denying, emphasised that, irrespective of the aims pursued and the related "metaphysical questions", the method of civil disobedience (Satyagraha) put forward by Gandhi strikingly corresponded to the Indian conditions.

Despite the differences in views, in the ideological legacy of Gandhi and Nehru, one can single out common features which one way or another determined the formation of the positive, progressive ideological tenets and slogans of the INC that secured this party great popularity and influence among the broadest sections of the Indian people.

First of all, a significant achievement of Gandhi and Nehru was their acknowledgement and insistent stressing of the decisive role of the popular masses in the struggle for national liberation and in the creation of new India. Gandhi's conclusion came prominently from his intuitive foresight, while Nehru arrived at it after a serious theoretical interpretation of the experience of world history and especially the Indian national liberation movement. The recognition of the decisive role of the popular masses by the INC leaders enabled this party to launch active organisational, political and mobilising work in the very depths of the millions of peasants, artisans and workers suffering from national and social oppression. Correctly seeing in them the main social base of the national liberation movement, the INC became the major political force that proved capable of awakening their national consciousness, inspiring them to bold actions against colonial oppression and enlisting them in the mass Satyagraha campaigns of Gandhi, which ultimately forced the colonialists to give up their rule in India.

Another aspect of the recognition of the primacy of the popular masses in social and political life was the bringing forward by Gandhi and Nehru of the idea of a social emancipation of the masses. On this question, they adhered to different views. Gandhi put forth the concept of Sarvodaya, a society of general welfare based on class cooperation according to the principle of wardship. To Gandhi's credit, it must be stressed that he, while remaining an advocate of Sarvodaya, did not ignore the ideals of socialism, although he interpreted them entirely in his own way. Nehru pointed out that Gandhi described himself as a socialist, but that he put into this word a special meaning almost or totally unconnected with the economic structure of society that is usually called socialism.

I have been asked what made Jawaharlal Nehru the leader of the Congress—which qualities of his, and through what contributions he made. I do not think the question can be answered briefly. That is why I have attempted in a general way to explain the role of Jawaharlal Nehru in the early years of struggle under Mahatma Gandhi's leadership. The qualities which really endeared him to the rank and file of the Congress all over the country, and made him a hero in the eyes of the nation's youth, were his sincerity, his dedication to the great cause, his impatience with the slowness of the then leadership to react to the vast changes taking place all over the world, his readiness to make any sacrifice, and his fearless and persistent efforts to convert the conservative sections of the Congress leadership to his own way of thinking. He did not believe in going it alone and fighting a frustrating battle from the wilderness. On the other hand, he believed in the possibility of changing the direction of the dynamic national movement represented by the National Congress. He symbolised not only the revolt of youth but the determination of youth to assume leadership and take the country forward to the cherished goal of a society in which equality would be a reality, of a nation which would be as great as any in the world and would serve as a model for other peoples struggling for liberation. Gandhi, as the supreme commander of the people's struggle, was the first to see that Nehru represented the forces of the future which could not be held back. And he named him his political heir.

It was Jawaharlal Nehru's emergence as the second biggest leader of the Congress that created faith among the people as a whole in the ability of the Congress to remove social and economic barriers and disparities. Even in the thirties he had begun to symbolise for the masses of our people the era of prosperity which freedom would bring in its wake. He was also the bulwark of the people against the reactionary and communal trends which had begun to show themselves in the country, and even in the Congress organisation. The people had watched him at work and had seen him succeed step by step in his efforts to introduce fresh thinking in the Congress leadership. The address delivered by Jawaharlal Nehru as President of the Lucknow Session of the Congress is a momentous pronouncement which deserves to be deeply pondered not merely by the members of the Congress Party but by all politicians and publicists, by the people and the Government. The speech is remarkable not merely for frankness and courage, but also for the clarity with which it expounds the political and social ideals of the President and the policy which he desires the country to pursue. His speech is further remarkable for its directness in brushing aside all issues which he considers to be of secondary importance and focussing attention on the two issues which, in his opinion, are fundamental. Political independence and socialism, or rather, communism, are the two vital issues which count. He is not much concerned with constitutional questions which are the pre-occupation of the Moderates. The Pandit is an admirer of the Bolshevik regime of the U.S.S R. and his speech is a perfervid appeal for the achievement of independence and socialism. He does not leave us in doubt as to the meaning and implications of socialism as conceived by him. It implies the abolition of private property and the dictatorship of the proletariat. Though he thinks that revolutionary leadership comes from middle class intellectuals and that our political weakness today is due to a decay of the middle class elements, he is, on the whole, inclined to look askance on the connection of the middle class intellectuals with the popular movement. He is an advocate of vast and revolutionary changes in the political and social structure alike. He favours revolutionism and catastrophic changes and is opposed to what he calls reformism. He has no place for the Indian States in his scheme of political organisation and would gladly see them abolished. The communal problem has no interest or significance for him as a matter of practical politics. The political structure of a united India must be fashioned by a Constituent Assembly elected by universal franchise. The device of such a Constituent Assembly for the making of a constitution has been a pet idea of many constitution makers, and especially so in revolutionary epochs. The faith which the Congress Party places in this method of framing any workable constitution is little justified by past experience. The Round Table Conferences which were held in England on the subject of Indian Constitutional Reforms failed to elicit any agreement among the delegates with regard to electorates and the representation of the various communities. How far the policy of the President remains to be seen. It is not likely that the policy of Communism will command acceptance in the country at large in the immediate future. There can be no doubt, however, that there is an extreme left wing in the Congress which will follow the lead of Pandit Jawaharlal. The problem of unemployment among the middle class and the grinding poverty of the masses are factors likely to swell the ranks of the extremists. The attitude of the Government with regard to constitutional reforms, their reluctance to make timely concessions to the demands of the moderate elements in the country who were looked upon as a microscopic minority with no claim to represent the masses, and the contempt with which they have treated the demands set forth in the famous memorandum of thirteen gentlemen headed by His Highness the Aga Khan, have brought about a sense of impotence and a feeling of distrust of the Government and have strengthened the conviction of the people as to the necessity for organising the masses and awakening their political consciousness. No mass movement can be successfully started or carried on except by an appeal to issues and watchwords which the masses can understand. The diversion of the attention of the people from political to economic issues may perhaps be welcome to the Government, but we do not know whether their appreciation of this aspect of the Congress activities will lead them to the length of alienating the sympathy and support of all the classes who may come under the description of the 'have'. Few people are satisfied with the new Constitution and a great majority of people believe that the fetters and safeguards provided by the Constitution will seriously interfere with the economic development of the country and retard the attainment of Dominion Status. The letter of the new Constitution does not justify much confidence in the possibility of making any great advance under it. But the spirit in which it may be worked by the Government may, to some extent, dispel the present feeling of pessimism. If the Government are guided by an exclusive regard to the interests of India and its political, economic and military development, and are not swayed by a regard for British or imperial interests inconsistent with the progress of India, and if they give up the time-honoured policy of 'divide and rule' and the encouragement of communal tendencies, they may be able to create a spirit of confidence in the sincerity of their intention to speed the progress of India.

Apart from the personal views of the President of the Congress the real question of importance at the present moment is the attitude of the Congress towards the new Councils to be brought into existence in the provinces. While the moderate school of politicians has also declared its willingness to reject the new Constitution, the Congress Party has declared the wrecking of the Constitution as its policy. It is strange that people who hold this view should seek to enter the Councils. But strange and illogical as it may appear, and difficult as it may be to reconcile the policy of Council-entry with the desire to wreck the Constitution, it has been declared from the Congress platform that this difficulty oppresses only the minds of those who believe in constitutional logic and that revolutionary logic is not troubled by such inconsistencies. Whether the Congress Party sincerely believes in the possibility of wrecking the Constitution by getting into the Councils is open to doubt. Fortunately for the interests of peaceful administration, the Constitution is absolute proof against all attempts at sabotage. The administration cannot possibly be overthrown or paralysed by any peaceful means, and even Pandit Jawaharlal is obliged to admit that he does not understand the talk of militant programme and militant action and that, of direct action on a national scale or civil disobedience is meant, he sees no near prospect of either. What does the Congress Party propose to do after it secures entry into the Councils ? Upon the question of acceptance of office there has been a conflict of opinion within the Congress. Pandit Jawaharlal is opposed to the acceptance of office and his reason for advising the Congress to enter the Councils is to secure a platform for propaganda to wreck the reforms from inside the Councils. He is not in favour of leaving the question of acceptance of office to the option of the provinces in which the Congressmen may win a majority of seats. The Congress has shelved a decision upon this point for the purpose of securing an apparent unanimity. The postponement of the decision is a strategical move of both the parties who hope that delay will work in their favour. It is to be hoped that the ultimate decision of the Congress will be in favour of acceptance of the responsibilities of office wherever its candidates obtain a majority of seats in the Councils.[8]

We live too close to the epoch straddled by Nehru's charismatic personality to assess him as a man or as the undisputed leader of the world's largest democracy. People still speak of him with a feeling not far short of idolatry; many still utter his name like a mantra. But few saw beyond the trappings of greatness and power to his frailties.

Dr. S. Radhakrishnan, who laid down the office of President in 1967, was closely associated with Nehru for seventeen years or more. His last homage to Nehru was a panegyric. Yet, to those very near him, Radhakrishnan once confided that Jawaharlal was a "poor judge of men" and often extended his confidence and protection to unworthy persons. He had in mind Pratap Singh Kairon and Dharma Teja. Kairon was the "strong man" and Chief Minister of Punjab who had to quit when a Commission of Inquiry pronounced him guilty of some of the numerous charges of corruption and mal-administration levelled against him. Dr. Teja caught Nehru's fancy as a "dynamic figure" and was able to wheedle out of the Government a loan of Rs. 200 million to finance a shipping company he floated. It was not long before the company was in difficulties and Teja and his wife fled from the country to avoid arrest.

Morarji Desai might justifiably have had harsh things to say of Nehru, for after being reckoned heir apparent he was dropped from the Cabinet in a purge euphemistically labelled the "Kamaraj Plan". But Desai spoke of Nehru's failings without a trace of rancour. He would not agree that Nehru was a bad judge of men. When Nehru sketched the character of a man, he sized him up pretty shrewdly, Desai said. "He once gave me an analysis of Krishna Menon's personality that no one else could improve upon", he added. Nehru utilised the men around him for his own purposes and they in return exploited him fully.

Nehru and Azad were intellectually and emotionally very close. Their friendship was based on two factors: First, they found themselves in agreement on most of the political issues that came before the Congress Working Committee. Secondly, Azad believed Nehru was an idealist with intellectual integrity and a progressive outlook and above all he was free from religious bigotry. At the same time, Azad was not unaware of Nehru's weaknesses. He blamed him for giving Jinnah the opportunity to win the leadership of the Muslims.

But Azad revised his opinion of Nehru in the last two years of his life. Indeed, he went to the extent of expressing regret for being unfair to Patel and asserting that he was sure that the country would have been better off if Patel had been Prime Minister. What motivated this change? Towards the end of his life, Azad realised that the best protection for the Muslims was the goodwill of the Hindus and a strong government. He told me he had come to the conclusion that Nehru's policies had weakened the administration and that his economic theories had failed to improve the living condition of the people, especially the Muslims.

"You know, my attitude towards him is one of complete adoration", Mrs. Vijaya Lakshmi Pandit once said of her brother Nehru. Nevertheless, her assessment of him was outspoken. "I used to think, as many others seem to do, that he was a bad judge of men. But I am sure now that he was not. Of course, some people did fail to measure up to the jobs assigned to them. But Nehru was tolerant to a fault; he was anxious to give everyone a fair deal, every reasonable chance to make good. I agree, though, that no leader should abdicate his authority completely. If my brother had asserted himself, Sheikh Abdullah (Jammu & Kashmir) would not have developed ideas of grandeur. Neither would Bakshi Ghulam Mohammed (Jammu & Kashmir) have strayed from the strait and narrow path had Bhai (brother) retained firm control in his own hands."

Lal Bahadur Shastri, who succeeded Nehru as Prime Minister in 1964 was a man of few words. One day, when he was told that with his rapport with Nehru he should be able to speak to him frankly, he confessed: "I know Panditji is wrong. He is not practical. He has strong likes and dislikes. He has little contact with the people; he mistakes the worship in their eyes for a complete endorsement of his policies. He has never known what poverty or human suffering is. Yet his heart is in the right place. He wants to see people happy and prosperous."

Shastri was critical of Nehru's plans and projects. "They only serve to strengthen the bureaucracy. When you take too much on hand, you do too little. Look at me. I have my limitations, both educational and administrative. I do not go for grandiose schemes." Shastri candidly admitted, "We have to submit to all he says and does. My loyalty to him therefore is unqualified. I keep my counsel to myself and carry out his wishes. I look for the greatest common denominator in all political and party disputes entrusted to my care by the leader. He has developed confidence in me, for he knows I am utterly loyal to him, and useful too."

Nehru had few personal friends. Prominent among these was Miss Padmaja, the daughter of Sarojini Naidu and later Governor of West Bengal, who always brought him good cheer. She laughed and joked with him and affectionately called him a "bald-headed old man". Her elder sister, Leelamani, said more than once that Nehru would have married Padmaja after he lost his wife but for considerations of political expediency.

To Nehru, his image as a democrat and secular being was of the highest importance. Once M.C. Chagla, who was Education Minister in Nehru's Cabinet and Ali Yavar Jung, Ambassador in the U.S., conveyed their concern and chagrin over the fact that whereas Nehru backed progressive Muslims among the Arabs he lent his ear to Conservative Muslims in India. They saw no reason, for instance, why there should not be a common civil code applicable to all citizens alike. When someone asked Nehru why he seemed to have adopted double standards, he replied his friendship with Nasser and other progressive Arab leaders was designed to counter-balance the Conservative Muslim bloc, which stretched from Pakistan to Jordan and posed a threat to India's security and its secularism. But he was hesitant to attempt reforms in the domestic sphere for fear that Muslim obscurantists would raise the cry "Islam in danger".

Mahatma Gandhi's outlook on life was based on economics. Patel understood that money was a very powerful motivating force. He encouraged capital and bent it to his purpose. Gandhi created an organisational alternative before he started to destroy what existed. Patel mastered the organisation and used whatever instrument was available and reshaped it to suit the need of the hour. Nehru had no experience of organisation. He did not understand economics, nor did he bother to face facts. He wove fantasies round his ideals and believed that somehow his preachings would make the people do the things he wanted.

Taking democracy in the political aspects, the functioning of Parliament, there is little doubt that Nehru established conventions and traditions which if followed will tend to put our parliamentary government on a sound and durable footing. So conscious was he of the supremacy of Parliament in all matters that when he heard a senior minister in his cabinet assert in Parliament that he would not adopt a certain course even if Parliament asked him to do so, he, it is reported, said that the minister concerned, however experienced, could never be entrusted with the responsibility of being a Prime Minister. Indeed Nehru has been described by his foreign biographer as "a supreme democrat". However so overshadowing was Jawaharlal's great personality that notwithstanding his ardent desire to be true to all parliamentary tradition he not infrequently ignored Parliament and disregarded the norms governing cabinet responsibility. His personal loyalty to friends frequently led him to continue as his colleagues inefficient, outworn or even undesirable politicians. His policy of trust in China made him withhold from the Parliament important facts relating to Chinese aggression which he was ultimately forced to admit when information from other sources had reached the Parliament. Indeed his policy towards China and his blind and unreasoning trust in a colleague brought the country almost to the brink of disaster at the time of the Chinese aggression in 1962. Equally unparliamentary and undemocratic was his dogged persistence in continuing in his cabinet colleague against whom allegations of corruption had been openly made and his continuance in office of a Chief Minister who had been guilty of persistent acts of maladministration while in charge of an important state. His loyalty to and trust in colleagues frequently made him ignore the well-accepted doctrine of ministerial responsibility. Notwithstanding however all these counts against him it must be acknowledged that Jawaharlal, the father of parliamentary democracy in India, fostered its growth and development to a remarkable degree.[9]

Planning, so dear to Nehru's heart, was a more serious business than being lyrical about the picture of an industrially transformed

India travelling with dignified steps towards socialism. Jawaharlal knew it very well himself; no one could put it so beautifully as when he said that his generation of Indians had been sentenced to hard labour and that to take one's ease was sin. His strong point was the capacity to offer his people fresh, evocative goals and "to take the vision a notch higher every time". Between enunciation and implementation of policies, however, there would always be a wide divergence which he could not eliminate. Even so, new dimensions would flash before the mind's eye when he spoke in Parliament on the plans. "In the final analysis", he said in 1956, "any effort is an act of faith", and then—as with a flash, he would add: "I have faith in the capacity of our people." This kind of thing was something to be thankful for whatever his shortcomings and the failures of his administration, he was, even in his most passive moments, seeking tirelessly to push India forward in the direction of a secular and socialist future and had made a personal commitment to dynamic perspectives which he never ceased to expound and defend before his people.

The understanding of India's underdevelopment displayed in the writings of Nehru and in the plan documents makes it clear that poverty was regarded as one of its major aspects. Question of low level of productivity, widespread unemployment, technological backwardness, non-progressive role, of social and economic institutions, the legacy of colonial rule, etc. were also considered closely related to the problem of poverty. Similarly, the size and growth of population, the role of financial institutions, agrarian relations and regional imbalances were considered issues very closely related to endemic and widespread poverty in India. While the breadth of issues related to poverty was quite comprehensive, it is not clear whether a total analytical picture emerging from these analyses was considered an organic whole capable of suggesting a policy framework in which the attack on the problem of poverty could emerge as the primary task. In fact, the problem of poverty was viewed as one emerging from the faulty working of the system of distribution, which could be corrected and restructured later on once plentiful production is ensured. Thus the primary task was the creation of conditions in which the problem of poverty can be tackled. It was a very frequent Nehruvian refrain that without increasing production and national wealth, one can only distribute poverty. From this the inference drawn was to assign primacy to the task of increasing production by means of capital formation and industrialisation which would increase the domestically produced supply of goods and services essential for relating the living standards and for self-reliance. In this scheme of things the attack on the problem of poverty and unemployment was considered a task to be tackled in the long run and indirectly by creating a powerful and extensive production structure. In fact, some economists have traced the origins of the concept of trickle-down to Jawaharlal Nehru in his writings even during the pre-independence period. Thus the familiar mechanism of capital formation, industrialisation, improvement in agricultural productivity, setting up of an extensive network of modern qualified manpower with access to modern educational and medical facilities, participation in international economic relations from a position of strength, etc. were the primary tasks adopted as a part of the planning and development policy initiated under the stewardship of Nehru. It goes without saying that in a plural democracy there cannot be any question of consigning the problem of poverty entirely to the agenda for the future and concentrate exclusively on production-oriented policies under the existing inequitous system. Given the size of agriculture, cottage and artisan industries and the work force, it was not even possible to carry out a programme of increasing national income without involving the poor masses. Their resources, motivations and constraints become crucial to the growth of output in agriculture, decentralised industries and myriad conventional and non-conventional services. Hence for agricultural and rural development, a scheme of community development was initiated with a view to catalysing co-operative self-help and increasing the use of improved production practices in agriculture. The state was to undertake improvement of basic facilities in the rural areas as a complementary exercise. The vast reserves of rural labour power was to be the main source for accomplishing these tasks and the State was to catalyse these processes by setting up a net work of extension services in each block.

Alongside this an ambitious programme of agrarian reforms involving abolition of zamindari, security of tenure, imposition of ceiling on land holdings, consolidation of land holding, etc. was initiated. A number of important social services in the field of education, health, welfare of Scheduled Castes and Tribes environmental sanitation, supply of potable drinking water, etc. were initiated. A limited programme of preferential discrimination in political representation, allotment of public employment and access to education was taken up. However, despite the constitutional mandate, the task of universalisation of free primary education was not taken up. These schemes were to operate under the framework of a national plan. Attempts were made even to set up *Gaon Sabhas* and institutions of democratic decentralisation for involving grassroot participation in the planning process. The regulation of private industry and investment was introduced partly with a view to avoiding the wastage involved in the operation of unregulated market mechanism and partly to prevent concentration of income, wealth and economic power. These too can be construed as a step for benefiting the poor insofar as the benefits of development were sought to be prevented from getting concentrated. Thus one can say that the planning and policy framework during the first three plans attempted to alleviate poverty in a gradual and indirect manner by means of raising public investment, growth of public sector, introduction of modern import-substituting industries, regulation and control of the private sector, agrarian reforms, community development and large public investments in irrigation and power projects for supplying water and electricity to the villages. A number of schemes were initiated for the growth and strengthening of cottage and village industries as well. A limited programme of special dispensation for overcoming social disabilities was also initiated. Even during Nehru's lifetime the realisation came about that very little might be achieved for improving the conditions of masses. The problem of unemployment kept on worsening as reflected in the figures of backlog of unemployment at the beginning of each plan. This period witnessed an intense controversy whether per capita daily income was three annas or a little more, thus underlining the fact that acute rural and urban poverty persisted. It was as a result of this realisation that a committee was appointed by Jawaharlal Nehru under the chairmanship of Prof. Mahalanobis to find out how the fruits of the development have been shared, what has happened to the living conditions of the majority of the poor people and how far concentration of the wealth and income has increased. As is well-known, the findings of these and other studies brought out, even though not in very clear terms, the worsening of the incidence of poverty and deformation of the content of development during the period. One would say that all this was quite expected. After all, the exercises carried out by the Planning Commission during the early 1960s revealed clearly that even for making a modest dent into the problem of poverty, a sustained rate of growth of seven per cent per annum in GDP for a period of 25 to 30 years is required. Since this rate of growth was not realised by a margin of as much as fifty per cent, agrarian reforms could not be carried out, the scheme of progressive taxation was introduced faultily and could not really be enforced, the market forces continued to retain their force and basic logic. Even then there was little indication of any basic re-thinking.[10]

Historically speaking poverty eradication has been a major objective of planning right from its inception. The strategies for achieving this goal, however, have been changing over the years. Though the planners adopted a kind of trial and error approach in this respect, one can see an evolution process in the approach. This evolution process can be broadly divided into three phases, namely, the phase of idealism (the First, Second and Third Five Year Plans), the beginning of disillusionment (the Fourth and Fifth Five Year Plans) and a move towards realism (the Draft Plan 1978-83, the Sixth and Seventh Five Year Plans). As the root causes of the weak planning links lie in the process of evolution, we shall examine it briefly. Phase one of the first three Five Year Plans under Nehru began with a note of idealism. In these early years of freedom the planners believed that economic growth will reach the poor if organisation are set up for common ownership of material resources, for their co-operative management and for democratic decentralisation in decision making. They assumed that constructive leadership will emerge in rural areas through these organisations which will not only work for the poor, but will also check concentration of power, cultural and economic, in the rural society. The First Plan, therefore, suggested that Co-operative Village Management (CVM) was the ultimate objective of rural development, which was to be achieved gradually with the help of Village Productivity Councils (VPC) to be set up in every village or in a group of villages, Rural Extension Centres to take care of the extension work of new programmes, and with the help of Co-operative Farming. The First Plan also set up Community Development Blocks in selected areas for the overall development of rural society. The Second and Third Plans carried on the idealism further and declared that the ultimate goal of planning was to set up a socialistic pattern of society. These plans introduced Panchayati Raj institutions and strengthened Community Development Programme to bring about participation of the masses in development. They also recommended setting up of Taluka and District Planning Councils involving people in planning. Thus the three Five Year Plans reflected immense faith of the planners in the goodness of human beings. They assumed that the new organisations will help not only in growth but also in poverty eradication. (It must be perhaps added that many of the organisations suggested in these plans did not see the light of the day).[11]

The Second Phase began when gradually planners started getting disillusioned about their idealism. They realised that economic growth was selective in terms of areas and people both, and that general developmental benefits were grabbed by relatively better off persons and areas, with the result that the people at the bottom perhaps remained as poor as ever. A new thinking about development emerged gradually from these realisations which accepted that an increase in GNP or in per capita income is not always likely to reach the poor and that a direct attack on poverty is needed to eradicate it. It was also accepted that basic human needs should be emphasized to improve the quality of life of the poor. Micro-level approach was recommended for this purpose. The approach paper to the Fourth Five Year Plan accepted this new ideology and recommended Special Programmes Strategy for poverty eradication. The Plan introduced Small Farmers' Development Agency, Marginal Farmers and Agricultural Labourers' Agency, and later on Drought Prone Area Programmes to take care of target groups and target areas. The Fifth Plan continued this approach and added a Minimum Needs Programme to improve the quality of life of the poor. Introduction of micro-level planning was another step taken to take care of the space dimension of development. In short, during the second phase, there was a shift towards special programmes strategy and micro-level planning which paid special attention to the need of the poor people and backward areas.

The third phase of the evolution of programmes for poverty eradication in rural areas began with the Draft Plan (1978-83). This phase introduced more realism in the approach. The Draft Plan, to start with, admitted that there were fundamental failures in planning in the past and that the most cherished goals of development had remained almost as distant as they were in the beginning of planning. The plan proposed that radical changes were needed in the poverty-eradication programmes and introduced (1) employment planning at the block level, (2) Integrated Rural Development Programme which extended the scope and content of SFDA, MFAL, etc. and which aimed at real integration of various programmes, (3) revised Minimum Needs Programme, (4) special area programmes for hilly and forest areas and for other backward areas, and (5) emphasized distributive justice through land reforms, extended public distribution system for mass consumption goods, etc.

The Sixth and Seventh Plans followed, more or less, the same approach. The Sixth Plan introduced some modifications to intensify the efforts: (1) First of all, it introduced an operationally integrated strategy by putting major rural development programmes under one programme namely IRDP. (2) It also adopted family approach which considered the family and not the individual as a unit for the purpose of giving benefits. Each beneficiary family was given a small family card which noted down the total benefits received by the family. (3) The Sixth Plan adopted antyodaya approach in IRDP which implied that the poorest families should get the top priority in IRDP. The plan also introduced other programmes to help the rural poor. These programmes include emphasis on land reforms, implementation of legislations like Minimum Wages Act, Bonded Labour Act, Inter-state Migrants Act, etc., programmes for credit for the weaker sections, wage employment programmes like NREP, RLEGP, etc. The Seventh Plan Approach Paper states that the strategy adopted so far is basically sound and should ultimately lead to achievement of the objective of poverty eradication and rural development. The Plan, therefore, recommends the same strategy with marginal changes to improve the efficiency of the programmes. The major anti-poverty programmes in the Seventh Plan are IRDP, NREP, RLEGP, DIC, SLPP (Special Livestock Production Programme), and programmes pertaining to land reforms, credit and marketing, training and technology. The plan also recognise the need for organising the poor and recommends some schemes in this area.

At the present stage of the evolution process (the process is still going on) of planning for poverty eradication in rural areas, we have a set of approaches, such as, largest group approach, special area development approach, minimum needs approach and micro-level planning approach. A large number of anti-poverty programmes are formulated under these approaches and a number of schemes are incorporated under each of them. The process of evolution which emerges from the trial and error approach of the planners shows clear improvements in certain areas. First of all, there is a definite move towards realism in the diagnosis of rural poverty. The idealism (or naivety) of the planners has given place to some realistic views of the situation. For example, there is a realisation that general growth does not reach the poor persons or poor areas and therefore they need special attention. Secondly, the anti-poverty programmes are now superior in terms of their technical content as lessons from the past, better quality of data and sophisticated methods of analysis of data have improved the designing of the programmes. And thirdly, the contents and scope of various programmes, have also improved over the years. For example, National Rural Employment Programme (NREP) of the Sixth Plan is broad-based and is better designed than the Rural Works Programme (RWP) of 1961. There is an improvement in the understanding of rural poverty and in the designing of anti-poverty programmes over the years. The process of evolution, however, is also responsible for the weaknesses of the programmes. First of all, the problem solving approach of the Planning Commission which takes care of various individual problems, fails to create an integrated or a total approach of poverty eradication. Consequently there is poor co-ordination among various programmes. And secondly, planners have ignored certain sensitive but crucial issues throughout the process of evolution. For example, positive steps to reduce the economic and political power of the rural rich or to reduce their influence on decision-making were never emphasised though it was always realised that this class does not allow the benefits to reach the real poor. Also, while formulating or evaluating a programme, asset distribution was hardly emphasized enough either as an objective or as an impact. For example, IRDP is evaluated mainly on the basis of the amount spent, on the number of beneficiaries covered and, at the most, the increase in the income levels of the beneficiaries. The same is the case with NREP and other programmes. Thus it seems that the diagnosis of rural poverty under the various anti-poverty programmes is not yet bold enough to recognise the role of these sensitive factors. The major weak links in the planning of anti-poverty programmes are mainly three: (1) poor diagnosis of poverty and absence of a total approach at the strategy level, (2) poor coordination of the programmes at the micro-level, and (3) weak planning component of individual programmes.[12]

Poor Diagnosis of Poverty and Absence of a Total Approach

Though low level of economic growth is an important cause of rural poverty, the deprivation of the masses of their due share is mainly due to the socio-economic power structure in rural areas. That is, the distribution of economic growth among the various sections is influenced largely by this structure. An important implication of this would be that anti-poverty strategy in rural areas should try to change the assets structure and the power structure in favour of the poor. The present set of strategies do not emphasize this aspect enough. First, no positive steps are taken to curtail the economic and political power of the rural rich and their influence over decision-making in anti-poverty programmes. In fact, their influence has been increasing over the years. For example, in SFDA, MFAL and DPAP programmes of the Fourth and Fifth Plans the role of panchayats and their elected members was not important. Project Officers carried out these programmes. But in the present IRDP and NREP they have a very important role in the decision-making as the Governing Body of District Rural Development Agency, which plans and monitors these programmes, is dominated by these power groups. In the case of NREP the guidelines clearly state that Panchayati Raj Institutions should be actively involved in the planning and implementation of the programme at all the levels. Though a number of studies have shown that elected leaders of panchayats do not represent the interest of the weaker sections, their role has not been reduced by any direct step. Secondly, asset redistribution also has not received enough attention in the present set of anti-poverty programmes. Except for land reforms, which have had a limited impact, no programme emphasizes asset redistribution directly. In fact, NREP and RLEGP, which are going to be major programmes in the Seventh Plan, are likely to have a negative impact on the asset distribution as they tend to strengthen the asset base of only those who have at least some asset. In short, the diagnosis of poverty underlying the anti-poverty programmes does not recognize the importance of the root causes of poverty. Apart from the above, another weakness at the strategy level is that there is no integrated total approach for poverty eradication. Anti-poverty programmes are neither integrated with overall planning (sectoral planning) nor with each other. Each anti-poverty approach is conceived independently, planned independently, and implemented as such. For example, when it was realised that the poorer sections of the society were by-passed by general economic growth, special programmes for target groups were designed; when the Scheduled Castes and the Scheduled Tribes were found lagging behind in development, the Component Plan (for the Scheduled Castes) and Tribal Sub-plans were introduced; when women and children were found to be remaining outside the mainstream of development, special programmes for them were designed. In the same way, when the need for improving the quality of life of the poor was felt the Minimum Needs Programme was introduced and when the need for providing extra employment for the unemployment was felt, NREP and RLEGP were introduced. As each programme is planned and implemented independently, there is poor coordination among these various approaches. Like the story of the blind men and the elephant, each strategy sees only a part of the problem and designs a suitable programme. The resultant set of programmes, therefore, is like a collection of patches rather than smooth fabric.

Poor Coordination at the Micro-Level

Second major weak link of the planning of anti-poverty programmes is that there is a large number of schemes which are covered under more than one programme. This has resulted in the multiplicity of planning which is very confusing. To give an example, a buffalo can be purchased by a poor person under IRDP, under ICDP, under DPAP, DDP, the Component Plan, the tribal sub-plan, the Antyodaya plan, etc. A well can be constructed under IRDP, DPAP, NREP, Component Plan, tribal sub-plan, etc. As each of these programmes are implemented by different agencies which have strong vertical linkages, there is no systematic horizontal coordination possible. The final result is that the total efforts in an area under all the programmes are neither planned nor known. Such a situation hardly helps in the planning or monitoring of anti-poverty programmes.

Weak Planning of Individual Programmes

The third major weak link in the planning of anti-poverty programmes is the poor planning component of individual programmes. It appears that the individual anti-poverty programmes are designed in such a fashion that the planning aspects has not received enough attention. To illustrate this point we shall examine two major anti-poverty programmes, namely, IRDP and NREP.[13]

Integrated Rural Development Programme (IRDP) which is a target group programme, is a major programme for poverty eradication in rural areas. Its basic economic philosophy in simple words is that special preferential treatment is necessary to enable the poor to participate in economic development. The policy mechanism of the programmes can be briefly described as follows :

(1) Precise identification of the poor household on the basis of asset (land) and income. (2) Examining the problems of the poor households and identification of suitable schemes for raising their income and employment in the present or in new occupations. (3) Provision of special extension facilities so that the poor are not informed but are also helped in participating in the programmes. (4) Provision of credit for undertaking the schemes in such a way that credit is easily available, it meets all the types of credit needs, and is available at a low rate of interest with easy instalments. The asset purchased is also subsidised. (5) Providing the complete package of supporting facilities to the poor to enable them to run the scheme successfully.

IRDP covers a large number of sectors like agriculture, minor irrigation, fisheries, animal husbandry, poultry, cottage industries, small trading activities, etc. and covers all the weaker sections, *viz.* small and marginal farmers, agricultural labourers, rural artisans and others. Though IRDP has now adopted the cluster approach, the antyodaya approach and the family approach, the programme suffers from a number of weaknesses. First of all, IRDP emphasizes self-employment rather too much. It assumes that the poor and especially the poorest of the poor are capable of taking up self-employment and managing independent enterprises successfully. This assumption is not realistic as many of the poor are illiterate, have poor risk capacity, possess poor entrepreneurial abilities, and have no or little assets and therefore not credit-worth. They are not capable of managing enterprises independently. Many of them would be better off if they are given wage employment. Secondly, IRDP assumes that the poor need a subsidised income generating asset and when it is given, the needs of the poor are largely satisfied. This assumption also is not fully correct as the asset will perhaps meet part of their needs, but it will not help them in reducing their exploitative dependence on the rich. To put it differently, the credit given to them will buy an income generating asset, but it will not help them in meeting other urgent needs like consumption loans, seed loans, loans to meet social functions, etc. In this sense IRDP is a partial approach which tends to create leakages in the working of the asset based schemes and in running of the programme successfully. Thirdly, IRDP assumes that the special arrangements made for poor will reach them. When one realises, however, that the implementing agencies are the same development administration, credit institutions and panchayati raj institutions, it is difficult to accept that the benefits will percolate to the poor. It is indeed difficult to accept that IRDP, which does not attempt to change the system in which it operates, will change the process of percolation of economic programmes in favour of poor. Apart from the above, the planning component of IRDP also is found to be weak. First of all, there is no systematic approach regarding allocation of IRDP funds among various schemes, various areas and households. There is no provision in IRDP which provides for allocation of resources among talukas or villages on the basis of their needs and resources. To allocate specific schemes to the poor households mainly on the basis of their own demands is definitely not a sound way of planning.[14]

National Rural Employment Programme (NREP) was introduced during the Sixth Plan with three major objectives, namely, employment generation for the unemployed, construction of durable assets and improving nutritional level of the poor. The main responsibility of planning and implementation of NREP is with the DRDA at the district level. The rationale of wage employment programme in a labour surplus economy like ours can be briefly explained as follows: The economy has, on the one hand, surplus manpower which is described by various terms such as disguised unemployment, underemployment, etc. and which needs more employment as well as higher incomes, while lags behind in social overheads such as economic and social infrastructural facilities which are often described as a minimum condition for economic growth. If the surplus labour is utilised in the construction of the required capital stock or social overheads, these economies will gain in terms of reduction of employment/underemployment as well as in terms of capital formation, the labour absorbing capacity of the economy will gradually expand and the surplus labour will be utilised gainfully. With the passing of time, the economy will reach a stage when the total labour absorbing capacity of the economy will have been expanded to such an extent that there will be little surplus labour left and the surplus labour will have constructed at least some infrastructural facilities in the economy by then. Wage employment programmes on public works (or even private) are thus essentially a transition programme which are expected to lay an important role in the growth process of an economy like ours. They contribute substantially as an anti-poverty programme in the initial stages and provide increased income levels to poor households. The transition process, however, is not as simple as it appears. There are number of issues that need special attention: (1) First of all, the programme should be designed in such a way that the supply of labour, that is, the extent and nature of unemployment, matches with the demand for labour, that is, the requirements for capital formation in each area. It is necessary, therefore, that the demand and supply factors are examined carefully before decisions about works for wage employment are taken. (2) Massive wage employment programmes are likely to create inflationary pressures in the economy as they will generate purchasing power of the workers but not immediate supply of consumption goods. To minimise these pressures, therefore, suitable steps will have to be planned out carefully. Some of the steps could be using surplus labour in the production of consumption goods in the sectors with under-utilised production capacities, taking up works with short gestation periods, modifying overall planning to increase the production of wage goods, setting up public distribution systems for basic consumption goods, etc. (3) Wage employment programmes on public and private construction works may not have favourable long term impact on employment as they may increase the total consumption in the economy (the income distribution will change in favour of the poor) and reduce the rate of investment. In order to avoid this, it is necessary to see that the works taken up under these programmes increase the capital stock in the economy in such a way that the labour absorbing capacity of the economy expands gradually. In other words, these programmes should not be treated as pure welfare measures, but should be planned carefully for capital formation also. (4) Wage employment programmes on public or private works are likely to generate assets (such as roads, wells, tanks, land levelling, etc.) which will benefit those who have at least some assets. Thus, these programmes will tend to strengthen the asset-base of those who have assets and will result in the deterioration of the assetless poor. This implies that if these programmes have to have any favourable impact on distributional aspect of development, they will have to incorporate the idea of collective ownership of these assets by the workers that constructed them. The workers should then be given a share from the returns of these assets, and (5) the wage employment programmes will have a favourable impact on the levels of livings of the poor only if (a) the employment of workers is continuous on these works, and (b) wages are high enough to provide the poor with a minimum Continuous employment of workers implies a well-planned shelf of living, projects for each area.

When we examine NREP, which is a major wage employment programme today, in the context of the above discussion, it becomes clear that the programme is designed very poorly.

First of all, the programme does not mention anywhere that its major role is to use surplus labour for capital formation in such a way that the extent of surplus labour gradually declines and that it is a transitional programme in that sense. Though a significant achievement in this transition is a distant dream, the focus of the programme should be on this goal right from the beginning so that the programme advances in the right direction.

The second major weakness of the programme is its very weak planning component: (a) The guidelines of NREP do not show as to how to identify infrastructural gaps of capital requirements of an area or how to assess the extent of unemployment and how to match both the sides for NREP planning, (b) the guidelines do not show as to how to integrate NREP with IRDP or with other rural development programmes (it merely mentions that such an integration should be brought out), (c) the programme does not mention as to how to bring about coordination among the various functionaries of NREP, such as the forest department, irrigation department, roads and buildings department, land development department, taluka and village panchayat offices, etc. and how to allocate resources among them in a systematic way, (d) the selection of works is not expected to be done on the basis of any cost-benefit analysis or any such systematic method, and (e) the allocation for afforestation and for SC/ST works are 10 per cent each in all the areas of India irrespective of the need for forestry or the size of the SC/ST population.

Thirdly, NREP pays no attention to its inequitable impact on the asset distribution in rural areas. The fact that it strengthens the asset base of those with assets and that it puts the assetless poor in a relatively worse situation in asset and income distribution is completely neglected. There is no provision of any collective ownership of these assets by the poor. Such a negative impact may worsen the asset distribution pattern in our rural areas.

Fourthly, NREP does not take into account the inflationary pressures which are likely to be created by it. Though the planners have raised the allocation to these programmes substantially in the Seventh Plan (the total outlay on NREP and RLEGP in the Plan is Rs. 10,500 crore) they have not taken care of these pressures at planning level.

And lastly, the allocation of NREP funds on the basis of the strength of marginal farmers and agricultural labourers (75 per cent weightage) and the incidence of poverty (25 per cent weightage) does not seem to be fully acceptable. The underlying assumptions for the 75 per cent weightage that the incidence of un-employment is high in the areas where the strength of AL/MF is high and that such areas are backward in their socio-economic infrastructure are not at all realistic. Studies have shown that the facts are just the reverse. It is clear that such an allocation pattern will widen the regional disparities rather than narrow them. In short, NREP is not a well-conceived and a well-designed programme.[15]

Some of the steps which are likely to help in this context are suggested below:

(1) The first need is to develop an overall logic or a total approach for poverty eradication. Independent approaches like household-based approach, resource-based approach (or sectoral approach), and spatial approach should be linked up with each other systema-

tically. These approaches are supplementary to each other and therefore should be planned as such. (2) Strengthening of the planning process at the district level will help considerably. If all the development efforts undertaken in a district are covered under one (and only one) agency, the total picture will be planned and monitored effectively, for example, identification of schemes for poor households should not be done only on the basis of the skills available with them or their preferences, but it should be done in the context of the overall development of the area also. (3) The problem of coordination among various schemes at the micro-level will become less formidable if there is one agency at the apex to look after all the programmes. If necessary, a number of programmes should be scrapped. For example, if IRDP is asked to take care of the SC/ST population, the need for the component plan or the tribal sub-plan will be very limited. (4) The role of "felt needs" of people's representatives must be reduced in anti-poverty programmes. If each programme is designed systematically and the importance of objective analysis of facts is accepted in its planning, the role of felt needs will automatically become less important. We believe that instead of involving "people's representatives" in planning in the initial stages, they should be consulted after the plans are formulated. Representatives may be, then, asked to suggest modifications along with the justifications. (5) It must be seen that the impact of anti-poverty programmes is reflected in asset-redistribution in favour of the poor. Each programme should be evaluated from this angle also, and should be monitored in such a way that it has favourable impact on asset-distribution for the poor, and (6) planners should be clear about their goals and about the translation of the goals into programmes. Once this genuineness is emphasized, it will take care of a number of problems like target orientation, interference of the rural rich asset-distribution, etc.

It needed no little courage, if the condition of those times be remembered, for Nehru to aver as he did from Delhi in November, 1947: "We intend cooperating with the United States of America and we intend cooperating fully with the Soviet Union." Some time later he said: "India is too big a country to be bound down to any country, however big it may be." Late in 1956, in the Parliament he condemned the cold war, then current, for creating "a bigger mental barrier than brick walls or iron curtains do", and added, "we are not obsessed by fear. We are not obsessed by hatred of any country. Our minds are a little more receptive than those of others—communists, anti-communists or socialists. I do think that is a virtue in us and it is in the good democratic tradition. When that goes, it is bad for the world."

In foreign affairs, which Nehru cared more about and felt more fully understood, he did often show firm leadership. In fact, Nehru had lack of commitment on many of his programmes and that may have been due to his being unsure about what he wanted in foreign policy.

John F. Kennedy was the first President to put aid to India on a long-term basis of five years. He was able to get Congress to endorse his policy. Johnson knew on the other hand that Congress was not favourable to foreign aid and asked for annual grant linked to performance. I learned that President Johnson was a man with a golden heart, but moody and whimsical.

There was much excitement in the Kennedy camp when Nehru agreed to visit Washington in 1961. But his first meeting with Kennedy was a flop. Nehru did not respond to what Kennedy said and it was left to Bijju-Nehru to carry on the dialogue. The Prime Minister was fatigued, probably by his heavy schedule of engagements. The same thing happened when he flew to Kennedy's holiday resort. There too, as they went sailing, Nehru would not react to Kennedy's conversational gambits and Kennedy again felt disappointed. They did not talk politics. This happened in 1961. Nehru was apparently a tired man. Finally, they had a quiet talk, mostly on Vietnam. Here again, Nehru would not state his view; he asked Morarji Desai to tell the Americans that they should not go into South Vietnam as they would get bogged down there. Kennedy was really worried about Vietnam and wanted to know Nehru's mind to help him determine his own policy.

Basically, Nehru was allergic to Americans, my informant said, and narrated an interesting incident. When Dulles visited Delhi in 1954 some people decided to hold hostile demonstration in front of the U.S. Embassy. Nehru came to know of this and sent for the Chief Commissioner, who told him that popular feeling against Dulles was strong and that a demonstration may prove a safety valve. Nehru said: "I know this fellow Dulles is conscientiously stupid. But I do not want any hostile demonstration."

Two senior I.C.S. officers who worked as Nehru's principal private secretaries found Nehru accomplished in his public relations. Once the correspondent of an American newspaper asked for an interview. The Principal Private Secretary put up with his letter clippings of the man's writings from Karachi which wholly supported Pakistan and criticised India violently. Nehru turned down the request, but a little later, as the Secretary was drafting a refusal, Nehru came into his room and said: "We are going to Kashmir tomorrow. Ask this man to join us on the flight." Nehru hardly devoted ten minutes to the correspondent in the plane, but that he should have had the privilege of flying with Nehru completely changed his attitude. After that he wrote in glowing terms about Nehru and also wrote a life of Gandhi.

As Prime Minister, Nehru was methodical and punctual and ordered his life carefully. He took notes of conversations with important visitors and filed them for reference. He was extremely hostile to certain countries and was accordingly curt to their diplomatic representatives in New Delhi. He had no stomach for administrative details and niceties. He was satisfied with issuing broad directives and expected his subordinates to put them into practice. However, he went into details on particular problems of foreign affairs when they interested him.

In the early stages of his prime ministership, he was firm against corruption of any kind. He used to come down heavily on anybody, whether an official or a politician, if any charge of dishonesty or misdemeanour was brought to his notice against the person concerned. This was the pattern from 1947 to 1951, but he gradually began to acquire a tolerance for the malpractices of politicians. He thereupon substituted political expediency for principle in dealing with his ministerial colleagues. Unhesitatingly, he turned a blind eye to a demand by C.D. Deshmukh for the appointment of a high-power Tribunal to eradicate corruption when one of the cases listed by him related to the son of a close colleague.

It was not difficult for a Civil Servant to get Nehru to do what he wanted. There was the instance of an officer, whom Girija Shankar Bajpai, the Secretary-General of the Ministry of External Affairs, wanted to have person appointed as an Ambassador in Europe. When the papers proposing the appointment were taken to Nehru, he hurled them to the floor saying he would never sign them. Next morning, his Private Secretary told him the man might make good in this post. Nehru, however, still refused to sign. A day or two later, the Private Secretary brought up the matter again and Nehru said: "Are you sure he will make good? All right, I shall sign the papers." The man was not a success, but his sponsor was pleased that the appointment had been approved. The day after Nixon's arrival in Delhi (December, 1953) the first Indo-Soviet trade agreement was signed. This was a rebuff to Washington. It meant that the U.S. would lose India and Asia if it followed a policy of divide and rule and tried to build up feudal Pakistan against democratic India.

Canada's Prime Minister, Louis St. Laurent, came in February, 1954 and received a warm welcome. He made it clear soon after arrival that "North America does not mean the United States. Canada attaches great importance to India's role in world affairs." He was asked: "Please tell Washington that by isolating India it will weaken the democratic forces." "Be assured", he responded. "They take from us what they will not take from anyone else."

Tito came in December and was the first head of state to visit India. He travelled like a monarch and the ceremonial platform in New Delhi was found inadequate for the purpose. No protocol was possible, for nothing had been rehearsed. Tito was then isolated and Nehru had attained the status of a world leader. The two found much in common in their outlook and views and the friendship struck between them became a force in global politics. Anxious to develop relations with India, Tito had earlier sent a high-power delegation headed by Vice-President Colakovic. During Tito's visit, Yugoslavia agreed to enter into a trade agreement with India on the basis of payment in rupees.

Nehru, I discovered, was considered pro-communist and anti-U.S. Some Europeans, especially the French, showed a sneaking admiration for Nehru as the man who had ticked off the Americans. They added: "We cannot afford to differ with America."

The only statesman in Europe who appreciated Nehru's constructive role was Chancellor Adeneur. He used to say that Nehru alone was in a position to create confidence between Russia and America. He felt that German reunification and future of Berlin were tied up with the cold war. It was only when both sides accepted co-existence that tension would relax. India and Nehru, he said, were a great factor for peace.

Nehru sponsored the Asian Relations Conference in New Delhi in 1947, with a view to evolving a counter to the United Nations, a whiteman club then. The Conference was designed to express Asia's political viewpoint in the post-war world. But rift amongst the members to the Asian Conference set in right from the outset. According to Werner Levi, a noted writer, "the Conference marked the apex of Asian solidarity and the beginning of its decline, the reasons for this were many and varied; the two major sources of discord were the intense rivalry in-between India and China in the conference and the growing distrust of the two Asian giants among smaller countries of the region."

"The Chinese began protesting against a map displayed at the conference dais which showed Tibet as a separate state; throughout the conference they were found to be more interested in pressing claim for leadership than helping to build up common decisions."[16] Another meeting was held at Delhi with a view to conceiving ways and means of assisting Indonesia in its armed struggle against the Dutch. The same leaders met again in Colombo in 1954 to examine the peace terms regarding Indo-China. The Bandung Conference of 29 Asian nations held in 1955 was the apogee of Pan-Asian solidarity. The Chinese delegates at the Asian Relations Conference had struggled hard to prevent it from coming under Indian patronage. Their efforts met with success at Bandung which was the Achilles heel of India. China's triumph was due to its endeavour to win over Pakistan, Indonesia and other small countries by fluting before them its revulsion of hegemony. India, on the other hand, was unable to manifest any specific goal during the meet. Nehru in his disappointment sentimentally expressed thus: "I say that Europe has been in the past a continent full of conflicts, full of troubles, full of hatred. Europe's conflict continues, its wars continue and we have been dragged into these wars because we were tied to Europe's chariot wheel. Are we going to be tied to Europe's trouble, Europe's hatred and Europe's conflicts? I hope not." Nehru's biographer Michael Brecher complains of his sentimental outlook thus: "the hangover of emotional hostility to the West because of its colonialism affected even a convinced rational like Nehru." Another writer puts it: "flair and feeling take the place of facts and thinking."

The basic objective of each country is the preservation of its territorial integrity, maintenance of its political independence and attainment of a reasonable standard of living for its people. Its foreign policy is based on its ideological aim, its historical ambitions and its physical conditions. The basic factors that contribute to the formulation of its foreign policy are its geographical location, internal homogeneity, economic stability, tradition and technological advancement. Although a country endeavours to attain its foreign policy objectives by peaceful means, yet it may have to resort to war when necessary. It is, therefore, relevant to cite some of the factors that matter in a country's preparation to meet all exigencies. They were enumerated in the Report of the sub-committee of the preparatory commission of disarmament of the League of Nations in 1926: (1) "The extent to which it (the state) is self-supporting (for instance as regards fuel, foodstuffs, raw materials and manufactured goods), and the extent to which, as a result of its means of transport and the freedom of communications, especially its communications by sea, and of its financial strength, it can obtain the commodities of every kind in which it is deficient from abroad. (2) The geographical situation, the configuration of its territory, and the development of its system of means of communication of every kind which might enable or prevent it from rapidly moving and supplying its forces. (3) The capacity of a country to produce or import war materials in war time . . . ."

India's pivotal position in Asia is strategically crucial for world peace because of its close proximity to the Soviet Union and the People's Republic of China. It has a key role to play in the new situation when it has emerged as a centre of potential power in the region where it has significant stakes. It cannot opt out of the power game except at the cost of its freedom and sovereignty. Nehru appreciated this as far back as March, 1949 when he declared in the Constituent Assembly: "If you have to consider any question of affecting the Middle East, India inevitably comes in the picture. If you were to consider any question of South-East Asia, you cannot do so without India. So also with the Far East While the Middle East may not be directly connected with South-East Asia, both are connected with India." But he did not supplement this appreciation. After the two Asian Conferences, he felt and said, "some people talk rather loosely, and, if I may say so, rather foolishly, of India becoming the leader of this or the leader of that or the leader of Asia. Now, I do not like that at all. It is a bad approach, this business of leadership. But it is true that, because of the various factors I have mentioned, a certain special responsibility is cast on India. India realises that and other countries realise it also. The responsibility is not necessarily for leadership, but for taking the initiative some time and helping others to co-operate." Unfortunately India has not developed the status in world power politics commensurate with its location, size, population and potential strength. The American and West European telescope envisages that the future of Asia lies more with Communist China than with India. As a sequel it is Peking's military and diplomatic posture which appears to be the determining factor in shaping the future policy in America and West Europe. India which stands on the cross-roads of the East and the West is far too big to remain in ivory tower or to be blinked by the world powers. It is a massive populous country which has the potential of becoming a powerful nation provided its resources and man power are properly exploited and channelized. The Indian leadership during the Nehru era viewed foreign policy through the global periscope rather than pursuing a more realistic regional approach to make it immune from foreign intervention. The accordance of low priority to its immediate neighbours in South and South-East Asia led to the overseeing of far-reaching economic and political changes. The security of the countries in South and South-East Asia to India is no less important than her own. Compulsion of geography determines that India should be more concerned about its neighbours, particularly in view of its economic stakes, being herself a major economic power in the region. It dawned much later on Nehru that economic, cultural and political cohesion with her neighbouring countries commensurate with the pursuit of a uniform foreign policy for the creation of a zone of peace was more important than expounding grand eloquent sermons on global matters. This he conceded in a letter addressed to the Chief Ministers on 30 December, 1955 when he wrote that "a country like Nepal, although weak is most important to us in the long run than some distant country, however, big or powerful it might be." He added, "geography leads to closer contact with neighbouring countries, unless there are very significant reasons to the contrary. . . . "

China is the most powerful of all of India's neighbours (the Soviet Union does not have common boundaries with India, though its territory is only a few miles away from Kashmir) and Pakistan could be classified as the most hostile. Nepal, Burma, Bangladesh and Afghanistan are other neighbours. To the north, India is separated from China, Tibet and Sinkiang by the great Himalayan wall, which has very few overland passes which are open for only a short while each year. A large scale movement of men or material through these passes is quite arduous if not impossible. Hence, despite the Chinese attack of 1962, "the fact remains that the Himalayas present a mammoth barrier to armed attack, and behind the Himalayas, for a thousand miles, stretches a vast barren plateau with an average height of twelve thousand feet."[17]

Regardless of the protection afforded by its physical features, India's northern frontiers have assumed a great deal of importance since the Communist occupation of China and Tibet and attack on India in 1962. The frontier which is not completely impenetrable is now shared with a powerful neighbour, bigger in size and population and engaged in industrialization and building up its military power. The eastern frontier of India, except for Bangladesh, is almost completely shared with Burma, a country with which India has reasonably friendly relations due to past religious and cultural ties. Most of the western boundary of India is shared with Pakistan —except for a small strip along the Pakistan occupied Kashmir border which is shared with Afghanistan. The boundary lines between India and Pakistan were drawn on a religious basis, and hence do not follow any natural division.[18]

The hostilities which have developed between India and Pakistan since their independence—August 15, 1947—have forced both nations to keep a watchful eye on each other and deploy most of their forces to safeguard their extensive frontiers. This situation led Pakistan into forming closer ties with the Western bloc by joining the South-East Asia Treaty Organization in September, 1954, the Baghdad Pact in September, 1955, and by acquiring military aid from the United States. Pakistan was also successful in forming closer relations with China after the Indo-China conflict of 1962. One of the main reasons for strained relations between India and Pakistan is the Kashmir problem. Kashmir, with an area of 82,000 square miles, has a population of approximately five million; nearly three million of these are Moslems, while two million are Hindus and the rest are mostly Buddhists. On August 15, 1947, when India became independent, the State of Jammu and Kashmir —the official name—was governed by Maharaja Hari Singh,—a lineal descendant of Maharaja Gulab Singh who obtained Kashmir from the British over 100 years ago in exchange for the sum of $ 250,000 and his assistance in the conquest of the Punjab territory.

Under the Government of India Act of 1947, India and Pakistan were carved out of original British India and became two separate Dominions in the British Commonwealth of Nations. At the same time, almost 400 princely states also became independent with the option of acceding to India or Pakistan according to their territorial contiguity. Kashmir was contiguous with India and Pakistan, as well as with Afghanistan, Russia and China. The ruler of Kashmir elected to remain independent—at least for the time being. He offered to enter into a bilateral treaty with India and Pakistan to maintain the *status quo* regarding trade, communications, transportation, etc.

While the negotiations were still in progress, the Kashmiri territory was attacked on October 15, 1947, by Moslem tribesmen from the Pakistan frontier. The raiders quickly overran a considerable part of the territory and were within a short distance of Srinagar, the capital, in the few days.

To gain public support, the Prince established a popular government under Sheikh Abdullah which, in turn, appealed to India for help in defence of the state. In accordance with the British India Act of 1947, an Instrument of Accession was formally signed by the Prince as head of the state, and the accession was accepted by Lord Louis Mountbatten who was then the Governor General of the Indian Dominion. By this act, the State of Jammu and Kashmir became an integral part of the Indian Union, and India was legally able to send her troops to protect her territory. However, at the same time, "India assured the people of Kashmir that after restoration of normal conditions in Kashmir, India would agree to the holding of a free and fair plebiscite to allow the people to decide whether they wished to continue the accession to India or terminate it."[19]

On October 27, 1947, Indian troops arrived in Kashmir while Pakistani regulars joined the tribesmen in their attack (it must be understood that Pakistani troops had no legal status in Kashmir and for a while, Pakistan completely denied the presence of its troops there). "The raiders made large scale sorties and then retired into Pakistan territory. The Indian forces could not follow them for fear of creating an international incident. Discussions at the cabinet level between India and Pakistan failed to resolve the situation."[20]

By the end of December, 1947, Indian Prime Minister Nehru made an appeal to the United Nations Security Counil to consider the Kashmir problem "and to persuade the Pakistan Government to deny aid, personnel, transit, and facilities of all kinds to the raiders. Pakistan in reply characterized the conflict as a widespread popular uprising of the Kashmiri Moslems against the Maharaja's rule; the invading tribesmen and Pakistani nationals were pictured as unorganized volunteers rushing spontaneously and irresistibly to the succour of their endangered co-religionists."[21] The case was argued on the Indian side by Sir Benegal Rao and on the Pakistani side by Sir Zaffrullah Khan. However, in spite of all legal arguments submitted to the Security Council, together with those of political and economic nature, it completely by-passed the legal aspects of the case—the Indian complaint of Pakistani aggression as seen in the light of international law and of the law of partition. The Security Council, instead, concentrated on stopping the conflict, and on the plebiscite.

In 1948, the United Nations appointed a five-power commission, consisting of Czechoslovakia, Argentina, the U.S., Belgium and Colombia, to bring about settlement of the dispute.

In July, 1948, the United Nations Committee for India and Pakistan (UNCIP) was able to bring about a cease-fire agreement. However, it was realized that a plebiscite would not be possible before a truce agreement had been concluded and a plan of demilitarization effected. The Commission recommended that the Pakistan-controlled forces be withdrawn from "Azad Kashmir" and the northern territories, and that withdrawal should include all units of the Pakistan army, Pakistan nationals who came to Kashmir for the purpose of fighting, and tribesmen who had initiated the invasion. As soon as this was done, the Government of India would withdraw the bulk of her army from the other side of the cease-fire line. This was the UNCIP resolution of August 13, 1948.

On January 5, 1949, a second resolution in regard to the plebiscite was issued. The Security Council would nominate a plebiscite administrator who would be appointed to his office by the Government of Jammu and Kashmir. "Both resolutions were accepted by the Governments of India and Pakistan, but it was soon found that the plan was impracticable because after withdrawal of all forces enumerated in the plan, a force of 28 to 30 battalions called the Azad Kashmir Army would have been left on the Pakistan side which would have upset the whole balance of demilitarization."[22] The United Nations' background paper on the Indian-Pakistan question summarizes the situation in the following words: "When the Commission adopted the resolution of 13th August, 1948 the Azad Kashmir forces did not appear to constitute a regular force and it was believed that the disposal of these forces would not create a major difficulty once the regular Pakistan troops had been withdrawn. However, by the time the Commission adopted its resolution of the 5th January, 1949 it was realized that the Azad Kashmir force controlled a large part of the state."[23] Hence the implementation of the truce agreement under the prevailing circumstances was out of the question.

It is interesting to take account of the fact that if the truce agreement had been realized, the plebiscite administrator would have derived his powers from the State of Jammu and Kashmir. Hence, one could infer that from the legal point of view this acknowledged the lawfulness of the Government of the State, which should in principle administer to the whole state. However, a new administration under the name of "The Azad Kashmir Government" had been established on the Pakistan side of the cease-fire line. What status it should have is not clear and has never been clarified by the UN. It would seem that after the ruler of Kashmir acceded to India, only Indian forces would have *locus standi* in the State. But if one is to accept the UNCIP resolution of January 5, 1949, one would be startled to find that aggressors would have been allowed more troops in Kashmir than the Indian Government which is endowed with a legitimate title according to the Plan of Partition of India—The British India Act of 1947.

Negotiations between UNCIP and India and Pakistan soon broke down and the Commission was replaced by a sole mediator, Sir Owen Dickson. Sir Owen, for the first time, tried to define the situation from a legal point of view when he took the position that the crossing of the border of Jammu and Kashmir by hostile elements, and the later entrance by regular Pakistani forces, was contrary to international law. Sir Owen suggested a plan of outright partition or of partition combined with apartial plebiscite limited to an area which would include the Vale of Kashmir. This plan would have left Jammu and Ladakh—non-Moslem areas—permanently on the Indian side and would have transferred to

Pakistan all territories now under her *de facto* control, while deciding the fate of the Vale by plebiscite.

The Government of Pakistan immediately opposed this plan, while the Government of India agreed to discuss it on the basis of certain principles. "The negative attitude of the Government of Pakistan showed clearly that it aims at the inclusion of the whole State of Jammu and Kashmir into Pakistan. Pakistan .... (has been) . . . converted from a Dominion within the Commonwealth of Nations into an Islamic Republic. The inclusion of the Hindu provinces of Jammu and Buddhist Ladakh into this new religious state seems impracticable. In fact, it would be dangerous to leave Ladakh with its strategic and commercial importance, in such a position. Ladakh can find its proper place in the framework of the secular state of India, which controls already other sub-Himalayan territories of Buddhist compostion such as Sikkim and Bhutan. If the Buddhist population of Ladakh which is of Tibetan stock, is pushed into the hands of an Islamic regime, the Lamas of Ladakh who are its leading element may prefer to go back to Tibet[24] and be at least under the spiritual overlordship of the Dalai Lama in Lhasa. This would bring Chinese occupation forces into Ladakh and would make the whole of Kashmir strategically vulnerable. No such solution can be envisaged by the United Nations, India, even by Pakistan."[25]

Sir Owen was replaced by Dr. Frank Graham. Dr. Graham abandoned the plan of possible partition suggested by Sir Owen, and concentrated on a new plan of demilitarization preceding an overall plebiscite. However, Dr. Graham did not fare any better than Sir Owen. He could not bring about any agreement due to "the position of the two governments derived from their differing conceptions of their status in the State",[26] and since Dr. Graham was not authorized by the Security Council to go into the differences of this status from a legal point of view, he was unable to bring the two parties together.

After the unsuccessful efforts of Dr. Graham, the problem of Kashmir was shelved for the time being, due to the suddenly rising problems in the Middle East and Hungary. There were some direct discussions between the Prime Ministers of India and Pakistan, but these were also dropped in May, 1954 when Pakistan was given military aid by the United States. It was not until January, 1957, that Pakistan again revived the Kashmir question in the United Nations. This was due to the fact that in November, 1956, the Constituent Assembly of Kashmir adopted a new constitution making Kashmir a fullfledged state of the Indian Union. This constitution was to take effect on January 26, 1957.

The outcome of the new debate was the adoption of another resolution (S/3793) by the Security Council on February 21, 1957. The resolution requested the President of the Security Council for the month of February, 1957, Mr. Gunnar Jarring, the Representative of Sweden, 'to examine with the Government of India and Pakistan any proposals which, in his opinion were likely to contribute to the settlement of the Indian-Pakistan dispute, having regard to the previous resolutions of the Security Council and of the United Nations Commission for India and Pakistan.' He was further requested to visit the sub-continent for this purpose and to report to the Security Council not later than 15 April, 1957.[27]

Mr. Jarring accordingly arrived in Karachi on March 14, 1957, and held discussions with the Governments of India and Pakistan. The Government of Pakistan claimed that Part I of the UN Resolution of August 13, 1948, requesting Pakistan to withdraw its troops, nationals and tribesmen who had initiated the Kashmir invasion, and to disarm and disband the so-called Azad Kashmir forces, had been implemented. Hence they asked for the compliance of Parts II and III of the resolution, calling for a plebiscite by India. India, on the other hand, gave several reasons for not holding a plebiscite:

(a) It maintained that Pakistan had not complied with Part I of the UN Resolution since there are still about 28 to 30 battalions of the so-called Azad Kashmir forces on the Pakistan side of the cease-fire line.

(b) Secondly, if Clause 6 of the January 5, 1949 Resolution were to be acted upon, all citizens of the State who had left on account of the disturbances would be required to return to their original houses. "At the most conservative estimate, it would involve the movement and uprooting of at least 500,000 persons or more, who are by now settled in every way."[28]

(c) Thirdly, if holding of a plebiscite were to be announced, there would be large-scale migrations of the minorities on either side; the atmosphere would be surcharged with panic and fear, and under such conditions a single incident could cause a great deal of disturbance, which no amount of supervision by the UN would be able to prevent or control. There would also be a strong possibility of the recurrence of religious riots in India and Pakistan.

Upon returning to the UN, Mr. Jarring phrased the conclusion of his report in the following way:

> "While I feel unable to report to the Council any concrete proposals which in my opinion at this time are likely to contribute towards a settlement of the dispute, as I was requested to do under the terms of reference of the Council's resolution of February 21 1957 (S/3793), my examination of the situation as it obtains at present would indicate that, despite the present deadlock, both parties are still desirous of finding a solution to the problem. In this connection the Council may wish to take note of expressions of sincere willingness to cooperate with the United Nations in the finding of a peaceful solution, which I received from both governments.
>
> "The Council will, further more, be aware of the fact that the implementation of international agreements of an *ad hoc* character, which has not been achieved fairly speedily, may become progressively more difficult because the situation with which they were to cope has tended to change."[29]

Putting aside for a moment, the legal, religious and political aspects of the Kashmir problem, one is apt to notice the strategic importance of Kashmir to both India and Pakistan. Kashmir borders on China, the most powerful Communist country in Asia, and second only to the Soviet Union in the Communist world. The north-western border of Kashmir is only a few miles away from the Soviet-Afghanistan border. Hence, whichever country controls Kashmir will be able to watch carefully two of the most powerful Communist countries. The importance of Kashmir also lies in the fact that most of the rivers flowing through northwestern India and Pakistan originate in Kashmir. Hence, the controlling power can greatly diminish the water supply of the other nation. The results of this would be disastrous since both Pakistan and north-western India are agricultural areas. Hence, it is easy to understand why both India and Pakistan are trying hard to gain control of Kashmir.

Nehru was a staunch opponent of colonialism. In his view, the problem of the colonies and dependent countries thus is a vital part of the world problems and an attempt to isolate it results in other problems becoming far more difficult to solution. It was he who took up the issue of apartheid in the UN way back in 1948 : "Obviously there are large regions of the world which have suffered from this question of radical inequality. We also feel that there is no part of the world where it can be tolerated in the future except perhaps because of superior force." The Non-aligned Movement fostered by Nehru has today gained momentum. Many colonies have now liberated themselves. The struggle against recial discrimination is being pursued vigorously. The world will remember him for his sound internationalism.

The country was thrilled with the news that Nehru would visit Peking in response to a pressing invitation by Chou En-lai, who broke journey in New Delhi in June 1954 on his way back from the Geneva Conference on Indo-China. Since Chou had gone to the Geneva Conference in a Chinese-owned Dakota, Nehru decided to fly to Peking in an Indian Dakota. Peking had made great preparations to receive Nehru as the leader of 360 million people. But Nehru was asked to find answers to two questions: Is China Communist first and Asian next? Will it guarantee the safety of the smaller Asian states? Nehru trip to China was marked by an enthusiastic welcome wherever he went. But Nehru was not deceived by this show of goodwill. He said that for all their Communism the Chinese had not changed their traditional outlook. Their country was still the Middle Kingdom. He sensed in the protocol observed during his visit that he was treated as a visitor from an important state which paid tribute to China. That had put him on his guard. The Chinese, he added, talked little and depended on poetic allusions to drive their point home politely. "Time is on our side. They will take long to be a strong, industrial power", was Nehru's consoling conclusion.

Dr. Rajendra Prasad felt very strongly that India's diplomatic approach to China was riddled with weaknesses and a proneness to wishful thinking. The "Hindi-Chini Bhai Bhai (Indians and Chinese are brothers)" honeymoon, did not blind him to Peking's ultimate aims and real feelings towards India. He was greatly upset at the Indian Government's impassivity when Tibet was occupied by the Chinese Reds. His words of caution to Nehru, he said, had fallen on deaf ears. The Prime Minister had been misled by his Ambassador in Peking, Panikkar. With his eyes moistened, Prasad observed: "I hope I am not seeing ghosts and phantoms, but I see the murder of Tibet recoiling on India." Nehru, as everybody knew in Delhi, lost his nerve at the time of the Chinese aggression. His appeal to Kennedy for immediate help included a sentence which said that parting with some territory here or there did not matter in the face of the crisis. That was how Harriman and Sandys were successful in making him reopen the Kashmir question. The situation was retrieved later when Nehru sent them to Morarji Deasi, the hard-liner on Kashmir, who spoke to them sharply and thereby made an enemy of Galbraith. Johnson was also pro-Pakistan to begin with, but he changed his attitude after Ayub started flirting with China. Johnson told Ayub when they met in Washington a folksy story the purport of which was: "You are free to abuse me and America, but I am also free not to help." He was particularly annoyed at the personal abuse showered on him in the Pakistani Press. Ayub promised to set matters right and shook hands.

Egyptian President Nasser, whose enthusiastic friendship for India and regard for Nehru was most heartwarming. He candidly recognised that Israel had come to stay but felt there was a genuine fear that with backing of the Jewish wealth Israel might become a danger to the security of the Arabs.

Following the Franco-British attack on the Suez, the Soviet Ambassador delivered a letter from Khrushchev to Nehru saying that he was issuing an ultimatum to Britain that unless there was a cease-fire by a stipulated time he would attack that country. The threat was not taken seriously in London but Nehru was upset. He quickly drafted a reply to Khrushchev, observing that a second and bigger war was not the way to stop the first and he feared Khrushchev would precipitate a universal conflagration by his action. The letter was delivered to the Soviet Embassy, which at that time occupied Travancore House.

Around midnight, the British High Commissioner, Malcolm MacDonald, wished to see Nehru. But Nehru was infuriated at what he considered the British Government's provocative and irresponsible action in attacking Egypt and refused to see MacDonald, turning him over to N.R. Pillai, the Secretary-General for External Affairs. MacDonald handed Pillai a message from London saying that the British troops engaged in the operations had been asked to cease fire. This was a great relief to the Indian Government, because Nehru had convinced himself that a major clash of arms could not be averted. Nehru backed Nasser to the hilt and Nasser, in turn, accepted the formula prepared by Krishna Menon regarding the Suez Canal. But the British rejected it.

Ali Yavar Jung was India's Ambassador in Cairo at the time of the Suez crisis. His role was to support Nasser in public but restrain him in private. He found the Egyptian President a man of intelligence and common sense; but those around him indulged in bravado and bluff. The question of U.S. economic aid was under consideration. Dulles was very angry with Nasser for recognising China. He also did not like Nasser approaching the Russians for arms. U.S. Congress was against granting much economic aid to the UAR and undertaking the Aswan High Dam project.

Dulles said that Egypt, having pledged its cotton crop to Russia for armaments, was not in a position to pay interest on U.S. investment on the dam and that Washington had decided to drop the project. At that time, Nehru halted at Cairo on his way to Brioni. Jung mentioned this matter to Nehru, who advised Nasser to avoid hasty or drastic action. Nasser promised to do so, but soon after Nehru reached India he announced nationalisation of the Suez Canal. Jung, who had gone to Beirut on holiday, rushed back to Cairo and told Nasser that this would have grave consequences and that Indian public opinion would not favour this step. Nasser did not agree. That very day Jung received a cable from Nehru asking him to tell Nasser that he had acted hastily and that public opinion in India was likely to be unfriendly. Nasser thought Jung had inspired the message!

It is true that while India pioneered that concept of non-alignment and used it as its foreign policy framework even in its embryonic form and indeed demonstrated its efficacy in international affairs for over a decade, even without formally using the term non-alignment, yet it was left to Yogoslavia's Tito and Egypt's Nasser to take the final initiative in the sixties for the formal launching of the movement of the non-aligned and for persuading Nehru to recognise the necessity of establishing a forum and an organisation to build firm solidarity of the non-aligned countries. Nehru's hesitation in the matter of a regular formal structure for the NAM was mainly due to his fear that it might become on the one hand too large and amorphous a group for meaningful concerted political action, and on the other, too bureaucratic in its orientation and thereby lose its political direction. Nehru was temperamentally opposed to forming separate blocs, groups and factions in politics, national and international, hence his continuous word of caution against building a 'third bloc', 'third force', etc. . ., that tended to divide and fragment. To add to this, the trend of Chinese policies towards, and approaches to, international relations in the late fifties, revealing not only an animosity towards India but also opposition to the Soviet Union, resulting in their effort to divide working-class movements, communist parties and regimes in Asia and Africa, created a new and disturbing situation in the ranks of the de-colonized and developing countries, and alarmed India in its initial romantic zeal for some sort of Asian solidarity. Bandung had revealed that the overt and covert pressure of the US and the Western alliance system precluded the formation of strong bonds of unity and solidarity among the newly freed countries. They were divided on all the three major concerns of liberation, security and development. With China playing a different role, the prospects of unity became more bleak. This consciousness was also a factor in Nehru's initial less than enthusiastic support to the proposal for formal structuring of the non-aligned countries. At Belgrade, almost singly and much against the dominant anti-colonial trend of the speeches, Nehru sought to emphasize the other more important factor, that is, the increasing danger of nuclear war and the primacy of peace and peaceful co-existence as the basic challenge of the time. He warned that "if war comes, all is doomed", and underlined "the desirability of peace for ensuring welfare (even) in domestic spheres". While recognizing the fact that "this great movement of freedom from colonial domination (has met) with success, indeed proving that in so far as the historical perspective is concerned the era of classical colonialism is gone and is dead." Nehru said: "I submit that we must look at things in proper perspective today. *First things must come first* and nothing is more important or has more priority than this world situation of war and peace. Everything else, however vital to us—and other things are vital to us—has a secondary place."[30] The greatest factor in India's foreign relations and internal development has been her close ties with the Soviet Union. Their origin and growth were largely the handwork of Nehru and Khrushchev. Mrs. Vijaya Lakshmi Pandit's appointment as the first Indian Ambassador in Moscow pleased the Russians much as she was Nehru's sister. She was given a standing ovation at the Bolshoi Theatre.

Dr. Radhakrishnan, who followed Mrs. Vijayalakshmi Pandit, was liked initially by the Russians because of his reputation as a philosopher and scholar. He retained his Oxford professorship and shuttled between Moscow and London. Since he kept aloof, Stalin thought well of him and granted him two interviews. This pushed up Radhakrishnan in Nehru's estimation. During his tenure, New Delhi's role in bringing about a cease-fire in Korea and in Indo-China opened Moscow's eyes to its growing influence.

The climate in Moscow towards India changed considerably after Nehru visited China in 1954 and was received there, as films and television recordings showed. The Soviet Foreign Office immediately asked our Ambassador to get in touch with Nehru in Peking and ask him to visit Moscow on his way back to New Delhi. Nehru replied that he would visit Moscow separately and not incidentally. This pleased Moscow.

Nehru visited the Soviet Union in June, 1955 and the reception he received on arrival in Moscow was unprecedented—something no visiting head of state or government has received after him. The Russians went all out to fete Nehru. Before his arrival a special study was made of his diets and habit. Nehru travelled in an open car, something unheard of in the Soviet Union, and Bulganin and Khrushchev had to sit or stand with him in it. Thousands of roses were showered on them by the onlookers. The entire Politbureau of the Soviet Communist Party came to dine with Nehru at the Embassy. Proposing a toast, Khrushchev said: "Some say Nehru is a Communist. I do not want him to be a Communist. I want Nehru to be Nehru. So I propose a toast to Nehru".

This visit to Russia made the West feel that it would result in relaxing tension. The feeling in India was one of exultation over the triumphant tour of their national hero. Swept along by the wave, President Prasad decided to bestow the highest honour, 'Bharat Ratna' (Jewel of India), on Prime Minister Nehru. Convention was disregarded and the decoration was awarded at a banquet without a citation. Some felt it was an exhibition of subservience; others thought it was degrading to national pride that a visit to a foreign country, however successful should be so rewarded.

Dr. Prasad said: "Jawahar is literally a *Bharat Ratna.* Why not formally make him one? He has laid the foundation for peace and you will see the visit will prove of historic significance."

We observe with great satisfaction that more recently Nehru's vision has also found articulation in the seminal initiatives taken by Soviet leader Mikhail Gorbachev, on the all-important questions of nuclear disarmament and peace in the Asia-Pacific regions. The crucial issue of peace and freedom from the threat of nuclear warfare has, in our times, acquired a new urgency with the ominous prospect of the militarisation of outer space. Similarly, since the centre of gravity of the world has shifted from Europe to the Asia-Pacific Region over the past half a century, the question of a just peace in this region concerns not only those who reside there but the world as a whole. The recent pronouncements by Gorbachev regarding the issues under consideration, therefore, deserve to be seriously considered by governments and the people. These pronouncements combine realism with idealism in finely balanced proportions. They take a dialectical instead of a mechanical view of the world system. And most important of all, for India and the Third World, they seek to provide the basis of a world community in which the creative capacities of all people—and not only those of a privileged few—will find full scope for expression. Today, we are not far from a new century which offers the prospect of hope and fulfilment for mankind. The wisdom of centuries and the new vistas of science and technology hold out the promise of a new era of moral and material creativity for common men and women throughout the world. We, therefore, appeal to governments and the people to reflect upon the means whereby we can establish durable peace and harness man's productive capacities for bringing into existence a just world.[31]

Nehru seemed to treat every proposal for a presidential tour abroad with reserve, apparently feeling that President Dr. Rajandra Prasad did not project the image of a modern secular India. In the first term, he agreed to his visiting only the Hindu Kingdom of Nepal in 1955. Reluctantly, Nehru agreed to Prasad's visit to Japan in 1958 and thereafter to some South-East Asian countries. The visit was a grand success everywhere. In Japan, at the Emperor's banquet only vegetarian dishes were served 'as a symbol of the reverence in which we hold President Prasad'. At lunch in Hanoi on the day of the Indian festival of Holi, to celebrate Spring, Ho Chi-Minh suddenly rose, smeared Prasad's face with gulal (coloured powder) and embraced him warmly, exclaiming: "We do not differentiate: we follow India." In Sri Lanka, Prime Minister Bandaranaike told him: "India is our mother country; there can be no dispute between brothers."

Soon after his return from a visit to India in 1959, Eisenhower sent a pressing invitation to Prasad to visit the U.S. before he laid his office. He had described Prasad in Delhi as "God's good man" and was keen to take him personally around the country. But between Nehru and the External Affairs Ministry, the proposal was killed. While the Ministry felt the time was not opportune, Nehru went on record to observe: "So many of us have been to America that it does not seem necessary for you to visit the U.S. immediately." The President replied: "I will choose my own time." It was not much different when Queen Elizabeth, during her state visit to India in 1961, urged Prasad to visit Britain in return.

Prasad told me that Nehru studiously excluded foreign affairs from the scope of his talks with him, and even discouraged him from serious discussions with foreign dignitaries visiting India. Prasad's visit to the Soviet Union, in 1960, demonstrated, however, that his presence abroad could benefit India. Prasad avoided talks on foreign policy, but made an intensive and fruitful study of the Soviet educational system, of the country's agricultural development and of the manner in which the Russians had resolved the problem of a national language. He produced a twenty-page note for the Cabinet on language based on the lesson he had gleaned from his Russian visit.

The President was a man of erudition and had a firm grasp of national problems. He used to write to Nehru on a wide variety of subjects, political, social and economic. He did this because he could not speak freely in Nehru's presence. He did avoided a dialogue. He appeared to suffer from an inferiority, even fear-complex in the presence of Nehru. Wherever he was urged to convert his meetings with Nehru into a dialogue, he would say that would inevitably lead to disagreement and passionate argument.

The note to Nehru on corruption was perhaps the strongest Prasad ever penned. "Corruption", he said, "will verily prove a nail in the coffin of the Congress." Prasad strongly supported C.D. Deshmukh's proposal for a tribunal or an Ombudsman, directly under the President or as an independent authority to inquire into charges of corruption and maladministration. Nehru did not reply to the note in writing; instead, he complained to Prasad personally about what he called "an unfriendly suggestion." Prasad said that he was deeply hurt at this misinterpretation of his motives and abjured Nehru to look into the future and see whether such measures were not necessary.

While studying Nehru's socialism we were in search for a definition of the concept of socialism itself. In course of this search we came to the conclusion—tentatively perhaps, for there can be no finality about such a conclusion—that the three basic ingredients of socialism were (i) recognition of the existence of class conflict, (ii) belief in social ownership of the means of production, and (iii) acceptance of the goal of a classless society. We have since traced the development of Jawaharlal's thinking from the early days of his boyhood to the closing years of his life, and to an extent analysed his action both as a leader of the freedom movement before independence, and as Prime Minister after independence, leading the country to his avowed goal. Our focus has, of course, been on socialism to the exclusion of other aspects of his thoughts and activities, such as his inter-national outlook and consequently his foreign policy, and his views on a variety of national problems, such as religious sectarianism, regionalism, linguism, etc., except to the extent that these impinge on his social outlook and are relevant for understanding his socialist views. On the basis of this review, where does Nehru stand in regard to the three criteria mentioned above?[32]

On the first criterion, namely, recognition of the existence of class conflict, there is no doubt that till the end of his days he never denied the existence of classes, nor the fact that the interests of the classes clashed. A certain mellowness had indeed crept into his views in this respect, as in several other respects. It will be recalled that in April 1936, writing to Mrs. Agatha Harrison, Mahatma Gandhi, who knew Jawaharlal well, had said that 'he (Jawaharlal) does not believe it possible to avoid it' (class war). In his later days, as Prime Minister, however, he not only sought to avoid class war but believed it possible to do so. Speaking to R.K. Karanjia in his series of interviews during 1963-64, for instance, Jawaharlal stated: "Class struggle is always there. One cannot deny it or put it aside. But the solution need no longer be one of violence or struggle or hatred; and that's where Gandhiji's peaceful approach, friendly and constructive approach, comes in. . . Marx was conditioned by his times where there was no democracy or franchise, no working class movement and—well, simply no means of resolving inequalities and equalising society other than struggle . . . Now while the nuclear energy holds out tremendous hope for human advancement, the atom bomb threatens to blow up civilisation with one or two or three hangs—thus the emergence of such a destructive weapon makes conflict or war, be it in form of class struggle or capitalist-socialist conflict, simply so disastrous that it is impossible to think of solutions in terms of violence at all . . ."[33]

There is force in the view of Nehru that democracy, even parliamentary democracy of what the Marxist would call the bourgeois type, provides opportunities for class struggle to be resolved in a peaceful manner. It is also true that with the development of nuclear technology the alternative of a violent class struggle is too dangerous to contemplate. Nevertheless, the Marxist argument cannot be denied that a bourgeois democracy, that is, a democracy not preceded or followed by a social revolution, cannot usher in a classless society. There is indeed nothing to prevent a determined Socialist Party winning the confidence of the deprived classes who, specially in underdeveloped countries, constitute the majority of the electrorate, and thus going ahead with a socialist programme. This, however, needs in the words of Prof. Gyan Chand, quoted earlier, "a dynamic technique of social change not inherent in parliamentary democracy. The inadequacy of Jawaharlal's view lies in his belief that the democratic processes by themselves provide sufficient opportunities for resolving the class struggle peacefully.

The second criterion we have adopted is 'belief in social ownership of the means of production'. To what extent did Nehru hold this belief? The type of economy which he actually created in India is what is known as the Mixed Economy in which private ownership plays an important role. We have noted how Jawaharlal justified this role at the initial stages as a transitional phenomenon. Later, however, he felt that Mixed Economy was inevitable in a democracy, but all through it was his firm belief that the public sector should set the tone of the economy by occupying its commanding heights and that the private sector should function in accordance with the pattern set by the Five Year Plans. We have noted that neither of these actually happened, and that in fact the logic of the situation was such that the private sector continued to dominate the economy. Nevertheless, whether or not it could be achieved in practice, Jawaharlal obviously believed in social ownership of the means of production and accepted it as his objective, leaving private ownership to play a subsidiary role.

At the same time, Jawaharlal was apprehensive of centralisation of powers, whether it happened in private hands or in those of the State. Perhaps this was one of the considerations why he did not wish to eliminate private ownership of the means of production altogether. In a modern economy, centralisation was unavoidable, he reflected, but he had no intention to be submerged by it. State control of all economic activities certainly yielded certain results, but it also developed bureaucracy, he thought, in an extreme measure and suppressed individual freedom.

Our third criterion is the goal of a classless society. The socialists share this objective with the democrats, with the difference that while the former focus attention on classes in capitalist societies, and therefore yearn for a classless society, the latter do not view society as consisting of classes but recognise the inequality which exists between men and consequently put forward 'Equality' and 'Fraternity', the famous slogans of the French Revolution, as their ideal. In this respect, Jawaharlal would be included in the former category, for he believed in the existence of class struggle, as he often called it. To him, therefore, democratic equality was only possible in a classless society.

On all the three criteria referred to, therefore, Nehru can be adjudged a socialist, but such a judgement would at best be a partial one, an inadequate and unsatisfying view of his outlook. Indeed, it is difficult to classify Jawaharlal as an adherent of any definite set of ideas, or of an ideology, for perhaps the most prominent trait of his thinking was a dislike, almost an obsessive dislike, for any form of dogmatism. He liked Marxism because it gave a "scientific" explanation of the historical processes, but criticised the Communists because of their tendency to treat Marxism as a "holy doctrine". He emphasised the dynamic nature of society and considered some of Marx's conclusions out of date, not because Marx was wrong when he arrived at these conclusions, but because some subsequent developments, such as growth of democracy and technological advance, had invalidated these conclusions. He was anxious not to be left behind by history, and was keen to be abreast of developments, historical, technological and ideological.

And yet, it would be wrong to consider that Nehru had no basic convictions, no basic ideology. Certain values, both positive and negative, he adhered to all his life. Negatively, he was anti-fascist all his life with a deep dislike for totalitarianism. Positively, he believed in human values, in the dignity of the individual, and therefore in civil liberty. These made him a democrat, but he realised that democracy in the capitalist context could not ensure human dignity. There could be no human dignity without individual liberty—liberty, not merely in the form of absence of physical restraint, but perhaps, more importantly, in that of freedom from want, freedom to develop one's talent and one's personality as one pleases. It was this wider concept of liberty that attracted him to socialism and it was to this that he gave his unswerving loyalty all his life.

This approach to socialism from the humanistic, liberal point of view made Jawaharlal's socialism more progressive than the socialism professed by Social Democrats all over the world, not excluding the non-Communist socialists in India. "The a-outrance fight is between the communists and democrats the world over", declared Asoka Mehta, an eminent Indian socialist. Indeed, he lamented that "towards the communists he (Nehru) has an instinctive indulgence that has weakened the differences of democracy, particularly in his own party. In the result an indulgent attitude towards the communists is deemed to be mark of a progressive, of being loyal to the legacy of Nehru."[34]

Ashoka Mehta is right in his characterisation of Nehru, but not so right in holding that there is a basic fight or conflict between democracy and communism. The difference between socialism and communism, as Nehru was never tired of pointing out, was confined to the means or the methods adopted, not to the objectives or the ideals. No socialist, or for that matter, no democrat can, without being false to his own values, disagree with the communist ideals. The flight between the communists and the socialists cannot be extended beyond the field of methods without endangering the democratic values themselves. Unfortunately, this distinction has not been observed by Social Democrats of Ashoka Mehta's persuasion, and the fight has been carried by them to the extent of supporting reactionaries and neo-colonialists, with the result that the Social Democrats are in danger of losing their professed values. It is to the credit of Jawaharlal Nehru that in spite of severe provocations, first during the Quit India movement in 1942, and later after Independence in the form of the Telengana revolt, he never lost his perspective. While he pulled no punches against the Indian communists, whom he once described as the "stupidest party", who have done more harm to communism than their avowed opponents, he never made the mistake of denigrating the communist ideal or showed any sympathy for anti-Communism. "The universalistic content" of socialism, to use economist P.C. Joshi's phrase, is no different from the "universalistic content" of communism, and Nehru could not condemn the latter without giving up the former, which he never did. Indeed, the democratic views find fulfilment in socialism and it was to seek this fulfilment that Nehru adopted socialism from the democratic point of view.

This approach to socialism has given wide currency to an image of Jawaharlal as a liberal democrat with a certain romantic attachment to socialism. The image derives support because it is partly true. He certainly believed in liberal, democratic views all his life, but his attachment to socialism was much more than romantic. Liberalism lacks a social framework in which liberal values can be realised. Capitalism is an inadequate vehicle for the realisation of these values. Socialism provides an alternative framework. The liberal values of human dignity, of individual personality can be developed better in a classless society, where individuals are free from want and oppression, than in a *laissez-faire* economy where competition, fair or otherwise, exalts the strong, leaving the Devil to take the hindmost. It was this realisation that gradually grew on Jawaharlal from the early days of his Fabian association to the Congress in 1927 when the "Oppressed met at Brussels", as he put it in his *Autobiography*.

This was more than a romantic attachment to socialism, and in this respect he did not change till the end of his life. It is true that he took certain steps as Prime Minister which can find little support in the views he expressed in the thirties, and omitted to take others which consistent with these views he should have taken. These have been noted and commented upon in some detail earlier. Nehru can well be criticised for these acts of commission and omission, but such criticisms do not reflect on his allegiance to certain basic values, though they do indicate a change of emphasis.

Nevertheless, with age certain new trends were noticeable in his thinking. A trend which is discernible in his *Discovery of India*, as we have noted earlier, is a search for values, other than the material values offered by socialism, to make for a full life. There were certain matters, he felt as we have noted, beyond the sphere of science, like appreciation of good music or art where material values were of little help. Speaking to R.K. Karanjia much later in the sixties on the problem of leisure, he said: ". . . I wonder if a problem like this can be tackled scientifically to the exclusion of other values. What appears to be wanting is—I do not know how to put it—except to say that it is an ethical aspect which might be wanting some spiritual solution." To which Karanjia put the further query: "Is it not unlike the Jawaharlal Nehru of yesterday, Mr. Nehru, to talk in terms of ethical and spiritual solutions? What you say raises visions of Mr. Nehru in search of God in the evening of his life." Jawaharlal's reply showed his mind : "If you put it that way, my answer is: Yes, I have changed. The emphasis on ethical and spiritual solution is not unconscious. It is deliberate, quite deliberate . . . . I do not happen to be a religious man, but I do believe in something—call it religion or what you like—which raises man above his normal level and gives the human personality a new dimension of spiritual quality and moral depth. . . ."[35]

Another trend which grew with age was the feeling that subsequent developments had made many of the communist beliefs out of date. Never a believer in dogmas, Jawaharlal always tried to keep his views abreast of the latest developments, but it was in later years that he emphasised that such recent developments as democracy with wide franchise and full personal and organisational freedom, and also technological advances had invalidated several Marxist conclusions. In regard to democracy, for instance, he said in his Note on the "Basic Approach", to which reference has been made in Chapter 9, ". . . Capitalism allied to democracy has undoubtedly toned down many of its evils and in fact is different now from what it was a generation ago. ..." and then added, "Various democratic processes interfere which these normal trends (of Capitalism). Capitalism itself has developed some socialist features even though its major aspects remain." This view, though contrary to current communist belief, is not entirely a novel one. In an article little known and rarely quoted, which appeared in the New York Daily Tribune on 25 August, 1852, Karl Marx had observed : "Universal suffrage is the equivalent of political power for the working class of England. . . . . The carrying of universal suffrage in England would, therefore, be a far more socialist measure than anything which has been honoured with that name on the Continent. Its inevitable result here is the political supremacy of the working class."

A second factor which Jawaharlal referred to was the technological development in recent years. He was of the view that Marx had formulated his thesis in the context of an economy of limited productivity, if not of scarcity. In this context the struggle between the capitalists and the workers to share the limited product had naturally to be keen. The struggle has, however, lost much of its keeness with technological advances and this will happen more and more as technology advances further. Indeed, a stage can be envisaged when enough will be produced for all, and the need for struggle to ensure equitable distribution will cease to exist. Theoretically, such a possibility certainly exists, but with even a mature capitalist democracy like the United States suffering from chronic unemployment, which is specially high among the black population, and persistent inflation and the consequent hardship, it is far cry for underdeveloped economies like those of India and other Afro-Asian or even Latin American countries.

Another aspect of technological innovation which entered Nehru's thought was the tremendous destructive capacity of the thermo-nuclear weapons. This development, he thought, made any violent struggle, be it class war or international war, unthinkable. The Marxist theory of a violent path to socialism, whether within a country or outside, was therefore out of date.

With all these heterodox thought, Nehru still remains a socialist. He was a liberal, a democrat, a socialist and to an extent, a communist too. He was all these, but could not be labelled as any one of these in particular to the exclusion of the other. The difficulty of fitting in Jawaharlal Nehru's views into any of these accepted categories arises because of the definitions attached to these categories which are rigid and mutually exclusive. To Jawaharlal Nehru, who was almost allergic to any kind of rigidity, the values represented by the categories referred to were not mutually exclusive. Indeed, as has been noted earlier, Nehru saw no contradiction between individualism and socialism. Similarly, according to him there was no contradiction between democracy and socialism. On the contrary, socialism was the fulfilment of democratic values, and democracy was the vehicle for ushering in socialism. Nor was there any contradiction between socialism and communism, only the methods adopted were different.

Nehru was undoubtedly a socialist, but as P.C. Joshi has said, "Nehru's thinking implies a clear distinction between the univer-salistic content of socialism whish should guide socialists in all countries, and the specific socialism which would differ from country to country in accordance with the economic, social, cultural and political condition of each country."[36] It was to the former that he owned allegiance, while he retained the right not only to determine the form of socialism and the path to it in his own country but also to criticise the form and the path adopted in other countries. If a lable has to be attached to this thinking, the nearest approach would be that of a "Social Democrat" but with the important difference that he had no hostility towards the communists. Of this he gave ample evidence all his life, both in national and in international politics.

After more than three decades of independence India is still precariously perched on her path to socialism. Indeed, the forces of capitalist development, call them those of reaction or otherwise, have proved stronger than those of socialism. To this extent the social content of India's freedom movement, to which Jawaharlal Nehru often referred, has been belied, for the time being at any rate. Whether these capitalist forces, subject to their own contradictions, specially in a poor, harshly non-egalitarian society, will give rise to counter-forces which will overwhelm them is for the future to reveal. The fact, however, remains that in spite of the socialist vision of Jawaharlal Nehru the forces of socialism failed to entrench themselves during more than a decade and a half of his prime ministership, and have lost ground considerably in a decade and a half since his demise. What then was his contribution to socialism in India? Did he advance the socialist cause in the country, or with his powerful personality and immense popularity did he act as a brake on Indian socialism? Is socialism in India stronger because of him, or would it have progressed faster without Nehru?

On one point there is not likely to be any difference. Though not poineer of socialism in India, a claim which he himself had denied, he was one of the early socialists in the country. When he returned to India at the end of 1927, after a sojourn in Europe of a year and a half, the Soviet revolution was less than a decade old, and few in India, apart from students and intellectuals, had given thought to socialism. It was certainly not a popular creed. Jawaharlal had, however, by 1927 attained a stature in the Congress and in the country, and when straight from Europe he attended the Madras session of the Congress his views received attention, though not acceptance, at the highest nationalist level. Indeed, as we have noted, Gandhiji admonished him for proceeding too fast. He could be criticised, and he was criticised, but he could not be ignored.

The years that followed added depth to Nehru's socialist views. Some success also came his way. The Karachi session of the Congress in 1931 adopted for the first time a resolution advocating social ownership of key industries. Jawaharlal continued with his campaign for socialism, and this undoubtedly had considerable influence on the youth of the country. Socialism gradually got entwined with nationalism, and became a part of the ethos of the freedom movement of the country. The agrarian movement in the early thirties in U.P., which he led with the approval of the Congress and of Mahatma Gandhi, had a distinct social content, unlike the agrarian movement in Bardoli, which was purely political. On the other hand, the socialist movement sponsored by Nehru was essentially a part of the Congress nationlist movement, and suffered from the constraint which a nationalist movement, in which person professing different social outlooks participated, necessarily imposed.

Nehru has been criticised for not joining the Congress Socialists, who had formed a separate group in the thirties. The group had been inspired by the socialist ideals of Jawaharlal Nehru, and looked up to him for leadership. Jawaharlal, on the other hand, though he supported and often defended the group against the criticism of the Congress Right, never formally joined it. We have discussed earlier the reasons which held Jawaharlal back from the group, and we came to the conclusion that by remaining within the mainstream of the Congress movement Jawaharlal was able to project his socialist views from a position of authority, first in the Congress and later in the Government. This was a distinct gain for socialism in India, but we have also noted that both in the Congress and perhaps more so in the Government, even when he was in control of both, he deffered to and allowed himself to be influenced by the views of the non-socialist elements with whom he worked. Could this have been avoided? Could he have contributed more to socialism in India by joining the socialists who seceded from the Congress after Independence and assuming their leadership, or could he, by the authority that he enjoyed on the basis of mass support in the country, have made both the Congress organisation and the Government organisation fit instruments for a socialist transformation of the Indian society?

The answer to the first question, we have already suggested, is in the negative. The socialists who seceded from the Congress, as Jawaharlal had himself occasion to remark, lost themselves in semantics, unable to find a clear path between socialism and Gandhism and splintered themselves into groups. They ceased to be an effective force as their performance in successive general elections showed. It is difficult to believe that these men who, distrustful of Nehru's leadership, broke away from the Congress, would have listened to him even if he had offered to lead them. As Chalapathi Rau has remarked, "to depend on these elements and weaken the Congress did not seem to Nehru a service to the country. He had not thought of himself in isolation from the Congress, and there was no certainty that non-Congress socialists would listen to him if he were to be detached from the Congress . . . . . ."[37]

On the other hand, with the undoubted support he enjoyed in the country it is reasonable to suggest that Nehru could have attained greater success than he did in remoulding both the Congress and the Government machinery. As he had himself told R.K. Karanjia, the Congress and country would go as far towards socialism as he was prepared to lead them, but this required not only leadership but an organisation. It was in the latter respect that Jawaharlal failed. While he provided the ideology which was explicit and which made radical commitments, "practical politics", in the words of Gunnar Myrdal quoted earlier, "moved in a pragmatic and conservative direction." The commitments were distorted because the organisations which should have translated the commitments into action were still manned, both at the political and at the official levels, by individuals who had no such commitments themselves.

Nehru's comparative lack of success in this direction can be attributed to his style of functioning, indeed, in the words of P.C. Joshi, to "the apathy of Nehru and his like-minded followers to the painstaking work of socialist organisation, specially at the grass-roots." As Joshi has stated, "Nehru even during the period when he was a fighter rather than a ruler, was in the habit of functioning as an inspired individual, the hero of the masses, rather than their organiser or as an educator of socialist cadres from among the masses . . ." "Thus occurred the chronic schism", Joshi adds, "between idea and organisation. Fired by a 'grand idea', Nehru tirelessly carried on a national campaign for socialism and evoked wide response for a change in the socialist direction. But he did not create the supporting socialist organisation. So the response remained only amorphous and diffused and could not assume any solid, organised shape."[38]

This is precisely what happened. Nehru concentrated on "training people's mind" which, according to Gunnar Myrdal, "was a rationalistic variation of Gandhi's prescription of change of heart." He put in a massive effort to turn the country into "a land of Nehrus", to use R.K. Karanjia's phrase, but his democratic instinct, his code of conduct towards his colleagues, prevented him from forcing the pace even to the extent that the democratic processes permitted. He preferred to convert his colleagues rather than overrule or discard them, and refrained from building up committed cadres to implement his policies. Nevertheless, it would be wrong to think that he achieved no result, or that his contribution to the socialist cause in India was negligible. The basic ingredients of a socialist structure, the concepts of modernisation and secularism, and those that received institutional form, such as planning, the public sector, the harnessing of science and technology to economic advancement, have not only endured but have shown a resistance which reactionary forces dare not challenge directly.

And yet, Nehru's contribution to socialism in India suffers when viewed on the background of the potentialities the movement had after Independence. It is not so much the slow progress of socialism under Nehru's prime ministership that attracts criticism, but his failure to forge an effective instrument of socialist action which could ensure socialist development, irrespective of individual leadership. It does not detract from Nehru's idealism, his sincerity of purpose and his faith in socialism and democracy to point out that post-independence India offered him opportunities to realise his vision on an enduring basis which he failed to avail himself of fully.

Nevertheless, in assessing Jawaharlal's overall contribution one can fully endorse what a keen observer of world affairs and one who was closely associated with him in formulating and implementing his foreign policy, K.P.S. Menon, has said of him:

"The reason why the Chinese Revolution of 1911 was followed by a more bloody revolution is that the former was, or turned out to be, purely a political revolution. Our Revolution of 1947, on the contrary, was intended to be not merely a political, but a social and economic revolution. But for Jawaharlal Nehru our movement for independence, too, might have become a purely political affair. Gandhiji's supreme contribution was that he gave an ethical content to our movement for independence. Jawaharlal Nehru's contribution was that he gave an economic content. His goal, which has finally been accepted by the Congress and the nation, was a socialistic pattern of society."[39]

And K.P.S. Menon's warning in this connection also deserves to be heeded:

"The basic principles for which Nehru stood, namely, secularism, democracy, a socialistic pattern of society, and the policy of non-alignment, have sunk into the minds of the people. Yet raucous voices are heard doubting the wisdom of these principles and demanding that they should be modified, if not abrogated. If such voices prevail, the result will be a counter-revolution, which is sure to be followed as day is followed by night, by a second, gruesome revolution, destroying many of the values for which India has stood from ancient times."[40]

These "raucous voices" have become shriller in the decade-and-half since Nehru's death, and the socialist consciousness he sought to build up in the country so assiduously, first as a freedom fighter and later as the Prime Minister, is indeed in danger of being overwhelmed by those forces which had developed even during his lifetime but which undoubtedly gathered considerable momentum after his death. And yet there is no reason to despair and to hold that the socialist endeavour of Jawaharlal Nehru has left no lasting imprint on the Indian scene. In spite of all the faults that an analysis of his policies might reveal, and obvious weaknesses in the implementation of these policies, his general direction and broad strategy are as valid today as they were in his time. The growing millions of India, growing both in numbers and in consciousness, cannot for any length of time be held down to the humiliating state of poverty below the subsistence level, in which they live at present. A reversion to the Nehru framework is inevitable if a catastrophe is to be avoided, and India has both the genius and the resources to avoid such a catastrophe. Chastened by the experience of the Nehru period, it will be possible to build anew on his framework. Meanwhile, and until the democratic process works out the alternatives, there has to be a ceaseless effort to improve on Nehru's policies, to profit by his failures and, above all, to keep the flame of hope and faith in democratic socialism alive.

In a democratic country like India we cannot think of any social objective which does not touch the vast masses of the people. This is a profound statement that unfolds the life's purpose of the great son of India who laboured for the economic emancipation of his countrymen after freeing them from political serfdom. This traumatic declaration was made by Jawaharlal Nehru before a galaxy of industrialists and economists, both as a challenge and as an inspiration.

Nehru had the vision of the kind of socialism that suited the Indian environment on an enduring basis. An early votary of British Fabian socialism, Nehru's ideas were influenced by Sydney and Beatrice Webb, Harold Laski and Bernard Shaw. He intended to create a society in which every individual had an equal opportunity to develop and progress. There was a deep sense of history and an abiding commitment to a scientific secular outlook in him. For him, planning basically implied the extension of the domain of rationality from the individual to the area of social decision-making.[41]

At home, Nehru intended to create a society in which every individual had an equal opportunity to develop and progress. An admirer of Russian experiment, Nehru distilled his own brand of socialism with a deliberate attempt to effect a compromise between extreme totalitarianism and a system that would ensure freedom for the individual to develop his personality in his own way. And in this task, Nehru emerged as a heroic blender of opposites, with malice towards none and charity for all shades of ideas, he drew the best from differing political ideologies with great circumspection that was so characteristic of his own. Nehru believed in socialism not merely in the humanitarian sense but in its welfare ethos as well. On economic matters, for example, Nehru never tried to glorify the State at the expense of the common man. Rather, he wanted to utilise the State in order to glorify the cause of the common man. His socialism included nationalisation of the primary means of production, distribution and exchange. And yet, unfortunately, one of the abiding ironies of the Nehru phenomenon has been that his economic and socialist ideas were not easily grasped and rightly interpreted even as they were not that inscrutable. In the dithering economic situation that was yet to form its shape after the country's freedom from foreign rule, unwittingly our economic and socialist distorted his views by drawing an invidious cleavage between the philosophies of Gandhi and Nehru on vital economic issues. However, what Nehru was doing by unfolding his socialist ideas was nothing but taking the Gandhian ideology to its logical conclusion in the social milieu of India. The disciple of Gandhi did it because he believed in its strength and viability, and not because he was a blind follower. But Nehru's convictions created for him problems on his own road to socialism through nationalism. One difficult task for him was to take the Indian National Congress along with him. Besides he wanted to restructure India on the socialistic pattern by involving the inteligentsia, the scientists, the administrators, the economists and the common man. On the top of this all, people were not yet fully convinced of socialism which was looked at with scepticism. A down-to-earth social reformer, Nehru embodied in himself the humanity personified for whom no cause was dearer to his heart than wiping out the tears from the face of every citizen of India. Today, the Nehru philosophy serves as an inspiration and illuminated the right path more brightly. The economic conditions prevailing in the country in the present times do vindicate the strength and pragmatism in the density of Nehru's ideas. After his death, his ideas on issues like socialism, inequality of incomes, planning and the role of the states sector, somehow got overshadowed in fruitless quibblings in the wake of the impact of new economic theories propounded by western economists—theories that mere irrelevant for developing economies. Our planners also started fumbling for what the western economists and their deceptive experiences had to deliver by way of magic formulae. The result was that the pace of development could not match the efforts put in. Nehru saw planning as a powerful motive force which could liberate the latent energies of vast masses of people and deploy them productively in bringing about what he called the socialist pattern of society.

Nehru's pragmatism made him zealously adopt the middle path—neither complete communism which he abhorred, nor the free enterprise of a capitalistic order. In this exercise of a splendid compromise, Nehru achieved the best of both the world, *viz.*, the dynamism of capitalism and the discipline of communism, in the capitalistic system Nehru saw the evils of an acquisitive tendency but he gave the devil his due when he said, "The capitalistic system had undoubtedly served humanity well in the past, but today it seems to be out of date." The economist in Nehru put his finger at the right place when he remarked, "Capitalism having solved the problem of production, has failed to meet the greater challenge of distribution. That was inevitable because its basic inequalities and faith in the blind forces of the market made it impossible for the capitalist system to organise equitable distribution of wealth and purchasing power." The mischief of capitalism is thus analysed in the most rational manner with emphasis on organising a proper distribution system in the economy.

Through socialism, Nehru believed in the possibilities of the vast revolutionary changes in the national and international social structure. Socialists of all brands, from Utopian to Scientific, agree that socialism is a means for social reconstruction. Nehru starts from the same fundamental and as he proceeds, he finds his own way of working it out.

We may recall that Rousseau propounded the basis of inequality among men by pointing out that the progress of science degraded the morals of men. Proudhon declared property as robbery and found it as the fountain-head of inequality. Gandhi branded him a thief who ate without work. And when Nehru thought of the equalisation of wealth, he meant by it equalisation through plenty. His views tended to suggest at times that he would prefer inequality without poverty to equality with poverty. He wanted to fight inequality not because it was bad *per se* but because it had a tendency to breed poverty.

Nehru allowed both private and public sectors to grow as complementary to each other. His emphasis on heavy industries was the theme of an effort towards a self-generating economy, to make India capable of producing what it sought from outside and free it ultimately from the psychological and practical burdens of foreign dependency. With fast developments in science and technology, Nehru would have betrayed conservatism and lack of foresight had he not tried to modernise India's heavy industry sector. That the use of modern science and technology was unavoidable was the central focus of Nehru thought. The mighty industrial structure of today's India has not only raised the status in the eyes of the world but has also triggered off the development process at a much faster speed.

Truth must triumph, said Mahatma Gandhi. That mankind must survive in cooperation was the clarion call of Jawaharlal Nehru to the whole world. This international statesman gave as much wisdom to the world as he did at home on social transformation. His greatest contribution is the conviction that 'India will pull itself up by work and sacrifice, if it consents to do so, but never, never under the knout.' And thus, Nehru proved that he understood the 'seamy side of life' although no less a person that his father, Motilal Nehru, was sceptical in his life-time about this aspect of Jawahar's personality. Nehru the socialist craved to establish a society where the suffering people are fully covered by various social security measure. Nehru, the economist, would like to fulfil this dream only as a by-product of development, not as its prerequisite.

For Nehru freedom of the press consisted essentially of editorial freedom and not of freedom of the owners of the press. He disliked press barons and barons of all kinds and post-war developments in the Indian press oppressed him so much that he took interest in the appointment of the Press Commission. I saw on his table a copy of the report of the British Press Commission often in those days when he repeatedly challenged the foundations of the press in India. As President of the Federation of Working Journalists, I made the appointment of a Press Commission the theme of my presidential address at the Calcutta session in 1952 and got a resolution passed by the session demanding the appointment of a commission and suggesting the terms of reference, when no other organisation wanted such an inquiry. I forwarded the resolution to him before leaving for China as a member of the official delegation led by Mrs. Pandit. There I was pleasantly surprised to learn that the President's Address to the new Parliament indicated the appointment of a Press Commission. Jawaharlal took interest in the selection of the personnel and then followed closely the work of the Commission giving evidence, before it informally. If some of the Commission's recommendation have not yet been carried out, it was not his fault. He provided a Bible for the press, and he was a constant chastiser of monopolies. He knew the set-up so well that at his press conferences, which were free-for-all affairs, he knew who was behind each questioner and what was behind each question. He never failed to inspire fear in the vested interests. Jawaharlal was a passionate defender of press freedom, as a part of the larger freedom. He stood for tolerance, and there may be increasingly less of it. He stood for standards and values, and these may suffer gradually. He distrusted monopoly, and the monopolists are happy he is gone. He looked forward to mass circulations, but like the Press Commission, he wanted the press to develop on the basis of democratic, widely diffused ownership. For those interested in the legacy he left behind, there will be much in the heritage of values he left for the press.[42]

There were only three effective spokemen of the Opposition during the Nehru era. They were S.P. Mookerjee, Kripalani and Lohia. The first was a real leader because he spoke for the largest group which opposed Nehru's policies. In oratory and debating skill, he excelled all others who have followed him. Kripalani was always the dissenter and a lone performer. He would have been more effective had he led an Opposition bloc. Lohia ruthlessly attacked Nehru at every opportunity, repeatedly accusing him of spending Rs. 25,000 a day on himself as Prime Minister in maintaining a large retinue of assistants and body-guards and a "luxurious" standard of living. Lohia callled Indira Gandhi a "dumb doll".

Mookerjee used to say that the only way to create an alternative to the Congress was to demolish Nehru's image. He died while in detention in Srinagar in 1953, and a promising political career was thus cut short. Kripalani too believed the evils in the country emanated from the top and that Nehru was the pace-setter in abusing patronage and power. Lohia believed that the Nehru family's identification with the nation was not only undemocratic but harmful and that Nehru's acceptance of Anglo-Indian cultural values led to his opposing anything that would give the nation a sense of Indianness.

Lohia is reported to have said several times that the North, especially the U.P., had remained backward because the Prime Minister had always been chosen from this region. This made the holder of the office lean over backward to please the South in planning economic development and the allocation of important portfolios in the Cabinet.

Nehru had his own plans for his daughter—plans which some of us clearly discerned. That was the time when people at home and abroad had started asking: "After Nehru, who ?" All manner of guesses were being made. However, few realised then that Nehru was, in point of fact, building up Indu, as he affectionately called her, to carry forward the Nehru legend for the third successive generation. It was not without reason that he had welcomed her idea of retaining use of her maiden name after marriage to Feroz Gandhi and calling herself Indira Nehru-Gandhi.

In fact, Nehru's succession plan was disclosed in the *Hindustan Times* as early as 18th June, 1957. Someone stated: "It is wrong to suggest that Mr. Nehru is trying to build up Mr. Menon, or anyone else, as his successor. If Mr. Nehru is consciously building up anyone, he is building up his daughter." That was shortly after Nehru had gone to London for the Commonwealth Prime Ministers' Conference and taken Menon along. Menon was then a member of the Cabinet and the fact that a Minister was accompanying the Prime Minister for the first time to the Conference had encouraged talk that Nehru was building up Menon for succession.

Abul Kalam Azad had independently reached the same conclusion. Of course, I had good reasons for my surmise on the succession question. India's first Prime Minister Jawaharlal Nehru had tremendous faith in the youth of India and he always inspired them with his ideas. He loved children and the children loved *Chacha Nehru* (Uncle Nehru). Nehru was a superb performer and the people loved him. He always dramatised his role and was so sensitive to the reactions of his audience that he would change his act if even a few voices booed. He could not stand dissent or disapproval. When some people waved black flags at him in Belgaum, demanding reorganisation of the State on a linguistic basis, he yielded without a fight. If he stuck tenaciously to his stand on Kashmir, it was because he knew that the whole nation stood behind him.

Nehru enjoyed the company of intellectuals and picked Krishna Menon's brains. Menon served as his Alsatian and Nehru threw him to the wolves when, following the debacle in N.E.F.A , he realised that his own leadership was in grave danger. He liquidated every politician, Morarji Desai in particular, who he felt might destroy the Nehru legend. He knew India was still feudal and needed to identify itself with a leader and a family. He used his British-oriented education for intellectual fights based on Fabian socialism; he used his social upbringing to play the gentleman, the nobleman and the humanist; he used his inborn talent as a Kashmir Brahmin to outmanoeuvre his detractors and rivals. He excelled his contemporaries in statecraft.

Nehru was an aristocrat at heart. Like royalty in the feudal days, he was not averse at times to the company of jesters, and there were those among the top circles of the Government who fulfilled this role. But he had little communication with ordinary Congressmen or with the people. In general, too, his contact with his Cabinet colleagues did not extend beyond official routine. Kidwai was the only member of his Cabinet who was free with him, but Nehru ceased to lean on Kidwai after Patel's death.

The Indian people made a hero of Nehru. For ten years, he made them feel as the chosen people whose leader was the moral leader of the world. Indeed, they began to think that India had come full circle to the Vedic age, in which all wisdom was the privilege of the seers of India. Much of the charisma had worn thin towards the closing years of his life. The Chinese attack rudely awakened the people to the harsh reality that they had been living in a world of make-believe. Nevertheless, when Nehru passed away, he still enjoyed in the minds and hearts of the Indian people a place which few before him have had and few ever will.

The present book will give Nehru scholars and a wider public a feel of his aspirations for India and for humanity as a whole. It brings out his determination to make the Indian National Congress a historical instrument of change and social justice. He was proud of being a Congressman and above all an Indian. He regarded anything that weakened the Congress as a disservice to the motherland. Let the people of India follow his example and keep their feet firmly on the path made for them by Mahatma Gandhi, Jawaharlal Nehru and the other great leaders of India.

Delhi ATTAR CHAND

References

1. C.B. Muthamma. India in the Contemporary World. *Daily* (Bombay), 8 June 1988.
2. *Ibid.*
3. *Ibid.*
4. *Ibid.*
5. J.D. Sethi. Gandhi and Nehru: The Real Difference. *The Illustrated Weekly of India*, 12 June 1988.
6. Rasheeddin Khan. Peace and Security in Nuclear Age. *Secular Democracy*, November 1986.
7. *Ibid.*
8. See *Indian Review*, 37 (5) 1936, pp. 273-75.

9. M.C. Setalvad, 'Nehru and Indian Parliamentary Democracy', *Nehru Legacy: A Symposium*, p. 23.
10. K.N. Kabra, 'Nehru and Planning for the poor'. *Mainstream* (28 May 1988).
11. Indira Hirway. Planning for Poverty Eradication in Rural Areas. *Kurukshetra*, April 1988.
12. *Ibid.*
13. *Ibid.*
14. *Ibid.*
15. *Ibid.*
16. See Werner Levi. *Free India in Asia*, p. 217.
17. Chester Bowles. *Ambassador's Report*. London, 1945, p. 137.
18. Peter Pritam T. Merani. The Foundations of India's Foreign Policy Under Jawaharlal Nehru. *Asian Thought and Society*, November 1987, p. 331.
19. Kashmir. *The Atlantic Monthly*, January, 1954.
20. Allice Thorner. The Issue in Kashmir. *Far Eastern Survey*, 11 August 1948, pp. 177-78.
21. *Ibid.*
22. C.H. Alexandrowicz. The Kashmir Deadlock. *Political Science Quarterly*, July-September, 1954.
23. U.N. Background Papers on the India-Pakistan question. ST/DPI/Series-A 72.
24. See Kusum Nair. Kashmir Today. *Foreign Affairs Reports*, June 1957, pp. 54-55.
25. C.H. Alexandrowicz. The Kashmir Deadlock. *Political Science Quarterly*, July-September, 1954.
26. U.N. Background Papers on the India-Pakistan question, ST/DPI/Series--A-72.
27. Report of Mr. Gunnar Jarring on the Kashmir Question. *United Nations Press Release*, 30th April 1957.
28. Kusum Nair. *Kashmir Today*, op. cit., p. 54.
29. See UN Security Council S/3821 (New York), 29 April 1957, p. 6.
30. Rasheeduddin Khan. Peace and Security in Nuclear Age. *Secular India*, November 1986.
31. P.N. Haskar. *Secular Democracy*, November 1986.
32. R.C. Dutt. *Socialism of Jawaharlal Nehru*. New Delhi, 1981, pp. 256-73.
33. R.K. Karanjia. *The Mind of Mr. Nehru*, pp. 76-77.
34. "Planning for Progress" by Asoka Mehta in the volume, *A Study of Nehru*, edited by Rafiq Zakaria, p. 295.
35. R.K. Karanjia. *The Mind of Mr. Nehru*, pp. 32-33.
36. P.C. Joshi "Nehru and Socialism in India". *Socialism in India*, edited by B.R. Nanda, p. 131.
37. Chalapathi Rau. *Gandhi and Nehru*, p. 77.
38. P.C. Joshi. "Nehru and Socialism in India". *Socialism in India*, edited by B.R. Nanda, pp. 139-140.

39 "A Revolutionary who forestalled Revolution" by K.P.S. Menon, *Builder of Modern India*, p. 11.

40. *Ibid.*, p. 12.

41. N.C. Joshi. Nehru's Socialist Philosophy. *Young Democrat* (Bombay), 1-15 June 1988, p. 9.

42. M. Chalapathi Rau. Nehru and the Press. In *Nehru Legacy; A Symposium*, pp. 80-81.

Nehru and His World Order

Twenty four years (1964-88) have passed since the death of Jawaharlal Nehru, outstanding leader of our national liberation movement, ardent and untiring fighter for world peace.

Nehru was the architect of independent India which has taken fundamental measures for liquidating the consequences of its colonial first, for achieving economic self-reliance, for creating an indigenous industrial base, for solving the food problem. A number of socio-economic measures which enabled India to achieve considerable progress on independent lines were formulated by Nehru.

The contribution Nehru made to the elaboration of the fundamentals of India's foreign-policy course can hardly be overestimated. India continues to adhere to this course. Dynamic approach to world processes; struggle against imperialism, colonialism and neo-colonialism; untiring efforts for strengthening universal peace; achieving real disarmament; development of wide international cooperation—these were the key objectives of India's foreign policy. Nehru perceived that these objectives could be achieved if India was not aligned to aggressive blocs into which the imperialists, during the 40s and 50s, wanted to drag India.

A number of newly liberated Afro-Asian countries followed the example of India in choosing the path of non-alignment as their foreign policy course. If Nehru were alive today he would have witnessed not only the phenomenal growth in the number of non-aligned countries, but also in the efforts made by the NAM in safeguarding world peace. India remained the Chairman of the NAM (1983-86) and made a significant contribution to solving the most urgent problems facing humankind.

Nehru devoted all his energy and effort, influence and position, to serving the cause of peace as well as the cause of building a new India. He knew that the real threat to peace emanated from the aggressive circles of international imperialism which talked even then of "brinkmanship", of "limited nuclear wars", of "position of strength", etc.

Nehru, at the same time, witnessed how a mighty movement of all peace-loving forces of the planet grew against the aggressive designs of such "hawds". He was not just a spectator, but an active participant in the world-wide anti-war movement. It was at his initiative that India introduced in the United Nations and in other world forums major constructive proposals for curbing the arms race, for banning all nuclear weapons, for prohibiting use of force in inter-state relations. Continuing the noble cause of her father, Indira Gandhi followed the same course, and now his great grandson Prime Minister Rajiv Gandhi is adhering to the same principles for which he lived.

Nehru once said: "I love to be among children, talk to them. Then I forget that I am terribly old and that I was a child long, long time ago."

It is symbolic that Jawaharlal Nehru's birth anniversary is marked as Children's Day. He saw in children the future of a happy and prosperous India. And it was to the future of India that Nehru devoted his great life.

1. Abbas, K.A. Who was Jawaharlal Nehru? *Blitz*, 29th May 1982; 24.

2. Ahluwalia, B.K. ed. *Facets of Nehru.* Delhi, SES, 1967, pp. 97.

3. Ahluwalia, B.K. Nehru the man. In *FON*; 86-94.

4. Aney, M.S. Nehru. In *NAG*; 180.

5. Attar Chand. State of uncertainty. *Indian Nation*, 2 August 1987.

6. Banda, B.R. Nehru, product of many influences. *Patriot*, 14 November 1978; 2.

A Fortunate combination of circumstances had helped to mould Jawaharlal Nehru. He had an extraordinary father : Motilal would have made his mark in any country at any time. Motilal's westernizatian was not a pale imitation of the West, but a revolt against the superstition, obscurantism and parochialism of his own people. National pride, rationalism and secularism for which youngmen of his generation had to struggle were part of Jawaharlal's heritage.

The fact that he went to Harrow and Cambridge at an impressionable age did not alienate him from his country; indeed it lent a romantic touch to his nationalism.

7. Baxi, Upendia, Recovering the revolutionary Nehru. *Mainstream*, 28 December 1985; 13-14, 16.

Mahatma Gandhi, right or wrong, was one unified configuration; he evolved in thought and action and yet, wonderously, remained one and the same person. With Jawaharlal Nehru, we come across a chameleon personality so much so that this year many different persons seem to go under one and the same name. This is not to say at all that he was fickle or an opportunist. Far from it. But there was a young Nehru and Nehru who matured and a Nehru who grew in years—without ever getting senile, a rare achievement in human affairs. And, if we ignore the Hamlet-like continuities in the three Nehrus, the youthful socialist Nehru was in many senses quite distinct from the mature of late Nehru.

8. Bayur, Hikmet. Nehru. In *NAG*; 171.

9. Bhagat, H.K.L., Vision of Nehru. *Patriot*, Annual 1984; 24-25.

Nehru clearly perceived that the salvation of the world lay in peace, cooperation and development and never tired of vigorously and passionately pleading for this great cause. Even at the time he assumed office as Prime Minister in the Interim National Government in 1946 he clearly outlined what India's foreign policy would be.

10. Bhambri, C.P. Nehru : A critical study. *Mainstream*, 11 November 1967; 12-17.

11. Brecher, Michael. Nehru—A study. In *NCV*; 145-64.

12. Bright, J.S. *Great Nehrus*. Lahore, Tagore Memorial Publications, 1947, pp. 320.

13. Buck, Pearl S. Jawaharlal Nehru. In *LON*; 25-26.

14. Bunker, Ellamorth. Jawaharlal Nehru. In *LON*; 27-32.

15. Caveeshar, Sardul Singh. Man of action. In *NAG*; 17-20.

16. Cavell, R.G. India's man of destiny. *NAG*; 64-67.

17. Chakrabarti, A. *Nehru*. Calcutta, 1956, pp. 103.

18. Chalapathi Rau, M. *Jawaharlal Nehru*. Delhi, Publications Division, 1972.

19. Chalapathi Rau, M. Man for all seasons. *Swarajya* (Madras), 12 November 1978; 6-7.

Since Jawaharlal Nehru had much to do with the shaping of Indian democracy and with giving it content, his birthday this year too will raise the question: how far is he still relevant or irrelevant?

I knew him well for a quarter of a century, as a freedom fighter and as Prime Minister, and the question came up repeatedly even then: What manner of man was he? Was he a visionary or a man of action? Was he a domocrat or a dictator? Was he as plain and honest as he seemed to be or was there something deep within him? He was many men in one, a thinker, a writer, a man of action, a political leader, a Prime Minister, but what lay behind it all? These questions demand an answer even now.

20. Chalapathi Rau, M. Relevance of Nehru. *Socialist India*, 30 May 1970; 19.

21. Chase, Stuart. Nehru and the middle way. In *NAG*; 58-60.

22. Chattopadhyaya, Harindranath. Two sonnets to Jawaharlal Nehru. In *NAG*; 7-8.

23. Chaturvedi, Umesh. *Pt. Jawaharlal Nehru*, Jaipur, 1939.

24. Chitta Ranjan, C.N. Nehru behest, *Mainstream*, 12 November 1983; 17, 41.

To many of us now in our early or late sixties, Jawaharlal Nehru remains the symbol of youth of fresh and radical thought, of dedication and deep human concern, of impatience for action to further the cause of the impoverished millions.

The memory of those inspiring years of the freedom struggle is particularly poignant in today's setting, when we find large numbers of young men and women, especially those who have had the benefit of a good education and have not known poverty and suffering, less and less concerned about the fate and fortunes of the community at large—a trend towards unhealthy self-centrism.

25. Chopra, V.D. Nehru vision of an age of reason. *Patriot*, 15 August 1981.

26. Cousins, Norman. Jawaharlal Nehru. In *LON*; 33-52.

27. Cousins, Norman. *Talks with Nehru: Recorded interview*. New York, 1951. Bombay, Allied, 1954.

28. Crocker, Walter. *Nehru: A Contemporary's estimate*. London, 1966, pp. 186.

29. Damodaran, A.K. Nehru values, nation's touch stone. *Mainstream* Nehru special Number, May 1984; 19-23.

It was a fashionable thing among "friendly" critics within the Congress establishemnt during the thirties to snipe at Jawaharlal Nehru for his exaggerated interest in foreign policy at a time when the country was still far away from the achievement of authority in decision-making in domestic matters, let alone external relations. An impression was sought to be created that Nehru did this because of a certain feeling of inequality before the domestic challenges of the country; it was easier to fly away into theoretical speculations about the problems which had nothing to do with our day-to-day life.

30. Dasa, Rai Krishna. Nehru. In *NAG*; 207-9.

31. De Reincourt, Amanry. *Soul of India*. London, 1961.

32. De Valera, Eamon. Ideal itself. In *NAG*; 3.

33. Desai, Hiralal. Nehru. In *NAG*; 200-4.

34. Dhar, Somnath. Down memory lane. *Akashvani* (New Delhi), 1 October 1983; 3-5.

35. Durant, Will. Saintly stead fastness. In *NAG*; 32.

36. Edib, Halide. Only great Indian. In *NAG*; 28.

37. Ehrenburg, Flya. Jawaharlal Nehru. In *LON*; 53-56.

38. Farrell, Janies T. Jawaharlal Nehru. In *LON*; 57-64.

39. Feilden, Lionel. Nehru. In *NAG*; 184-85.

40. Gandhi, Rajmohan. Memory to cherish: Reflections on Jawaharlal Nehru. *Statesman*, 27 May 1984; 6.

Among the things about India that we can love and be proud of, the memory of Jawaharlal Nehru is surely one.

His appearance was striking. Integral to its magic was the white cap. When Laxman removed it in his cartoons Nehru suddenly seemed more vulnerable. The cap shielded him and raised him above the mortals.

41. Ganesh Prasad. Jawaharlal Nehru: A renaissance representative. *Mainstream*, 14 November 1970; 15-17.

Jawaharlal Nehru wrote in *The Discovery of India:* "The awakening in India was two-fold: she locked at herself and her own past."

This awakening was the Renaissance. Its highest products were modern nationalism and the national liberation movement. This was quite natural. A colony, as Shaw said, is like a patient of cancer; it can think of nothing else but its liberation. With Raja Ram Mohan Roy as its fountain-head, the Renaissance threw up its representatives at different times.

42. Ghosh, Aurobindo. Jawaharlal: Some impressions. *Mainstream*, 18 November 1967; 17.

We were at school then. At lunch once a friend, all excitement, came to our table, and opened out the magazine in his hand. "Look", he said, "Can you believe it? He smokes." We wouldnt' believe. So we forgot the food and pored over the photograph instead. He did smoke, but in our young, immature, idealistic minds the image of Jawaharlal Nehru was such that it took quite some time to get adjusted to this new idea. Once we did, however, we loved him more for that. He was our hero, our inspiration, after all, and whatever he was and did, good or bad, was immensely admirable.

43. Gide, Andre. Natural nobility. In *NAG*; 157.

44. Gill, Naranjan Singh. Nehru. In *NAG*; 181-83.

45. Glimpses of a fearless Nehru. *Statesman*, 26 March 1984.

It was on September 2, 1946, that the Congress formed the Interim Government and Nehru was sworn in as member in charge of external affairs and Commonwealth relations. The Muslim League joined it a few weeks later, but before doing so and even afterwards, tried to obstruct Nehru's each move to fashion his foreign policy. And the Viceroy, Lord Wavell, supported the League.

Nehru enunciated new India's independent foreign policy of keeping away from the power politics of groups aligned one against the other. Soon the troubles started.

46. Gopal Singh. Nehru we did not know. *National Herald*, 27 May 1980; 4.

47. Gorev, A. and V. Zimyanin. *Jawaharlal Nehru*. Moscow, Progress Publishers, 1982, pp. 340.

Soon after Jawaharlal Nehru died in May, 1964, the Government of India decided to convert the Teen Murti House, where he had lived for nearly sixteen years, into a museum and library dedicated to his memory.

Jawaharlal Memorial Museum, which was inaugurated by the then President, S. Radhakrishnan, on November 14, 1964, is today the most popular museum in the capital. People from all over India visit the museum to see the place where stayed their beloved leader. The living rooms at the Teen Murti House are preserved as they were on May 27, 1964 when Jawaharlal Nehru died. Foreign tourists also visit the museum in large numbers to pay their homage to the great humanitarian and world statesman that Nehru was.

48. Govind Das. Nehru. In *NAG*; 207-9.

49. Great visionary, *National Herald*, 27 1981; 4.

50. Gundevia, Y.D. Glimpses of the Nehru years. *Indian Express*, 27 May 1984.

In my retirement in Pune, 1,000 miles from Delhi, among other things, I found myself defending Nehru—why were we in the Russian orbit? I thought it was worth explaining that we were not in any orbit at all. Basically we were only rotating on our own axis every 24 hours, as part of the great galaxy of nations.

This done, a hundred memories came back to me: back from Burma in 1948, I had found Nehru allowing you any amount of initiative and always appreciating what little a junior officer could do in his ministry; there was the 10 years' exile to Moscow, Switzerland, London and Ceylon; back in Delhi, the last four years of Nehru's life, and then the last 100 days.

51. Gunther, John. On Nehru. In *Inside Asia*, London, 1948.

52. Gurupadaswamy, M.S. Nehru as I saw him. *Newstime*, 14 November 1987.

53. Gurupadaswamy, M.S. Nehru as I saw. In *NP*; 188-90.

54. Iqbal Singh. Several distinct lives. In *NAG*; 72-75.

55. Ismail, Mirza M. Spirit of Compromise. In *NAG*; 40-41.

56. Jha, S.V. and R.K. Sinha. Jawaharlal Nehru, man of the masses. *Searchlight* (Patna), 28 May 1980; 4.

Nehru's great contribution to international politics was the building up of an Afro-Asian personality. It was he who enunciated the concept of non-alignment which is an accepted principle of political science today. When Egypt was invaded by British and French commando units in support of Israeli forces in 1956, Nehru condemned the aggression in unambiguous terms.

The steel plants, the budding factories, the dockyards, the dams and canals and all what is today are what Nehru thought yesterday. Under his leadership India entered the modern industrial age.

57. Kalra, A.N. My encounter with Nehru. *National Herald*, 14 November 1985; 7.

By the early thirtees, Jawahar Lal Nehru had become the most popular national leader next only to Mahatma Gandhi. He attracted huge crowds whereever he went, and people, particularly from villages would walk long distances, just to have 'darshans'.

His influence on the youth of the country was phenomenal. He was their beloved and idol. His socialistic approach to the country's problems was greatly appreciated by them.

58. Kannan, K. Panditji remembered. *People's Comment* (New Delhi), 31 May 1987; 24-25.

It will be twenty-three years since Pandit Jawaharlal Nehru passed away. Those who might have grown up in the 30's and 40's may like to remember him as a leader of the Indian revolution—the great lieutenant of the Mahatma—implacable enemy of imperialism, hero of youth and the darling of the Indian masses. Even when he was well past middle age, he had an aura of youth. "Ritu Raj" that is what Tagore described him.

59. Karaka, D.F. *Nehru*. London, 1953.

60. Karan Singh. Jawaharlal. *National Herald*, 14 November 1972; 5.

He disappeared on a summer morning, he became a voice in the garden. We looked for him, passionately at first, then more deeply. We didn't find him, of course, except that in the garden, in the most unexpected nooks and crannies, in the leaping light of the mountain stream that runs along the top; in the sudden eloquence of the birds and the silence of the winter night; in the black thunder of the monsoon and the technicolor gaiety of spring, there suddenly would arise an aroma, a fragrance, which recalled him to us. We could almost see him, with his rosebud and thoughtful eyes. He disappeared on a summer morning and became a voice in the garden; his garden.

Jawaharlal Nehru's first reaction to the Mountbatten Plan for the partition of India was strongly hostile. When Mountbatten in May 1947 showed the plan in confidence to him at "The Retreat" in Simla—where Nehru was staying as his private guest—Nehru the very next day wrote a letter which the Viceroy, described as "a bombshell of the first order." In that letter, Nehru warned Mountbatten about the proposals for the transfer of power to India as they had been cleared from London: "Instead of producing any sense of certainty, security and stability, they would encourage disruptive tendencies everywhere and chaos and weakness."

61. Karanjia, R.K. *Mind of Mr. Nehru*. London, George Allen and Unwin, 1960, pp. 112.

62. Karanjia, R.K. *Philosophy of Mr. Nehru*. London, George Allen and Unwin, 1966, pp. 162.

63. Kaushik, R.M. Nehru: The mind and vision. *Northern India Patrika*, 22 May 1983.

Lenin once said, "Man's dearest possession is life and . . ., he must so live as not to be seared with the shame of a cowardly and trivial past . . . ., so live that dying he can say: 'All my life and my strength given to the first cause in the world—the liberation of mankind'." Jawaharlal Nehru sounds a true liberator on Lenin's touchstone.

64. Khan, Abdul Majid. *Jawaharlal Nehru and his ideas.* New Delhi, Indian Printing Works, 1951, pp. 102.

65. Khastgir, Sudhir. Nehru. In *NAG*; 210.

66. King, Martin Luther. Nehru: A tribute. *Indian and Foreign Review*, 15 November 1986; 8.

Jawaharlal Nehru was a man of three extraordinary epochs. He was a leader in the long anti-colonial struggle to free his own land and to inspire a fighting will in other lands under bondage.

He lived to see victory and to move then to another epochal confrontation—the fight for peace after World War II. In this climactic struggle he did not have Gandhi at his side, but he did have the Indian people, now free in their own great Republic.

67. King, Martin Luther. Jawaharlal Nehru. In *LON*; 65-68.

68. Lester, Muriel. Nehru. In *NAG*; 179.

69. Malkani, Sindhu. On Nehru. *Hindustan Times*, 8 December 1986; 8.

In my family papers I found a review of this book done by my uncle, the late Prof. N.R. Malkani, for *The Hindustan Times* (June 25, 1936), then the leading pro-Congress English daily of India.

The review paid rich compliments to Panditji but it also noted: "The book is an autobiography only by accident. It reads like a novel and is essentially political history of modern India in which Panditji happens to play an important part and for which he has leisure to write a review. It is an autobiography with part revealed and part concealed beauties of the author's life. The revealed part is delicious and then one hankers for more. At the end I have a sore feeling of deprivation, of a certain lack of intimacy, for I fear that even such an extrovert has after all great reserves and greater silences."

"I do not seem to know him well enough, not because he is a perplexing personality but because he denies me some of his confidences. The veil is slightly lifted from his domestic life and we proudly join him in his admiration for his father or share tender sorrows for his wife. But even here we know nothing that we did not, or could not, know otherwise. Whole chapters, almost divisions of his life, seem to be hidden from our view—he is so silent about his personal ambitions, so reticent about his attitude to sex, so cautious about the mention of monetary affairs."

"I would love to see him waging battles royal within his breast to be able to glory over his victories and feel over his defeats. The book is not subjective enough, for I sadly miss the biography of his soul. And Panditji does not even tell me that he has, or had, a friend. Of all the thumb-nail impressions of well-known personalities with which the book abounds, there is not one which could be called as one of his friends."

The reviewer also thought that Panditji showed a certain "lapse of good taste" in attacking the Liberals the way he had. He added: "But there is a real deficiency which I realise when I close the book. The book is great but not profound. Gandhiji has set us a standard and we judge thereby. The chapter 'What is Religion?' lacks the religious sense."

Interestingly enough, Mr. Mahadev Desai reacted to this review immediately and enthusiastically. In a letter from Wardha (dated 27-6-1936) he wrote to Prof. Malkani:

"I happened, just by chance, to read your article on Jawahar's autobiography. I say ditto to everything you have said, and you have said it so well, and without offence. It is the first oasis in the desert of fulsome appreciation one sees everywhere. May I congratulate You? I rarely write to you about your writings, but this one so very much echoes my own feelings that I could not help exclaiming 'I am glad'."

Was Mahadev Bhai echoing the thinking of the Mahatma? I don't know. But perhaps Mr. Nanda could throw some light on the subject.

70. Martin, Kingsley. Gentle colossus. *Illustrated Weekly of India* (Bombay), 27 May 1984; 46.

I knew Nehru for 30 years and in many moods. He first came to see me when he was just out of prison. Surprisingly, he bore no grudge against the British. He had learnt in goal to live with himself and by himself. He often thought too much. His greatest weakness was not to be able to build up a team of younger men with whom he could have exchanged ideas and who have been inspired by him. Smaller plants did not easily grow underneath this old-tree. He was loved and revered, but no group grew up pledged to carry on his work when he retired. As a result, he could not retire even when he was ill and everyone knew he ought to retire. He was surrounded by men of conservative, capitalist and national mind who did not dare oppose him, but could not be relies upon to carry out his wishes.

71. Martin, Kingsley. Interview with Nehru. *New Statesman* (London), 21 December 1962; 893-94.

72. Mathai, M.O. Nehru's adherence to truth. In *MDN*; 229-33.

Nehru was a man who dedicated himself for a great cause; but he did not believe in renouncing the world and all it contained. To him power was an intrument to do good, and political freedom was but the beginning of a prolonged struggle for economic development and social change. The crudities of politics did not infect Nehru. Undoubtedly Nehru was one of the most truthful politicians in history. This was largely due to the absence of fear in him.

73. Mehta, Ashok. Knight sans Peur. In *NCV*; 137-40.

74. Mehta, Asoka. Nehru and India. In *FON*; 44-49.

75. Michael, Eduard. *Nehru.* London, 1971.

76. Misra, K.P. Nehru, Indira, Rajiv : Their roles. *World Focus* (New Delhi), (88) April 1987; 26-28.

In a significant manner, Jawaharlal Nehru provided ideological basis to Indo-Soviet relations by enunciating the basic framework of our foreign policy, the pillars of which were nonalignment, peaceful coexistence and anti-colonialism. These were the concepts which were closer to the foreign policy principles of the Soviet Union also.

What helped the initial growth of the Indo-Soviet relations was Jawaharlal Nehru's concern about the cold war politics and its effects. During the 1950s, when the United States and its friends and allies attempted to create a network of military alliance systems in different parts of the world in order to contain what they called the "communist menace", it was not to this country's liking. The creation of the NATO and the SEATO was seen in India as steps towards increasing tension in international relations.

Referring to this situation Nehru said in Parliament on September 29, 1954: "Honourable members may remember the old days when the great powers had spheres of influence in Asia and elsewhere. . . . it seems to me that particularly Manila Treaty is inclined dangerously in the direction of influence to be exercised by powerful countries. . . . After all, it is the big and powerful countries that will decide the matters and not the two or three weak and small Asian nations that may be allied to them."

It was in this general context that soon after the Bandung Conference, Nehru visited the Soviet Union for seventeen long days in June 1955. This was a significant visit in cementing the relations between the two countries. It led to greater understanding between Nehru and the Soviet leaders, some of whom had already visited India earlier.

During Nehru's Prime Ministership, the attitude of the Soviet Union towards the Kashmir issue became a factor of some importance in the relations between the two countries. The Soviet Union gave significant support to India and this was greatly appreciated by the Government and the people of India. Right from the early 1950s, the Soviet Union openly recognised Kashmir as an integral part of India. When the UN Security Council in February 1957 debated the proposal put forward by the US and the UK about stationing UN troops in Kashmir, the Soviet Union stalled a decision by exercising a veto. On India this had a good impact.

77. Moraes, Frank. *India Today*. New York, 1960.

78. Moraes, Frank. Jawaharlal. In *Nehru: Sunlight and Shadow*. Bombay, Jaico, 1964; 149-79.

79. Mukherjee, Hiren. *Gentle Colossus--A study of Jawaharlal Nehru*. Oxford, 1987. Book Review in *Daily* (Bombay), 16 August 1987.

Quite a number of books have by now come out on Nehru, where rich tributes have been paid to him by his biographers. It appears we are still thirsty for more knowledge about the eminent statesman Nehru. Here, then is one more excellent biography on the Gentle Colossus, by the distinguished scholar and writer, Hiren Mukherjee. The title too is so aptly thought out by the author, indicating a towering personality, unwavering in his integrity and honesty of purpose and yet, the hard core mellowed by an aura of gentleness, a unique combination.

80. Mukherjee, Hiren. Reminiscences on Nehru. *Akashvani*, 1-15 November 1986; 4-5.

Too many things rush into my mind, but I must share the happiness I felt when, early during our Parliamentary contacts, Jawaharlal at a dinner in Constitution House asked me about my wife and children. Then, saying he always had time for children if not for adults, he asked us all to breakfast with him, an unforgettable experience for my wife and our two children—a girl of eleven and a boy of six—to sit with the great man who easily made friends with them while I took, metaphorically, a back seat.

81. Mukherjee, Hiren. Sculptor of our times. *Patriot*, 14 November 1981; 4.

82. Mukerji, D.P. Nehru. In *NAG*; 172-76.

83. Mullick, Situ. Rare glimpses of Nehru. *Hindustan Times*, 14 November 1986; 23.

One of my lifelong regrets has been that I never saw Gandhiji alive. But on January 30, 1948, late in the evening I got a glimpse of Pandit Jawaharlal Nehru for the first time in my life, at Birla House, New Delhi. His was then a gravely saddened, young, handsome face that stood out in a seething sea of stunned humanity as he spoke out haltingly those immortal words "The light has gone out of our lives."

84. Munshi, K.M. Peerless Nehru. *Bhawan's Journal*, 16-30 November 1987; 17.

85. Murthy, S.N. Remembering Jawaharlal. *Akashvani*, 11 February 1979; 35.

During the three decades of my career in Indian Broadcasting, both Radio and Television, it was always a rare and stimulating experience handling Jawaharlal Nehru as a broadcaster. As poet Wordsworth put it in his immortal lines:

Bliss was it in that dawn to be alive,
But to be young was very heaven.

It was winter morning in Lucknow and the place was Government House. India's Nightingale, Sarojini Naidu, State Governor, had passed away a few hours earlier. Morning papers came out without a mention of it. Radio was the only source of news for the city and the rest of the country. Jawaharlal, Rajaji, Azad and many others including Lady Mountbatten arrived in no time to join the milling crowds on the sprawling lawns of Raj Bhavan.

86. Narasimhaiah, C.D. *Jawaharlal Nehru*. Mysore, 1960.

87. Narasimhachar, K.T. *Profile of Jawaharlal Nehru.* Bombay, 1960.

88. Narasimhachar, K.T. *ed. Quintessence of Nehru.* London, 1961, pp. 271.

89. Natwar Singh, K. Jawaharlal Nehru. In *LON*; 69-74.

90. Nehru, Tito, Nasser. *National Herald*, 14 March 1988; 6.

The Non-Aligned Movement has come a long way since its launching in the early years of the post-World War II era and become a major factor in world politics. From being viewed with suspicion by both the dominant military blocs in its nascent years, the movement has grown steadily to a position where its ideology holds the key to the solution of knotty international issues like Afghanistan and Kampuchea and even South Africa's differences with Angola. As the Minister of State for External Affairs, Mr. Natwar Singh, noted at a seminar in New Delhi on March 11, 1988, the Non-Aligned Movement "remains a vibrant, dynamic force in international relations. Its relevance and importance has, if anything, increased over the years." The seminar, organised by the Indian Institute for Non-aligned Studies had as its theme "Nehru, Tito and Nasser: Non-alignment and the Contemporary World", affording a wide scope for discussion to the 100 participants from India, Yugoslavia and Egypt, the countries of the three eminent founding fathers. As Mr. Natwar Singh and other speakers pointed out with a sense of pride, few new question the relevance or *raison d'etre* of the movement which emerged as the response of the newly freed nations to the division of the world into two dominant military blocs. Its membership has increased to more than four-fold since the Belgrade Conference of 1961 attended by 25 countries. Besides Nehru, Nasser and Tito, the participants in that conference included President Soekarno of Indonesia and President Nkrumah of Ghana. Interestingly, also present were Prince Sihanouk of Cambodia who is hoping for a come-back along the non-aligned trail and the then Prime Minister of Afghanistan, Sardar Mohammed Daud, whose association led his country to a long period of crisis from which salvation appears to be round the corner through a reassertion of non-alignment.

91. Norman, Dorthy. *Nehru the first sixty years.* 2 Vols., Bombay, Asia, 1965.

92. Pandey, N.K. *Jawaharlal Nehru : The man and the myth.* Calcutta, 1964.

93. Patkar, B.S. *Jawaharlal Nehru : Jewel of India.* Poona, B.S. Patkar, 1942, pp. 155.

94. Pattabhi Sitaramayya, B. Life of sacrifice. In *NAG*; 27.

95. Pauling, Linus. Jawarharlal Nehru. In *LON*; 75-80.

96. Pillai, K.M. Kumara. Nehru. In *NAG*; 189-91.

97. Radhakrishnan, S. Jawaharlal Nehru. In *FON* ; 1-4.

98. Radhakrishnan, S. Jawaharlal Nehru. In *LON*; 13-18.

99. Radhakrishnan, S. *On Nehru.* New Delhi, 1965, pp. 70.

We wish to place on record our very high appreciation of the devoted services he has rendered to our country and to humanity at large. We are all passing through a period of crisis. The only way in which we can show our respect to Jawaharlal Nehru is by adopting an attitude of freedom from every kind of prejudice in dealing with affairs which are brought to our notice.

100. Rao, Raja. Jawaharlal Nehru. In *LON*; 81-96.

101. Ravinder Kumar. Vision of Jawaharlal Nehru. *Congress Varnika* (New Delhi), 1984; 3-10, 19.

What was the vision of Jawaharlal Nehru? What were the distinctive constituents of this vision? How did it influence the course of the freedom struggle before 1947? Equally, how did this vision shape the policies which he adopted as Prime Minister.

Even as a young scholar in Harrow, Jawaharlal Nehru took a close interest in British politics, and a passionate interest in the course of the freedom struggle in his country. His political views at this juncture are reflected in his letters to his father—Motilal Nehru, letters which reveal his conviction that a militant struggle would have to be waged against the British Government before India became a free country.

102. Ravinder Kumar. Vision of Nehru. *Blitz*, 4 November 1987; 12, 15.

103. Reddy, B. Sarojini Pulla. Nehru: The moulder of destiny. *Deccan Chronicle* (Secundrabad), 27 May 1980; 4.

Nehru was the architect of modern India and the moulder of her destiny. He strictly followed in the footsteps of his mentor, Mahatma Gandhi, and ever believed in the motto that nobility of ends does not justify resort to means that are base.

Jawaharlal Nehru, a worthy son of a worthy father, did not hesitate to give up a life of comfort and luxury in his yearning to free his motherland from the shackles of bondage. He gave utmost priority to principles and cheerfully faced all odds to uphold them.

104. Rudra, S.K. Nehru. In *NAG*; 163-70.

105. Russell, Bertrand. Jawaharlal Nehru. In *LON*; 97-102.

106. Saksena, Mohanlal. Jewel of man. In *NAG*; 138.

107. Sen, G. Emerson. Nehru. In *NAG*; 192-97.

108. Seth, Hira Lal. *Red Star of the East*. Lahore, Hero Publications, 1942.

109. Seton, Marie. *Panditji*. London, 1967.

110. *Shri Pt. Jawaharlal Nehru*. Madras, Kishit Publishing House, 1965.

111. Shukla, Ravishankar. Country's brightest jewel. In *NAG*; 84.

112. Sinha, Umesh. Down memory lane with Nehru. *Pioneer*, 24 May 1987.

Once I was on duty in the official gallery of Rajya Sabha. Panditji (Nehru) came out of the Lok Sabha to the outer lobby, then to the Central hall, outer lobby of Rajya Sabha and wanted to go to the Chamber of the Chairman of Rajya Sabha, Dr. S. Radhakrishnan. He knew the short cut to his room but as per security arrangement Prime Minister's route is always well defined. I was on duty in the passage of the official Gallery of Rajya Sabha (Upper House of Parliament). I got up and stood there like a rock blocking his way. Panditji as usual in a hurry told me "I have to go to the Chairman." I replied very politely but firmly "Sir this passage does not lead to his chamber." He ascertingly replied "Don't tell me that. I know it goes there through the room meant for general pool stenographers." I was determined not to allow him to go through this passage, due to the reasons best known to me. For a while his face flushed and became red, everyone there thought that I am going to get a smart slap on my face. I was ready for that, but the next moment he gave a childlike smile, which I will never forget till my last breath. He smilingly but sportingly said, "I know you will not allow me to go this way." The master of destiny of countless Indians bowing down so sportingly—can any one beat it.

As a security measure and also with various official reasons, a search is conducted in the morning, in the houses of Parliament, before they sit and in the evening, after they adjourn for the day. One evening it was past seven. Winter session of the Parliament, was ensuing. I along with so many of my colleagues, were conducting search. Incidentally, Panditji on way to his room from Lok Sabha happened to pass from the Central Hall where I was conducting search. He stopped and asked me, "You—people are still at work, it is very late." I replied, "Sir, Madam Deputy Minister of Finance, Mrs. Tarkeshwari Sinha has lost her Parker Pen here in the house, so we are searching it again." He listened to it carefully and went to his room near Gate no. 5 of the Parliament House. Next day, during our usual morning search, we came a bit earlier as the pen was not traced last night. Panditji was going to Lok Sabha from his room. He asked me, "Could you find the Pen?" Before I could reply, to her ill luck the concerned Deputy Minister appeared and told us that the pen was lying in her purse. It was the beginning of the episode. Panditji, very much annoyed, gave her a bit of his mind and patted me and said, "Does not matter." To this day, I still feel vibrations on my back, who says, Nehru is dead.

113. Sri Prakash. Nehru. In *NAG*; 211-28.

114. Stephens, Ian. Nehru. In *NAG*; 161-62.

115. Stevenson, Adlai E. Jawaharlal Nehru. In *LON*; 103-6.

116. Stone, S. Nehrus. *Times of India*, 30 July 1980; 8.

No country, especially a country as large and complex as India, can benefit from the sort of weak central leadership and its far-reaching effects that India experienced under the Desai government when, to cite but a few critical areas, labour unrest and caste and communal violence intensified. The Nehrus have not necessarily had all the answers to India's problems, but they have been a continuous elite upon whom the country could rely for strong, honest leadership. The Nehru political dynasty will not be prepetuated through Sanjay Gandhi, as some had hoped and many had feared; we hope, however, that other leaders, as strong and honest as the Nehrus will emerge from various sectors (industry, military, etc.) to form an elite to serve the nation.

Although the democratic inclination is to frown upon an elitist approach, one need only look to the U.K., the mother of parliaments, to appreciate the prominent role of generation after generation of the Churchills, for example, or to the USA, the nation with the world's oldest constitution, to observe the service of the Roosevelts, Kennedys and Rockefellers. Why shouldn't India have their own elite families in public service?

117. Tandon, P.D. Epistolary portrait of Nehru. *Pioneer* (Lucknow), 13 November 1983.

For Nehru no one was big or small. He treated every one on a human level. Before the independence of India, there were too many communal riots and this greatly distressed Jawaharlal. Once Allahabad was on the verge of a fierce communal riot and Nehru dreaded the prospect. He wanted to stay in his hometown and ease the situation, but he had to leave for Calcutta because he had to attend an important meeting of the Congress Working Committee.

118. Tandon, P.D. My days with Nehru. *Searchlight* (Patna), 25 May 1986.

I had walked with Nehru in the city and in the villages of Allahabad, cycled beside him when he pedalled Purnima Banerji's tricycle. I had travelled with him by the ekka, car and aeroplane. I have many memories of those exciting days and some of them still haunt me. After his release from Ahmadnagar Fort in 1945, he toured U.P. extensively. I shadowed him wherever he went and stayed with him.

119. Tandon, P.D. Tea and sympathy with Panditji. *Statesman* (New Delhi), 26 May 1987; 6.

"Why are you here at this meeting? Its proceedings are not to be reported in the Press. I think you had better go out," Jawaharlal Nehru said brusquely. Used to his kindness and patronage, I was stunned at his command. I went and stood outside, stupefied. I had been invited to the meeting as both a Congressman and as a representative of the National Herald. Nehru was the paper's chairman.

Suddenly, a friend came up and said, "Tandon, come in. Panditji is calling you." I accompanied him and took my seat. The meeting had begun. After about five minutes, Nehru rather harshly said, "Tandon, I think you should go out. I do not want anything to be published anywhere regarding our discussions here today."

120. Thakur, H.K. Nehru: Man of Compassion. *Socialist India*, 27 November 1976; 29-31.

"Let us make obeisance to our great men and salute them" is not a repetitive ritual or a mechanical formality on sacred days like the birthdays of Gautam Buddha, Mahabir, Gandhi and Nehru or several such days held sacred in our country. It is not for their sake that we place verbal flowers on the pedestal of their memory but for our own well-being, for as Ecolesiastes enjoined, they have left us a very precious 'inheritance'."

121. Thant, U. Jawaharlal Nehru. In *LON*; 107-110.

122. Thomas, Norman. Jawaharlal Nehru. In *LON*; 111-114.

123. Toynbee, Arnold J. Jawaharlal Nehru. In *LON*; 115-22.

124. Toynbee, Arnold J. Foreword. In *Nehru* By Walter Crocker. London, 1966; 9-14.

125. Upadhyaya, Haribhan. Nehru. In *NAG*; 184-85.

126. Varma, Ravi. Light of Asia shines brighter. *Madhya Pradesh Chronicle* (Bhopal), 5 December 1979; 4.

127. Viswam, S. In recollection of Nehru. *Mainstream Nehru Special Number*, 1984; 17-18.

In the field of foreign policy, the decision to make non-alignment its cornerstone was Nehru's. The world has graduated from a bi-polar to a multi-polar polity, but the validity and relevance of non-alignment for India persevere.

128. Yudin. *Jawaharlal Nehru*, New Delhi, CP Publication, 1968.

Abdullah, Sheikh Mohammad

129. Mathai, M.O. Sheikh Mohammad Abdullah. In *MDN*; 234-43.

Sheikh Abdullah came into contact with Nehru after the formation of the National Conference. He brought the National Conference into the mainstream of Indian political developments by making it an affiliate of the All India State's Peoples Conference started by Nehru. He became its President in 1946 and kept the National Conference independent of the Indian National Congress.

Aesthetic

130. Tewari, U.N. Nehru as an aesthete. *Young Indian* (New Delhi), 11 November 1971; 7.

Nehru loved children. He loved flowers. He spent more than half of his life in the 'battlefield' and the rest in construction of a nation damaged not only by the century-old colonial rule but also paralysed by mental backwardness, superstition, disunity and lethargy. No other contemporary politician comes in mind when one thinks of Nehru's aesthetic sublimity.

Agriculture

131. Gujral, M.L. Food and agriculture. In *EFNIG*; 131-64.

132. Joshi, P.C. Nehru and the land of problem in India. *Patriot*, 15 November 1982; 2.

133. Libel on Nehru. *National Herald*, 1 September 1977; 6.

One of the present libels on Jawaharlal Nehru, sought to be sedulously propagated, is that he neglected agriculture and village economy and over-emphasised the importance of heavy industry. Mr. Charan Singh is a champion of this propaganda, and he seems to have misled mass media to give him a helping hand. According to *Samachar's* summing up of Mr. Charan Singh's views: "Nehru preferred huge, expensive, capital intensive schemes which were time-consuming and extravagant in the use of scare resources such as steel and cement and foreign exchange and required sophisticated technical expertise," and "India's present plight is largely due to the grievous decision taken after Independence to go industrial immediately." This is a complete misrepresentation. Apart from the fact proven many times that Nehru's economic strategy made the country withstand aggression more than one quarter, it is not from disjointed quotations from Nehru or from random samplings from the "Selected Works of Jawaharlal Nehru" that his views or policies can be correctly and comprehensively presented but from an understanding of his total perspective.

134. Mathai, M.O. Agriculture and community development. In *MDN*; 136-46.

Nehru was worried about the severe strain caused by continuous foodgrain imports. He made innumerable radio broadcasts on the subject, and more than once hinted at stoppage of imports. But his choice of Food and Agriculture Ministers was far from happy. Rajendra Prasad was more interested in pinjarapoles (cow ashrams) than anything else. Jairamdas Daulatram, who rightly belonged to pinjarapole, was wrongly appointed Minister of Food and Agriculture. Rafi Ahmed Kidwai was lucky in the short term, but circumstances conspired against him in the matter of finding a lasting solution. K.M. Munshi and Ajit Prasad Jain were birds of passage. Nehru further complicated the situation by bringing in a man as Food Production Commissioner in the Food and Agriculture Ministry during the tenure of Jairamdas Daulatram, thus creating a fifth wheel in the coach.

135. Nehru's concept of land reforms. *National Herald*, 14 November 1982.

Astrology

136. Mathai, M.O. Stranglehold of astrology. In *MDN*; 17-24.

In modern times no people are under the influence of astrology and palmistry as the Indians from the villages to the nation's capital. Muhoortam (auspicious time) is invariably determined by pandits and astrologers for every marriage or important ceremony. Before a marriage is decided, the horoscopes of the boy and girl are examined by astrologers and pandits to determine compatibility as is done in regards to "blood groups" in several Western countries. In some parts of India no one will get out of his house during Rahu-Kaalam which extends to 90 minutes daily during day-time.

Early in the fifties Dr. Sampurnanand, who was a remarkable character in many ways, wrote to Nehru about astrology suggesting that he should stop making fun of it publicly. Nehru replied to say that he did not wish to ridicule astrology but that it was a dangerous thing for people to condition their minds on the basis of astrological predictions.

Autobiography

137. Chaudhary, Ram Narayan. *Nehru in his own words*. Ahmadabad, 1964, 218 pp.

138. Naik, M.K. Discovery of Nehru: A study of Nehru's autobiography. In *SON*; 387-400.

139. Nanda, B.R. Nehru's autobiography: Various British reactions. *Times of India* (New Delhi), 14 November 1986; 6.

Fifty years ago, when Jawaharlal Nehru's autobiography was published, it was an instant success. The success was anticipated neither by the author nor by the publishers. Indeed, until almost the last moment, fears were entertained that the book might be banned.

On 18 March 1936, M.K. Rahman of Kitabistan, publishers and booksellers of Allahabad, who had published Nehru's Glimpses of World History in the previous year, addressed a letter to the Secretary, Home Department, Government of India, stating that they had received from John Lane, The Bodley Head, London an announcement of the publication of Nehru's autobiography. "Before we place our indent with the publishers," Rahman wrote, "We would like to be sure that the book is not objectionable and will not be proscribed."

140. Nehru, Jawaharlal. *Autobiography*. Bombay, Allied, 1936.

141. Wasi, Muriel. Exile and autobiography. In *NAG*; 113-16.

Azad, Maulana Abdul Kalam

142. Nehru and Azad. *National Herald* (New Delhi), 22 February 1988; 6.

The publication deadline now is marked by interesting controversies with legal, commercial and political angles. Some people are said to have served a legal notice on the publishers, seeking to regulate the publication. The critics of the Congress-I and the government are known to be looking for any "anti-Nehru" angle in the writings which could be exploited for political purposes. The controversy has served to heighten public interest in the contents, but the generation that has firsthand knowledge of the personality of the leaders and of the later phases of the freedom struggle would take what is said in the 30 pages in its stride, knowing of the greatness of the leaders and their liberal attitudes. Jawaharlal Nehru as well as Maulana Azad, who had the distinction of heading the Congress organisation for several terms at a momentous phase of the country's history, were known to have high regard for each other. They got on well both in the party and in the government. None of the leaders of the time shied away from expressing their views freely at party and Cabinet meetings or giving vent to any honest differences they had.

Backward Classes & Scheduled Tribes

143. Kidwai, Anser. Nehru's new deal for scheduled tribes. *National Herald*, 14 November 1982.

Jawaharlal Nehru's policy for the amelioration of the lot of the Scheduled Tribes formed an integral part of his overall concern for the welfare of the neglected and poverty-stricken people of the country. This policy hinged on bringing about the socio-economic emancipation of India's tribal population—constituting seven per cent of the total populace—without interefering with their traditional and cultural heritage. Also, this policy aimed at ensuring a process of their peaceful transformation to modernism as part of the national mainstream through pursuasive and educative methods. Obviously, this entailed gradual steps towards the overall goal through a well thought out programme of planned development and radical reforms without "dislocating" the traditional pattern of the tribal culture.

Bibliography

144. Sharma, J.S. *Jawaharlal Nehru: A descriptive bibliography.* Delhi, 1955, 421 pp.

Biography

145. Attar Chand. Remembering Nehru. *National Herald*, 28 May 1968; 5.

146. Mehta, N.C. Nehru: A Study in biography. In *NAG*; 238-314.

147. Nehru, Jawaharlal. *Builders of tomorrow*. New Delhi, 1959.

148. *Nehru abhinandan granth: A birthday book*. Nehru, 1949.

149. Ramakrishnan, S. Jawaharlal Nehru. *Bhavan's Journal* (Bombay), 16-30 November 1987; 18-24.

150. Sarin, L.N. Early career. In *Jawaharlal Nehru*. Delhi, 1968; 13-33.

151. Sarin, L.N. *Jawaharlal Nehru*. Delhi, S. Chand, 1968, 98 pp.

Bose, S.C.

152. Mathai, M.O. Subhas Chandra Bose, 1897-1945. In *MDN*; 56-60.

Bose ridiculed Nehru of practising "sentimental politics". Once he described Nehru as the supporter of all lost causes such as China and Spain.

For his re-election as President of the Indian National Congress in 1939 Bose went to the extent of inducing Rabindranath Tagore to lobby for him. Bose was never assailed by thoughts of "means and ends". In fact he did not have such thoughts. Bose's approach to Tagore was repugnant to Nehru.

153. Sharma, S. D. Jawaharlal Nehru. *Women on the March* (New Delhi), November 1973; 3-5.

Bureaucracy

154. Chopra, V.D. New ruling elite and Nehruism. *Patriot*, 16 November 1987.

155. Mathai, M.O. *My days with Nehru.* New Delhi, Vikas, 1979, 270 pp.

156. Mathai, M.O. Nehru and administration. In *MDN*; 118-30.

A statesman need not necessarily be a good administrator. A combination of the two is devoutly to be wished, but how rarely does this occur! Neither Winston Churchill nor Nehru were good administrators. But unlike the Prime Minister in the United Kingdom, Nehru saddled himself with more than one portfolio—External Affairs and Atomic Energy and Scientific Research—on a permanent basis.

157. Mathai, M.O. Nehru's mail. In *MDN*; 44-52.

Innumerable Indian children also wrote and saked the Prime Minister far autographs, autographed photographs and postage stamps. Some of them sent leaves from their autograph books and some sent whole books. Nehru was generous with his time for these children; and all their requests were attended to. Many Indian and American children sent their pocket-money to Nehru when they heard of floods and other natural calamities in India.

158. Mathai, M.O. Some dispointed facts. In *MDN*; 147-63.

Nehru was particular that he should not spend money lavishly on himself. He would go on darning his old clothes including cotton Khadi kurtas and churidar pyjamas. Whenever he left a room he would put off the fan and lights himself instead of leaving it to the servants. When an old overcoat belonging to his father became totally unserviceable, Nehru turned down a proposal to buy an overcoat in London. Instead he bought some rough woolen material from the Khadi Bhandar and his tailor Mohammad Umar made the coat. I never discovered what D.P. Mishra was quick in discovering "Nehru was extremely fond of European dress." It is true that until the mid-fifties he wore European clothes whenever he went to western countries. The reason was that he did not want to appear different and attract attention.

159. Saxena, A.F. Nehru and administration. *National Herald*, 14 November 1973 & 15 November 1973; 5.

160. Sharda Prasad, H.Y. Nehru observed. *Mainstream* Nehru Special Number, 1984; 31-32.

In their long history, the Indian people have had two great love affairs. One was with Krishna of legend. The other was with a flesh-and blood man of our own times, Jawaharlal Nehru. Nehru knew how much he had received. He worte about it in his will and testament. To deserve what he got, he gave abundantly. He wanted to be remembered as a "man who with all his mind and heart, loved India and the Indian people."

161. Trivedi, K.D. Nehru and administration. In *SON*; 322-32.

Cabinet

162. Mathai, M.O. Some ministers. In *MDN*; 244-61.

Barring a few exceptions, more especially after Sardar Patel's death, Nehru's colleagues were not men who would frankly speak out in his presence. Many were tongue-tied before him, some were ever anxious not to displease him, and some tried to find out in advance what was likely to please him. Nearly all had an awe of him. The net result was that Nehru was not well served by his colleagues. This has also happened to other great leaders who towered over their colleagues in parliamentary democracies. A striking recent example was Winston Churchill.

163. Mathai, M.O. N. Gopalaswami Ayyangar and son G. Parthasarthi. In *MDN*; 259-61.

Parthasarthi is an Oxford graduate. He was a good sportsman. He joined the editorial staff of the Hindu which is owned by his close relatives. For a time he was the PTI representative in London for liaison with Reuters, and was later the General Manager of the PTI with headquarters in Bombay, and after some time reverted to the Hindu. I have known him as an agreeable and level-headed person.

When the International Control Commissions were created for the Indo-China states of Vietnam, Cambodia and Laos, India was to provide their Chairmen. Krishna Menon had recommended Foreign Secretary M.J. Desai for Vietnam. The posts for the Control Commissions for Cambodia and Laos were open. I spoke to the Prime Minister and suggested the name of G. Parthasarthi for Cambodia. He liked the suggestion. He asked me to ring up Parthasarthi in Madras and ask him to come over to Delhi. He also asked me to mention the matter to Krishna Menon.

Parthasarthi came. The Prime Minister offered him the Chairmanship of the Control Commission in Cambodia—a post carrying the status of ambassador. Parthasarthi accepted.

Centenary Celebrations

164. Musical chairs. *Newstime* (Hyderabad), 17 May 1987; 4.

During Indira Gandhi's time the Chairmanship of the Congress (I) Centenary Committee underwent rapid changes with Dr. Shankar Dayal Sharma going as Governor to Punjab and B.N. Pande taking up the Orissa governorship and Mr. Uma Shankar Dixit being made the West Bengal Governor. Finally when the celebrations came around Mrs Sheila Dixit was heading the committee. The post was considered a jinxed one as none stayed there for more than six months.

165. Nehru commemoration becomes party affair. *Current* (New Delhi), 30 May 1987; 7.

The 40th Independence and Nehru Centenary Commemoration committee is in the throus of a controversy. Chairman Amitabh Bachchan had to make a quiet exit last fortnight because of the consistent flat it got. The main criticism was its leading lights had nothing to do either with Nehru or with independence. Though Amitabh has slunk out, to be replaced by Minister of State for Parliamentary Affairs Sheila Dikshit, Romesh Bhandari (Vice-chairman), Romi Chopra and Sam Pitroda (general secretaries) are holding out.

166. Plans for Nehru birth centenary fete: Jawahar peace corps to harness youth. *Blitz* (Bombay), 3 January 1987; 7.

N.G. Goray said, banning all *senas* (para-military forces) and specific measures to promote and preserve secularism would be the best homage to Nehru, and the most effective means to observe our independence anniversary.

Arjun Singh, Union Communications Minister, proposed composition of an inspiring poem on Nehru, and its rendering into an evocative song by Lata Mangeshkar (who is also a member of the committee and was present at the meeting).

Darbara Singh urged the school to propagate awareness that "we are Indians first despite our different faiths", in the anniversary year.

Mrs. Nandini Satpathy described Nehru as a "Philosopher King", and felt that Doordarshan must televise about a hundred serialised episodes on Nehru's life.

167. State BJP and Pt. Nehru. *Madhya Pradesh Chronicle* (Bhopal), 3 August 1987; 4.

The state Bhartiya Janta Party President Sunder Lal Patwa's stance that the celebrations of the 40th Anniversary of independence and the Jawahar Lal Nehru Centenary should be combined, separate committees be formed for the two and that if this is not done his party will boycott participation in the joint committee seems to be politically motivated. It is just another instance of opposition for the sake of opposition. It does not become a major national party like the BJP to behave in this fashion. There had been in every country, political leaders with such a towering personality, broad outlook and such a great contribution to the service of the nation that they cannot be rightly considered to belong exclusively to a particular party. They belonged to the entire nation and the nation belonged to them. Abraham Lincoln in the United States of America, Sir Winston Churchill in England, Marshal Tito in Yugoslavia and Col. Nasser in Egypt were such all-time great leaders, and so also were Mahatma Gandhi and Pt. Jawaharlal Nehru who had become synonymous with the Indian freedom movement. To say that Nehru was merely a Congressman only reflects BJP's anti-Nehru bias. Nehru has been rightly called the "Father of Modern India" and the harbinger of industrialisation in the country. It was he who laid a solid foundation of a secular democratic Republic in India and took the country ahead on the road of progress and prosperity. It was due to his painstaking efforts that India today stands among the front-ranking countries of the world.

Challenges

168. Chopra, V.D. Nehruism—the main rudder. *Patriot*, 27 May 1985; 4.

169. Chakraberty, Atulnanda. *Nehru flings a challenge*. Bombay, 1943.

170. Contemporary Nehru. *Link*, 15 November 1987; 3.

171. Kamath, M.V. Nehru steered India to stability. *Pioneer*, 26 April 1987; 4.

In the weeks from 1 January to 6 April, 1948 communal tension reached unprecedented levels in India and resulted in the assassination of Mahatma Gandhi. The country's independence, at the beginning of 1948 was hardly five months old. The Prime Minister, Jawaharlal Nehru was beset with problems from all sides. How was communalism to be tackled? What was to be done about the incoming refugees from Pakistan? Relationship with Pakistan had to be sorted out, there was the problem of restoration of abducted women, the rehabilitation of refugees, the integration of Hyderabad, Kashmir at the United Nations and just the question of governing an unmanageable country. We get a glimpse of the magnitude of the issues confronting Nehru and the manner in which he handled them from his voluminous correspondence with colleagues, friends and officials. Volume 5 of the second series of the Selected Works of Jawaharlal Nehru is just out (ed. S. Gopal, Oxford University Press, Bombay, pages 610; Rs 150) and it provides us fresh glimpse into his personality.

172. Mehta, Asoka. Glory and tragedy of Nehru. *New Socialist*, November 1959; 4-6.

173. Moraes, Frank. Nehru: Sunlight and shadow. Bombay, Jaico, 1964, 208 pp.

174. Nehru and the future. *National Herald*, 14 November 1977; 6.

175. Nehru harbinger of change. *Madhya Pradesh Chronicle*, 16 November 1985; 4.

Shri Jawaharlal Nehru was the focal-point of India's policy for over forty years. With his debut in Indian politics in 1924, he continued to be the architect and builder of modern India.

Nehru was the harbinger of a change which transformed a feudal, hierarchical polity into a modern country. This change was brought about by him with perseverance, dedication, wisdom and courage. It was Pt. J.L. Nehru who laid out the foundation of a secular and democratic State. Not only that. He was the first national leader to evolve the concept of national consensus and self-reliance as the corner-stone of national resurgence towards a definite national identity.

Nehru was the architect of an independent, non-aligned foreign policy for India. It was an element of faith for him. During his life-time, he never compromised on the policy of non-alignment. He vigorously propagated it along with his trusted friends, Nasser and Tito.

176. Nehru phobia. *Free Press Journal* (Bombay), 10 November 1979; 4.

177. Satinder Singh. Forty-years of Nehru dynasty: the decades of decadence. *Newstime*, 15 August 1987.

178. Sinclair, Upton. Man of action. In *NAG*; 6-7.

179. Singh, A. Nehru and India's future. *New Republic* 106, March 1942.

Children

180. Anand, Mulk Raj. *Chacha Nehru*. New Delhi, Sterling, 1987.

181. Chacha (Uncle) Nehru. *Deccan Herald* (Bangalore), 14 November 1985; 6.

If Mahatma Gandhi was, as Nehru designated him, "the Father of the Nation", Nehru himself was the universal "chacha" of India's young. Come to think of it, no world leader has been identified so much with children as Nehru. At the height of the Cuban missile crisis of 1962, when the balloon really seemed about to go up, President Kennedy remarked to his wife that it was for the children of the world that he was concerned since "we adults have had our innings". Nehru respected the autonomy of children and would have nothing to do with the strategy of "catching them young" much favoured by some of our revivalist brethren.

182. Ghosh, Atulya. Tryst with chacha's love. *Economic Times*, 15 November 1981; 4.

Jawaharlal's debut in politics was not spectacular, rather slow and gradual. But once in it, he became a whirl-wind. No checks and balances for him. A combination of Gandhiji and Jawaharlal, the two opposite forces, opened a new chapter in the country's struggle for independence. Jawaharlal has himself admitted that in many matters he opposed Gandhiji, but ultimately in most of the cases Gandhiji was in the right.

183. Menon, K.N. *Children's Nehru.* New Delhi, Caxton, 1960.

184. Nehru and Children. *National Herald*, 14 November 1985; 4.

November 14, Jawaharlal Nehru's birthday, is Children's Day. To the children all over the world 'chacha' Nehru was more than a friend, philosopher and guide. Despite his hectic day-to-day schedule, Nehru found time to be with children and those moments were to talk to them a out what he called this 'beautiful world' of ours—flowers, trees, birds, animals, stars, mountains and glaciers.

Communalism

185. Communalism and the minority problem. In *NFC*; 72-85.

186. Ganesh Prasad. Approach to Communalism. *Mainstream*, 21 June 1969; 13-15.

Jawaharlal Nehru was the child of the Indian Renaissace. By temperament, training and conviction he was opposed to obscurantism, medievalism, communalism and sectarianism. Reading his thoughts on communalism is refreshing, instructive and fruitful, especially at the present time when Indian nationhood is threatened by all sorts of narrow creeds, irrational norms and fissiparous tendencies. His views and works foster scientific understanding of social phenomena. His failing represent the weakness of the link-generation in solving national problems. A study of relevant references to communalism form the works of this Descartes of modern Indian politics can indeed be a fruitful exercise in understanding the robust aspect of Indian nationalism.

187. Goyal, D.R. Affront to Nehru legacy. *Mainstream*, 12 November 1983, 15-16; 37.

Nehru's contribution to the making of modern India is many-faceted; his ideas compel wider and wider appreciation as science is being exploited more and more for destructive purposes by those who fear the changes that science and comprehensive democracy entail. Specifically for India, the most important part of Nehru's framework of thought was secularisation. It stands out because the circumstances in which he assumed office in 1946-47 were most uncogenial for establishing a secular state.

Partition and the immense suffering it imposed upon millions of people made the ideal of secularism look almost like a luncatic's dream. RSS led by Golwalkar had mounted a big campaign for 'Hindu-Hindi-Hindusthan'. The Jamaat-e-Islami chief, Abdul Ala Maudoodi, counselled that leaders of India should consult the Hindu scriptures to evolve a Constitution for themselves while Pakistan developed into an Islamic state. Many of Nehru's colleagues in the Congress and even in his own Cabinet agreed with that way of thinking. And yet he did not yield.

188. Khan, Abdul Majid. Communalism and Imperialism. In *Jawaharlal Nehru and His Ideas*. New Delhi, 1951; 52-57.

189. Nehru, Jawaharlal. Hindu Mahasabha and communalism. In *REW*; 43-44.

190. Nehru, Jawaharlal. Hindu and Muslim communalism. In *REW*; 45-59.

191. Patil, V.T. Hindu Muslim relations and partition of India: the Nehru approach. In *Nehru and the Freedom Movement*. New Delhi, Sterling, 1977; 179-224.

192. Pillai, K.M. Hamara Nehru and the Hindu Muslim question. In *SON*; 266-85.

193. Raghib, A.R. Communal crescendo: Nehru's vision splintered. *New Wave*, 19 April 1987; 5.

This cursory look at the states shows that the slogan of national integration has ceased to have any impact. The reason is, as "New Wave" has been consistently pointing out, the policy of secularism cannot succeed in isolation. In Nehru's vision of India, socialism, secularism and democracy formed integral parts of the whole. All the three elements of this vision reinforce each other and can succeed, if pursued together.

191. Vijai Singh. Relevance of Nehruism. *Hindustan Times*, 27 May 1981; 9.

Communism

195. Mitter, J.P. Nehru as a Communist. *Statesman*, 20 December 1969; 6.

It is pertinent to let the public know that Jawaharlal Nehru in those days was castigated as a "reformist" of the worst type by the Communist Press. Subsequently, much later, when Nehru made a statement in December, 1933 that he believed the choice before the world lay between Communism and Fascism and that he chose the former, his articles started being published in some of the Communist papers.

196. Nehru, Jawaharlal. Fascism and Communism. In *Recent essays and writings*, Allahabad, 1934; 125-26.

The Indian press has been very kind and considerate to me and has given me numerous opportunities of giving publicity to my opinions. I must express my gratitude to it. But sometimes it gives me a shock and one of the biggest shocks that I have recently had has come today from the report of a so-called interview in Delhi given to certain foreign visitors. The National Call of Delhi first gave publicity to this and I was amazed to read what I was supposed to have said. The Free Press Journal of Bombay has now gone a few steps further and in a seven-column headline announces that I have put my cards on the table and declared that I prefer Fascism to Communism.

197. Verma, P.S. Nehru and the communist movement. *Link*, 15 August 1987; 33-39.

A very considerable amount of literature has grown around Nehru yet there exists no systematic work which discusses and delineated the pattern of relationship between Nehru and the Communist movement in India. Incidentally, both Nehru and the Communist movement had appeared on the Indian political scene almost simultaneously during the years immediately following the First World War.

The national and international factors which influenced the growth of the Left movement in the country had equally affected his evolving ideas and political values, though he joined neither the Communist movement nor the Congress Socialist Party in the formation of which he played a significant role.

Communist Party of India

198. Gupta, Bhupesh. No good reviling us, Pandit Nehru, meet us, on the plane of politics. *New Age*, 29 January 1957.

199. Mishra, R.K. Nehru's concept of Left in Indian politics. *Patriot*, 24 January 1976.

Nehru was aware that the building of socialism and ending of exploitation would lead to conflict and, therefore, it will be necessary for the Congress to decide whose side it will take in the case of a conflict. He was not prepared to push this issue under the carpet of "nationalism" and asked pointedly "whose freedom are we particularly striving for, for nationalism covers many sins and includes many conflicting elements?'.

200. Sen, Mohit. Nehruism and the left. *Mainstream*, Annual Number 1966; 73-75.

Some supposedly "Left" critics are thoroughly upset by the charge levelled against Indira Gandhi for deviating and even repudiating the so-called Nehru line. A few of these critics are annoyed that those making these charges should still continue to be under what is called the spell of the ineffectual angel. Others of the same circle wonder why Indira Gandhi should not be permitted the right of ideological parricide-socialism is not to be identified with Nehru's outlook and programme, they say.

201. Sethi, J.D. Nehru and the communist Left. *Indian Express*, 27 May 1983; 6.

Today the nation remembers Nehru as an architect of modern India which his successors have systematically dismantled. The Indian Communists would also like to remember him for his vision, anti-imperialism and policies which now are buried under a heap of ruins. The Communists between 1947 and 1953 called Nehru a running dog of imperialism, because that is how Moscow characterised him. They now take cover under Nehru for their sins of betraying the Indian revolution and of having become the discarded rump of international Communism.

Constitutional Development

202. Kashyap, Subhash C. *Jawaharlal Nehru and the Constitution.* New Delhi, 1982.

Cripps Mission

203. Patil, V.T. *Jawaharlal Nehru and the Cripps Mission.* Delhi, 1984, 132 pp.

204. Singh, B.N. *Cripps Mission.* New Delhi, Usha, 1979.

205. Venkatarami, M.S. and B.K. Shrivastava. United States and the Cripps Mission. *India Quarterly* 19(1), January-March 1963.

Criticism

206. Attar Chand. Degradation. *Daily* (Bombay), 3 August 1987.

207. Attar Chand. Nehru's failures. *Newstime*, 19 August 1987.

208. Dubashi, Jay. Irrelevance of Nehru. *Organiser*, 17 June 1984; 2.

Jawaharlal Nehru's 20th death anniversary was celebrated with marked lack of popular enthusiasm despite the fact that the family used the entire government machinery to drum up publicity. The professional sycophants did their bit of course bringing out special supplements and reviews and so did the family retainers in such well-maintained stables as Jawaharlal Nehru University and the Nehru Museum.

There was, however, little popular reaction and most of the meetings called by fellow-travelling worthies who come into their own on such occasions, went virtually unattended. It is, as if, twenty years after his death, Nehru had become irrelevant, just as Mahatma Gandhi had become, less than 20 years after his own death.

I have a feeling that the popular reaction is correct, that Nehru has, indeed, become irrelevant. It is not his fault of course. The country has changed so much since his death that it has no place for him in its pantheon. It has changed for the worst and my main charge against Nehru is that it is he who is responsible for the deterioration.

I am not one of those who believe that Nehru erred in going in for heavy industry on the Russian pattern or that everything would be fine in the garden if only he had taken the low technology route, giving priority to agriculture, village industries, etc., on the Gandhian lines. In my view, Nehru was right to reject the Gandhian path of development, whatever that is; for I do not think that it can ever be the right path for a country like India.

209. Durga Das. Nehru's critics. In *India* London, 1969; 373.

There were only three effective spokesmen of the Opposition during the Nehru era. They were S.P. Mookerjee. Kripalani and

Lohia. The first was a real leader because he spoke for the largest group which opposed Nehru's policies. In oratory and debating skill, he excelled all others who have followed him. Kripalani was always the dissenter and a lone performer. He would have been more effective had he led an Opposition bloc. Lohia was the debunker. He ruthlessly attacked Nehru at every opportunity, repeatedly accusing him of spending Rs. 25,000 a day on himself as Prime Minister in maintaining a large retinue of assistants and bodyguards and a "luxurious" standard of living. He called Mrs. Gandhi a "dumb doll".

Mookerjee used to tell me that the only way to create an alternative to the Congress was to demolish Nehru's image. He died while in detention in Srinagar in 1953, and a promising political career was thus cut short. Kripalani too believed the evils in the country emanated from the top and that Nehru was the pace-setter in abusing patronage and power. Lohia believed that the Nehru family's identification with the nation was not only undemocratic but harmful and that Nehru's acceptance of Anglo-Indian cultural values led to his opposing anything that would give the nation a sense of Indianness.

Lohia told me several times that the North, especially the U.P., had remained backward because the Prime Minister had always been chosen from this region. This made the holder of the office lean over backward to please the South in planning economic development and the allocation of important portfolios in the Cabinet.

210. Ghosal, Nirmal. Nehru's mistakes. *Amrita Bazar Patrika*, 26 July 1987; 6.

It is true that our first Prime Minister Jawaharlal Nehru was a great statesman, intellectual and a liberal democrat. But due to his enthusiasm in the first flush of independence he committed some grave mistakes for which the people in India are now suffering tremendously. These are as follows: First, he did not agree to Mr. Jinnah's proposal for exchange of population and properties as a natural consequence to the partition of India on the basis of religion. He was proved wrong, because we all know what happened in Punjab and East Bengal shortly afterwards. So much of bloodshed, killings and sufferings of the Hindus and Sikhs could have been avoided if he had agreed to the proposal, since several

Muslims were then for Pakistan and wanted partition on the basis of religion.

Second, it also did not occur to Mr. Nehru (being such a liberal Hindu) that the Muslim League which spearheaded the movement for partition on the basis of religion and obtained the same with so much jubilation should have been banned. Third, the formation of the linguistic states was a great blunder which is now threatening the integrity of India. Regionalism is raising its ugly head and confronting the Centre by all means which has a dangerous implication for the country.

Last, India's tacit approval of the Chinese occupation of Tibet, a buffer state of strategic importance, by brute force, had emboldened China to occupy the vast Indian territory. This shocked Nehru so much that he could not bear it and died a frustrated man.

211. Ghosh, Sankar. Nehruism in danger. *Amaita Bazar Patrika*, 12 November 1979; 6.

The critics of Nehru in the Congress could be broadly divided in two groups. One group thought that he did not go far enough along the socialist path the other alleged that he was too far gone on the path to the detriment of national interest. Normally, there could be no question of these two groups coming together for their politico-ideological commitments were different. The right and the left coming together was a rare spectacle some two decades ago though it is not so today. Patel could not have blessed both; maybe on many of the points at issue Nehru and Patel would have been on the same side.

The name of Patel is being used as a convenient flag for Patel died almost on the morrow of independence. He died full of glory. Had he lived a few more years the problems of independence would certainly have taken some of the shine off his image. Nehru was Prime Minister for 17 years—a period long enough to make younger aspirants resolve and bitter. There is no doubt that if Nehru had died early and Patel lived on, Patel's critics would have been as numerous as Nehru's were and they would have, irrespective of their political and ideological commitments, used Nehru's name as the rallying point against the rule and polity of the Sardar.

212. Mehra, Manmohan. Reversing Nehru is riversing history. *Patriot*, 27 May 1980; 2.

After independence, Jawaharlal Nehru dominated the national scene. From a militant soldier of the Congress, he rose to be its topmost leader. With his largeness of vision, cosmopolitan culture, and his constructive and radical approach to the multifarious problems confronting the country, Nehru took India a long way towards progress and prosperity. He was a great democrat who helped to build democratic institutions. He taught India the temper of democracy. He was the greatest parliamentarian of his time who upheld the dignity and decorum of the Parliament. Secularism was a natural corollary of Nehru's democratic faith in the right of every individual to attain his full stature.

213. Mishra, Girish. L.K. Jha opens a new front to subvert Nehru. *New Wave*, 5 April 1987; 7.

For quite some time Nehruvian policies and Nehruvian model of socio-economic transformation have been under attack from various quarters, some of which still swear by his name and thinking. These attacks are both covert and overt. In recent weeks these attacks have been in the context of the fast increasing defence spendings of the country.

214. Nayar, Kuldip. Nehru has no honest followers. *Current* (Bombay), 4 June 1983; 5.

Nehru was conscious of the existence of corruption but it had never reached the proportions it has reached these days. He did not try to shrug it off, unlike Indira Gandhi, by saying that corruption was a world phenomenon.

215. Nehru's power was never challenged.—Tarkunde. *National Herald*, 21 January 1979; 4.

Mr. V.M. Tarkunde feels elders have exhausted their creativity and all "they can do now is to wait and encourage the younger generation build a more human society."

He described nationalism as a "tribal sentiment". It did not require pre-thinking equality or fraternity. The movement was wholly negative but vested with democratic values.

After independence was achieved, large numbers of Indians wanted "Ram Rajya" rather than "Swarajya".

216. Patel, D.V. *Which Way Nehru*? New Delhi, 1961.

217. Patwardhan, P.H. *Jawaharlal Nehru : The ecstasy and the agony*. Poona, 1967.

218. Pillai, R.C. *Jawaharlal Nehru and His Critics*. New Delhi, Gitanjali, 1987, 279 pp. Book Review by T.S. Gill in *Tribune*, 8 August 1987; 4.

Tracing the growth of Nehru's political ideas from his interest in science and socialism, the author contends in the words of his perceptive biographer that he had "a radical rather than an ideological mind". As a result of his interest in science, Nehru professed the ideas of western rationalism and the impulses of democratic thought. Impelling him to grow into an agnostic, this thinking process made him indifferent to the subterfuge of mythology, religion and theology. This was in spite of the fact that in his later years he acquired deeper appreciation of Indian history and philosophy.

The author describes all this while tracing the evolution of Nehru's political ideas. What implication his scientific bent had on popular thinking is not, however, precisely dealt with anywhere in the study. This perhaps laid the basis of his good sense as distinct from the common sense of the people that subjected them to ignorance and alien rule, on the one hand, and sustained them in the face of deprivation and scarcity, on the other hand.

The trajectory of his good sense grew in diachronic as well as synchronic proportions though it did not realise its entirety in either direction. Evidence of its growth in the diachronic direction is provided by his study to history. Valuable for several of its materialist perceptions, it is regrettable for its idealistic evocations. A few in number in its historiographical aspect, they dispose his thinking to the Vedic-Upanishadic ethos, that even now forms the regressive core in the common sense of the Indian people.

That his good sense grew in the synchronic direction is provided by his interest in socialism. Besides giving an economic content to his political thinking, it turned him into a votary planning, of mixed economy and of socialist pattern of society. Anti-imperialist and anti-fascist to begin with, he became the founder of non-alignment. As a dynamic strategy, it was distinct from its passive connotation in terms of neutrality.

Nehru's good sense was meant to awaken the feeling of national independence, economic progress and modern outlook in the minds of the Indian people. That he assumed this responsibility in all its subtlety and sobriety is evident from the lifelong challenge that he posed to Gandhi's advocacy of the common sense of the Indian people. Regarding it as self-sufficient, Gandhi sought solutions to scarcity and deprivation in terms of anthropocentricism and anthropomorphism latent in it. No wonder he regarded non-violence, non-cooperation, trusteeship and village industry as imperative for the purpose.

219. Ranga, N.G. My differences with the great democrat. *National Herald*, 14 November 1987.

220. Sethi, J.D. Enormous unrealism. *Indian Express*, 8 November 1985, 6.

The realism that Rajiv Gandhi displays in handling domestic issues despite pressures from vested interests gets twisted as soon as he steps out of the country. South Block bureaucrats seem to have succeeded in convincing him that foreign policy is all a matter of image-building for populist rhetoric and that fundamental issues can be subordinated to the compulsions of global fame.

That was what Nehru believed and he came to a sorry pass when the harsh reality caught up with him. The military and economic power needed to sustain a global image was simply not there and Nehru's image lay battered in humiliation after the Chinese attack on India in 1962. The moral of Nehru's failure is to avoid the temptation of wanting to strut on the global stage while living on inadequate and borrowed strength.

221. Twenty-years after Nehru: they attacked Nehru, but he has triumphed over his detractors. *Link*, 27 May 1984; 14-15.

Nehru put the nation on the road of planned development and for this his detractors describe him a disguised Communist. Taking into account the correlation of social forces, he opted for mixed economy; the radicals criticised him as a defender of the bourgeoisie. He proposed to reorganise rural India on cooperative lines, and for this the vested interests within and outside his party organised a revolt against him.

Culture

222. Anand, Mulk Raj. Jawaharlal Nehru's idea of culture as a human right. *Indian and Foreign Review*, 30 April 1987; 8-11, 28.

That culture is human right was an emergent concept in Jawaharlal Nehru's quest, specially during the last period of India's struggle for freedom. He wished it to be possessed by every individual, in his or her own way, for development of the personality, by the exercise of creative talents. And he wanted when our country would be liberated for it to realise many freedoms, not only political freedom, but all the freedoms necessary for growth of the people into whole men and women.

223. Attar Chand. His love for India. *Madhya Pradesh Chronicle*, 20 August 1987.

224. Chelyshev, E. Nehru and culture. *Patriot*, 14 November 1972; 4

In Jawaharlal Nehru's works the development of Indian culture is stipulated by the historic process of the development of Indian society, and he does not isolate the development of his national culture from the history of world culture. An important place in his works belongs to the problem of appraising the influence of the national-liberation movement on the formation of democratic tendencies in Modern Indian culture.

225. Culture. In *QON*; 118-22.

226. Gracias, Valerian. Nehru: Man of two cultures and one world. In *Nehru and the modern world*. New Delhi, UNESCO, 1967; 8-22.

227. Jamuar, S.P. Pt. Nehru : Symbol of India's cultural identity. *Indian Nation*, 14 November 1986; 4.

Pt. Jawaharlal Nehru, who was born on November 14, 1889 at Allahabad and died on May 27, 1964 in Delhi, was a man of a very high order and endowed with an examplary gift of fine expression in English. He succeeded in making a great experiment in economic planning of our democratic polity so that it may compete with developed countries. He was very much keen to usher India in its industrial revolution in the existing socio-economic perspective of the country.

228. Karanjia, R.K. Philosophy of synthesis. In *Mind of Mr. Nehru.* London, 1960; 76-80.

229. Nehru, Jawaharlal. What is culture? *New Wave*, 26 July 1987; 2.

230. Nehru, Jawaharlal. Civic ideal. In *REW*; 137-39.

231. Nehru nursed nation's tolerant culture. *National Herald*, 26 May 1983; 4.

Prof. Khusro said Nehru was not only the chief architect of economic planning, but also piloted such crucial strategies such as industrialisation, import substitution, agricultural progress, infrastructure construction and scientific and technological development. Had he been alive today, Nehru would have noted with satisfaction the continuation of the growth process, though slow, but an occurrence which had put the country in a class by itself among the developing countries, he said. He would also have been satisfied with the process of industrialisation and the strides made in the field of science.

232. Rao, V.K.R.V. Nehru and India's cultural renaissance. In *FON*; 15-20.

Defence

233. Defence spending and Nehru approach. *Mainstream*, 25 April 1987; 7-8.

For quite some time Nehruvian policies and Nehruvian model of socio-economic transformation have been under attacks from various quarters. These attacks are both covert and overt. In recent weeks, these attacks have been in the context of the fast increasing defence spending of the country.

234. Gupta, Rakesh. Nehru model and defence production. *Patriot*, 12 May 1987; 4.

Any discussion on India's anti-imperialism would positively indicate the temporariness of its stability caused by the path of capitalist development pursued in India. The Nehruvian model is based on the sharp logic of a razor's edge. It was possible within the logic of following independent capitalist development to deviate from its "independence" and move towards shades of lesser or greater dependence.

235. Sarhadi, Ajit Singh. Nehru era. In *India's security in resurgent Asia*. New Delhi, Heritage, 1979; 236-71.

Nehru sponsored the Asian Relations Conference in New Delhi in 1947, with a view to evolving a counter to the United Nations, a whiteman club then. The conference was designed to express Asia's political viewpoint in the post-war world. But rift amongst the members to the Asian Conference set in right from the outset. According to Werner Levi, a noted writer, "the Conference marked the apex of Asian solidarity and the beginning of its decline, the reasons for this were many varied; the two major sources of discord were the intense rivalry in between India and China in the conference and the growing distrust of the two Asian giants among smaller countries of the region.

236. Subrahmanyam, K. Nehru's concept of defence. *IDSA Journal*, 15(2) October 1972.

237. Victor, Cecil. Subversion of Nehru's self-reliance. *Patriot*, 21 November 1984; 4.

In recent times there has been an acceleration of a process which goes against the grain of everything that Jawaharlal Nehru had advocated with regard to peace and security in Asia and the world. For one thing he saw the world in its totality; not broken up into region wherein developments could be insulated and not have effect globally to the detriment of world peace and security. Thus there was in his world-view both elements of rational peace and security and non-proliferation of nuclear weapons (indeed of disarmament).

Today, regional conflicts are being created, and nuclear weapons proliferation is being winked at by the very nations which want that the rest of the world must sign the non-Proliferation Treaty (NPT) and so we have racist South Africa and Israel as crypto-nuclear powers and Pakistan busy fashioning a bomb in its basement in the knowledge of if not active collaboration by the US.

The Asian dimension to peace and security in the nuclear age has, therefore, become paramount in any discussion of global trends. It is here that a systematic attempt is underway to subverts national sovereignties, undermine non-alignment to which most of the States of this region subscribe, create new regional military groupings and proxies to execute military plans formulated outside the region. Asia is, in short, a powder keg which will make all talk of peace and security in the nuclear age redundant if events are allowed to along present, predictable lines.

Nehru, in his lifetime, had begun to feel the pressures of neo-colonialism and when Chinese expansionism destroyed his dream of "bhai-bhai" across the Himalayan frontier, he set about giving content to self-reliance in defence material because national sovereignty and territorial integrity were obviously incomplete without a self-sustaining military capability. It was a military debacle that started the process of indigenisation of military technology.

But not that alone. It was the fearful vista of dependence and the concommitant subservience of national interests that Nehru perceived in the men bearing gifts who offered us a nuclear umbrella and all the trappings of servitude which went with it. It would have meant a fall from non-alignment and a duplication of the obliterating cultural experiences of Japan, the Philippines and the others who fell to invading armies. It would have also injected the virus of military dictatorship as happened in neighbouring Pakistan which had already lent itself as a handmaiden to military pacts.

So, the much-maligned Krishna Menon during his tenure as Defence Minister set about erecting an infrastructure for the production of military wherewithal, using licence production of foreign armaments as a first step towards eventual self-reliance. That it was necessary to begin that way was dictated by the time factor, the long gestation periods and the nascent nature of Indian science and technology. But that stage was never conceived to be as permanent as it has come to be.

Democracy

238. Baig, Tara Ali. Nehru and democracy. In *NP*; 97-102.

239. Bimal Prasad. Three pillars of Nehru's democracy. *National Herald*, 18 November 1981; 4.

240. Chakrabarti, A. *Nehru : His democracy in India.* Calcutta, Thackers, 1960, 438 pp.

241. Chalapathi Rau, M. Democratic process. In *Jawaharlal Nehru.* New Delhi, 1962; 1-5.

242. Chandy, K.T. Democracy. In Socialism, democracy and secularism: *A symposium in memory of Jawaharlal Nehru.* New Delhi, 1965; 32-47.

243. Das, A.N. Nehru's vision of parliamentary democracy. In *NP*; 67-80.

244. Democracy. In *QON*; 150-54.

245. Dinesh Singh. Author and guide of Parliamentary democracy in India. In *NP*; 43-46.

246. Diwaker, R.R. Nehru and Parliamentary democracy: Some thoughts. In *NP*; 34-35.

247. Gopal Singh. Jawaharlal Nehru: The democrat. In *NP*; 108-14.

248. Jakhar, Balram. Nehru: An ideal parliamentarian. In *NP*; 26-29.

249. Karan Singh. Nehru and Parliament. In *NP*; 153-54.

250. Kashyap, Subhash C. Jawaharlal Nehru and Parliament. *Indian Express*, 14 November 1985; 6.

Under Nehru's stewardship, the rights and privileges of Members were duly safeguarded, and the dignity and prestige of the House maintained. He asserted, "I am zealous of the powers of this House and I should not like anyone to limit those powers." He believed in the primacy of Parliament in Indian polity and in its supremacy within the field assigned to it by the Constitution. In the matter of the role of the judicial review, Nehru took a very firm stand and said that the courts could not become a third legislative chamber; their role was to interpret the laws made by Parliament and not lay down the law.

251. Kidwai, Anser. Nehru and working of democracy. In *NP*; 81-85.

252. Krishna Mani, P.N. Nehru era in Parliament: Some recollections. In *NP*; 171-81.

253. Mahtab, Hare Krushna. Architect of parliamentary democracy in India. In *NP*; 30-33.

254. Morarka, R.R. Father of parliamentary democracy in India. In *NP*; 47-58.

255. Nehru gave shape to democracy in India. *National Herald*, 14 August 1981.

256. Nila Kanta Sastri, K.A. Democracy in India. In *NAG*; 337-40.

257. Niraj. *Nehru and democracy in India.* New Delhi, Jain Book Agency, 1972.

258. Parashar, Narain Chand. Nehru and democracy at the grassroots level. In *NP*; 106-7.

259. Patnaik, Biju. Nehru and parliamentary democracy. In *NP*; 103-5.

260. Ranga, N.G. Democratic thinker. In *NAG*; 146-48.

261. Rasheeduddin Khan. Nehru as a democrat. In *NP*; 115-24.

262. Roy, Renuka. Nehru and parliamentary democracy. In *NP*; 59-66.

263. Setalvad, M.C. Nehru and Indian parliamentary democracy. In *Nehru legacy*. New Delhi, 1966; 14-24.

Taking democracy in its political aspect, the functioning of Parliament, there is little doubt that Nehru established conventions and traditions which if followed will tend to put our parliamentary government on a sound and durable footing. So conscious was he of the supremacy of Parliament in all matters that when he heard a senior minister in his cabinet assert in Parliament that he would not adopt a certain course even if Parliament asked him to do so, he it is reported, said that the minister concerned, however experienced, could never be entrusted with the responsibility of being a Prime Minister. Indeed Nehru has been described by his foreign biographer as "a supreme democrat."

264. Shah, K.K. Parliamentary democracy: Right means to achieve ends. In *NP*; 36-42.

265. Singh, Bhishma Narain. Nehru and parliamentary democracy. In *NP*; 93-96.

266. Singh, Raghuveer. Prolegeomena to a conceptual treat of Nehru's view of democracy. In *SON*; 49-60.

267. Smith, D.E. *Nehru and democracy*. London, 1958.

Desai, Morarji

268. Nehru's industrial policy valid: Desai. *I dian Express*, 17 February 1978.

Deshmukh, C.D.

269. Mathai, M.O. C.D. Deshmukh. In *MDN*; 244-48.

He was an outstanding ICS officer who ended up the Duputy Governor and later Governor of the Reserve Bank of India during British times. Nehru wanted to include Deshmukh in the interim government in September 1946. Deshmukh had just then retired from the Reserve Bank of India. He told Nehru about his family troubles and that he wanted to make a final effort at reconciliation with his English wife. After conveying his excuses to Nehru, he went to England where his wife was staying in estrangement. Deshmukh's mission ended in failure. He even suffered the humiliation of being called "blackie" by his daughter. Deshmukh ultimately returned to India after the final break with his wife.

Diplomacy

270. Mathai, M.O. Some foreign dignitaries. In *MDN*; 179-92.

Dynasty

271. Kothari, Rajni. Nehru dynasty. *Newstime* (Weekend), 23 August 1987; 2.

272. Maharishi Agnesh. Kingdom of the Nehrus. *Organiser* (New Delhi), 20 November 1983.

It appears as though we have pledged India to the Nehru family. True, Motilal Nehru did contribute some funds to the Congress during British rule. But so did the Birlas many hundred times more. Many other philanthropists and country-conscious people, including Dadabhai Naoroji, did so, and much more than Motilal. But Gandhiji preferred Jawaharlal to Patel and Subhash. The result is that the country has suffered immensely inasmuch as a new kingdom of Nehru has been established although constitutionally we are a republic.

The entire country today is spotted with Jawaharlal stadiums, Jawaharlal universities, Jawaharlal tunnels, Jawaharlal colonies, Jawaharlal shopping complexes, nagars, this, that and all. We have also Indira islands, Indira bridges, Indira nagars. Now sundry institutions are being named after Sanjay also. If this continues we may soon have the names of Rajiv, Sonia, Rahul and Priyanka prefixed to places and institutions.

In this race for immortality by Nehrus even Mahatma Gandhi has been reduced to a secondary position while not even a single institution or place has been named after martyrs like Bhagat Singh, Sukhdev, Rajguru, Chandrashekhar Azad, Udham Singh, V.P. Phadke, etc. Don't they deserve even this little bit from us ungrateful people.

273. Nehru and his heirs. *Telegraph* (Calcutta), 15 November, 1983; 6.

274. Nehru's heirs? *National Herald*, 15 November 1973; 5.

275. Pandit, Vijaya Lakshmi. Prime Ministers are lonely people. *Times of India* (Sunday Review), 30 August 1987; 5.

276. Rahul Singh. All in the family. *Indian Post* (Bombay), 18 August 1987; 7.

Except for four years and six months, India has been led by three generations of the Nehru family since Independence. We have perhaps in a sense taken this for granted but for outsiders, especially if they come from the democratic world, it is a phenomenon which causes them great wonder and often bewilderment. There is no parallel with any other democracy.

Earthquake

277. Nehru, Jawaharlal. Quetta earthquake. In *India's freedom*. London, 1962; 49-54.

There was no room for Gandhiji or Rajendra Babu or other popular leaders and well-known relief workers in Quetta, but Boy Scouts could be sent without danger of their catching disease or lessening the stock of food. If Gandhiji had gone there might have been a shortage of goat's milk and dates.

Quetta became one of the battle-fronts, enveloped as it were in the fog of war, a no-man's land which was out off from the rest of the country. The official megaphone boomed out its version of the news to us and told us of the wonders that were being performed by the official agency alone and unaided by others.

Economic Philosophy and Planning

278. Abid Husain, S. *Way of Gandhi and Nehru.* Bombay, Asia, 1959.

279. Activizing the base of Indian society. *Patriot,* 18 February 1978; 4.

Nehru considered planning essential for economic and social development. But, he warned: "Planning is a much more complicated process than merely drawing up some schemes and fixing a system of priorities. . . in planning we have to balance heavy industry. We want heavy industry because without it we can never really be an independent country. Light industry too has become essential for us, so has cottage industry. I am putting forward this argument not from the Gandhian ideal but because it is essential to balance heavy industry and to prevent the big gap between the pumping in of money and production. (New discoverers of Gandhian economics may please note).

Inaugurating production at the Integral Coach Factory at Perambur, Madras, on 2 October, 1955, Nehru said, "I am quite sure that if it had been our good fortune to have Gandhiji with us today, he would have been glad at the opening of this factory. This factory, like all factories, does not come in the way of his basic desire to develop the village industries and generally raise the standard of our vast rural and urban population. Some people take a rather narrow and lop-sided view of Gandhiji." How true, especially these days!

Speaking in the Lok Sabha on 11 April, 1955, Nehru said, "We talk about a socialistic pattern of society, industrialization, the removing of unemployment, of higher standards and so on. What is really necessary is somehow to activize and dynamize the base of the Indian social structure. I want the House to appreciate this phrase. No doubt there must be approaches from the top, but there has been too much activizing from the top layers of society all the time. We do not solve our problems unless we activize the base of Indian society, which means millions and millions of villagers, millions of workers and small earners, unemployed people and people on the land." Those who claim to be more genuine followers of Gandhiji that Nehru might well remember these words of Gandhiji.

280. Ajoy, Ghosh. *On India's path of development.* New Delhi, CPI, 1956.

281. Amrit Kaur. Wealth of human sympathy. In *NAG*; 139-40.

282. Appadorai, A. Nehru, the thinker: Importance of pragmatism. *Statesman*, 1 September 1979; 6.

283. Attar Chand. Need of the hour. *Hindustan Times Evening News* (New Delhi), 1 August 1987.

284. Attar Chand. Nehru and small industries. *National Herald*, 4 August 1987.

285. Attar Chand. Nehru's vision of new India. *National Herald*, 30 July 1987.

286. Attar Chand. Towards self-reliance. *Newstime* (Hyderabad), 2 August 1987.

287. Audichya, Janardan. *Economic ideas of Jawaharlal Nehru.* Jodhpur, Jain Brothers, 1977, 170 pp.

288. Bawa, T.S. Nehru's *India: An analytical study*. New Delhi, 1956.

289. Benjamin, N. Evolution of Nehru's economic thinking. *Economic Times*, 26 May 1974; 4.

Jawaharlal Nehru has emerged as one of the greatest personalities in Indian history. The period of his prime-ministership ending with his death in 1964 witnessed the laying of foundations of a new India. The deep impression made by his ideas is evident not only on the policies of his Cabinet, but also on the policies followed by Lal Bahadur Shastri and Mrs. Indira Gandhi. In view of this it would be in the fitness of things to recollect the evolution of his economic thinking for, May 27 will be the day of his tenth death anniversary. For the sake of brevity, only two of the most important aspects of his economic thinking will be covered in the present note viz., economic planning and socialism.

290. Bhave, Vinoba. Bounteous Providence. In *NAG*; 130.

291. Birla, G.D. Nehru. In *NAG*; 177-78.

292. Chakravarty, S. Nehru's concept of planning. *Akashvani* (New Delhi), 20 January 1974; 81-83.

To understand Nehru's concept of planning, one has to appreciate his attitude to the theory of problem-solving in human affairs. It is also necessary to recall his deep sense of history. Nehru's concept of planning arose from his deep conviction that if capitalism of the 19th century variety was a transient phenomenon, which must give place to a more rational and human society, then the best way of bringing about such a change would lie along a path of planned economic and social transformation which can resolve the inevitable conflicts and contradictions in a peaceful manner. He recognised the crucial role that the State had to play in this process. But he never showed any liking for "stateism" as such. Hence, he repeated emphasis that planning must be conceived in democratic environment.

293. Chandra, Bipin. Jawaharlal Nehru and the Capitalist class, 1936. *Economic and Political Weekly* (Bombay), 10 August 1975.

294. Clearing 'path' laid by Nehru. *National Herald*, 8 January 1986; 5.

India has chosen the path of a mixed economy right since Independence and the economic policy resolution specifically highlights this aspect. Jawaharlal Nehru was the first to declare that along with the government, private sector would be granted adequate scope for growth and development. In fact he was a strong votary of a synthesis of public and private sector, and he was a true socialist.

295. Dantawala, M.L. Economic ideology of Jawaharlal Nehru. *Economic and Political Weekly*, July 1964.

296. Dharia, Mohan. Nehru and public sector. *Young Indian* (New Delhi), 20 January 1972; 5.

We are deeply indebted to Nehru who, with his foresight and broad vision, enunciated the philosophy and strategy for the economic development of the nation. Nehru regarded the removal of poverty as a basic objective of economic growth. Development has, therefore, to be geared to creating more employment and elimination of poverty and this Nehru saw could be achieved only through the application of socialist principles. He attached great importance to rapid industrialisation of the country and believed "if we are to reap the full benefit of industrialisation and avoid many of its dangers, it is necessary to resort to careful planning." He stressed that "planning is essential and without it there would be anarchy in our economic development."

297. Dubashi, Jay. Myth of Nehruism. *Organiser* (New Delhi), 15 January 1987; 2.

Jawaharlal Nehru has been dead twenty-two years but the only persons who seem to be remembering him, apart from the pais hacks of the Establishment, are, Aruna Asaf Ali, the editor of Patriot (whoever he is) and P.N. Haksar. What the three have in common I do not know, apart from the fact that Patriot is the only paper whose entire readership consists of those who write for it, but it is surprising that a man who built himself up has a kind of father-figure of modern India should have been forgotten so quickly, and that too, while his progeny still rules the roost.

298. Dutt, R.C. Planned growth, a Nehru gift to India. *Business Standard* (Calcutta), 14 June 1979; 5.

299. Face to face (With Nehru). *Economic Times* (New Delhi), 16 August 1987; 3.

300. F.I.C.C.I. In *India* by Durga Das. London, 1969; 316-17.

One of the most interesting phenomena on the economic front since Independence is the eclipse of the Federation of Indian Chambers of Commerce and Industry. Under the British, the Federation was the economic wing of the Congress. Business leaders supported the freedom movement with money and moral backing and the Congress leaders supported the business community in the legislatures. In fact, the comments of the Federation on the Central Budget were awaited by Congress and other legislators to decide what line to take in the general discussion on it. F.I.C.C.I. also had a powerful lobby in the Central Assembly and successive Finance Members invariably consulted it before initiating action on important matters for fear that the Opposition would otherwise charge them with acting arbitrarily and promoting British business interests.

The situation changed radically after Independence. On coming out of Almora Jail in 1945, Nehru addressed a meeting at Ranikhet in which he declared: "Blackmarketeers and profiteers have flourished at the cost of the nation. All such persons will be hanged from the nearest lamp post when the Congress comes to power and the country becomes independent." The Congress Party adopted this declaration as one of its key talking points after Independence. Although it has not succeeded in punishing such men or stopping these evils, the Congress has by this attitude put itself and the business community in opposite camps. The role of the business community since Independence has, therefore, been defensive.

What mainly derailed businessmen politically was the action the Government took against firms suspected of evading taxes. Liaquat Ali had proposed a commission of inquiry and drawn up a list of about 150 business houses under suspicion. This action paralysed business leaders and most of them never recovered from the shock. Sardar Patel told me that businessmen offered their dues collectively by depositing Rs. 500 millon in the exchequer. This would have enabled them to bring out their black money and use it legitimately. Patel favoured the deal because he wanted business to play its full role in activating the country's economy. But Nehru, for reasons of ideology, would not listen to him. The result was that not only did black market money not come out but it kept multiplying.

Perhaps the most objective view of the business community on the economic and political health of our nation was given to me by a self-made leading industrialist of Bombay, K.C. Mahindra, who headed India's Purchasing Mission in the U.S. during World War II, and took keen interest in national affairs. Writing to me on 15th July, 1963, he stated that "the lapses in the economic determinants have become acute, and unless a drastic revision of the instruments of policy made, there may rapidly be drift to chaos." He added: "I feel it is becoming more relevant that the execution of policy should be left to technocrats. Social and economic objectives have been spelt out in great detail, but failure is writ large on the methods and procedures followed in implementing that policy. But who would listen? The P.M. is strongly entrenched in the party's forums; likewise in the affections of the people. It is, therefore, a personal decision along which could bring about healthy changes. If he shies away from a drastic proposed revolutionary change, one may have to wait until events and circumstances force his hands. I do not otherwise see any other light."

301. Fotedar, M.L. Nehru's vision and our task. *New Wave*, 25 October 1987; 11.

302. Ghose, Sankar. Jawaharlal Nehru and Planning. In *Changing India*, New Delhi, Allied, 1978; 3-19.

303. Gujral, M.L. Abject poverty. In *EFNIG*; 10-18.

304. Gujral, M.L. Foreign investment. In *EFNIG*; 235-40.

305. Gujral, M.L. Industry. In *EFNIG*; 165-193.

306. Gujral, M.L. Socialist Professions and the Plans. In *EFNIG*; 39-73.

307. Gyan Chand. Nehru and Planning. In *Nehru legacy*. New Delhi, 1966; 35-47.

Jawaharlal rightly stressed again and again the importance of occupying and utilising strategic positions or commanding heights as positions of vantage for bringing a socially dynamic planned economy into action and using all its levers for developing a socialist economy. A number of nationalised institutions and undertakings, like the Reserve Bank of India, the State Bank of India, Railways, airways and shipping services, basic public industries like steel mills, heavy-engineering undertakings, air-crafts-making factories and a number of other similar undertakings have been developed in the public sector, and given the will, they could be used as powerful instruments for shaping, developing and steering our entire economy and realising its potential.

308. Haksar, P.N. Relevance of Jawaharlal Nehru. *Mainstream*, 24 May 1986; 24-27.

What did Nehru seek to do? What did he seek to achieve? What was his design—socio-architectural design—for India? One can answer these questions by reading his books and speeches over a period spanning nearly half a century. One can gather a great deal about his vision by reading through the various significant resolutions adopted by the Indian National Congress, beginning with its Karachi session in the thirties, followed by the Avadi session in the fifties, and ending with the resolution passed by the Indian National Congress at its session in Bhubaneswar in the sixties. One can also get a clear picture of Nehru's thought and vision, of his passion, of his design for India by reading through the Constitution of India, more specially the Directive Principles enshrined as part of our Constitution.

309. Haksar, P.N. Relevance of Jawaharlal Nehru. *Mainstream*, 16 November, 1974; 16-21.

310. Importance of Nehru's ideas for development. *Patriot*, 14 November 1977; 4, 8.

Jawaharlal Nehru's ideas about the future of India began to take shape quite early in his life when he started thinking of the need to give economic content to the slogan of political freedom. After Independence, he was able to clarify the range of urgent problems facing Indian society and worked on the practical mechanism and methods necessary to implement pressing reforms.

In recent months, particularly after the Janata Party was voted to power at the Centre in March last objectives evolved after 90 years of India's struggle for independence have come under open attack.

311. Joshi, Navin Chandra. Nehru and new world economic order. *Hindustan Times*, 17 November, 1986; 9.

The need for a conciliatory approach on the part of the developed nations is quite crucial if the dictum 'poverty anywhere is a threat to prosperity everywhere' is rightly understood. This fact of life was forecast by no less a person than Jawaharlal Nehru whose insight recognised that the powerful vested interests of the world (the developed nations) would undermine any movement towards attainment of the sociali t objective of equality. In the capitalistic system, Nehru saw the evils of an acquisitive tendency but he would give the devil his due.

312. Joshi, P.C. Building new India. *Mainstream*, 12 November 1983; 11-12, 50.

313. Joshi, P.C. Nehru's vision of new India. *Patriot*, 14 November 1979; 2.

Nehru provided new categories of understanding of the Indian problem and gave an intellectual depth to the Indian response to the Western impact. From Western liberal thought he imbibed a scientific temper, deep humanism, and faith in the human spirit; and from Marxian he acquired a deep sense of history and an understanding of the economic forces in the historical movement. In particular, Nehru derived from these modern thought systems and understanding of the demands and compulsions of the industrial age. The role of ethics, morality and character in India's struggle for freedom—these were the elements on which Gandhi had laid the primary emphasis. Without underplaying the importance of these essential ingredients, Nehru upheld the role of ideas and of an intellectual or scientific approach to problems without which, he emphasised, life in the modern age was not possible.

314. Kapoor, Purnima P. *Economic thought of Jawaharlal Nehru*. New Delhi, Deep & Deep Publications, 1985, 266 pp.

315. Laski, Harold J. Remarkable record of achievement. In *NAG*; 21-22.

316. Mathai, M.O. Nehru and industrialists. In *MDN*; 88-90.

The one and only Indian Industrialist, with whom Nehru was personally friendly before Independence was J.R.D. Tata. They were on terms of calling each other by first names. This personal relationship between the two and Nehru's initial good opinions of the House of Tatas were primarily due to J.R.D. Tata's life-long passionate interest in aviation, the readiness with which he started the Tata Institute of Fundamental Research with a view to providing research facilities to the promising young scientist Homi J. Bhabha before Independence, and the contribution of the House of Tatas towards the promotion of science and medical research in India.

After Nehru entered the Government, J.R.D. Tata was correct and always observed properties in dealing with Nehru. For example, he never discussed with the Prime Minister any problem confronting the business house of Tatas. His dealings were confined to overall policies governing aviation and broad policies affecting industrial development and production.

317. Mathur, Girish. Nehru and the Congress' economic thinking. *New Wave*, 31 May 1987; 2.

The Indian National Congress which represented the National mainstream in the struggle against British imperialism was much more than a mere political party. It was a broad-based multi-class movement for national freedom and social, cultural and economic regeneration for the Indian people. It reconciled for more than six decades, conflicting interests and claims and focussed the attention on and channelled the entire energy and enthusiasm towards the central task of throwing away foreign rule. It impressed upon the people that without political independence no economic independence could be achieved and the task of building a new and better India could not be undertaken.

318. Mathur, Girish. Resolving contradictions in the Nehru way. *Patriot*, 27 May 1984.

319. Mishra, Girish. *Nehru and the Congress economic policies.* New Delhi, Sterling, 1988, 163 pp.

320. Mukerjee, Hiren. Planning and Impose. In *Gentle Colossus,* Calcutta, 1964; 140-49.

321. Narayana Rao, T. Surya. Architect of Indian planning. *Deccan Chronicle*, 27 May 1981; 4.

It will not be too much to say that Nehru showered parental care and concern on planning. He nursed it in its babyhood; and gave it all the protection needed in its infancy. He saw it grow into adulthood in his own way. He tried at the same time to take with him the people, the party, the experts and the Parliament and also the non-Congress state governments in all that he did in Planning Commission right from its meeting.

His last meeting with the Planning Commission was on May 10, 1964, just two weeks before his passing away, when he said he would be glad to give us much time as was needed because he was interested in planning. He gave to planning a fair degree of dynamism and a spirit or flexibility. His was never a doctrinaire approach or a closed dogma.

322. Nargolkar, Vasant. Nehru and Gandhian economics. In *SON*; 117-35.

323. Nehru, Jawaharlal. Importance of tomorrow. *New Wave*, 9 August 1987; 2.

324. Nehru Jawaharlal. *Community Development, Panchayat Raj and Cooperation* . Delhi, 1965.

325. Nehru, Jawaharlal. Economic security and progress. In *India's independence and social revolution*. New Delhi, 1984; 118-42.

326. Nehru, Jawaharlal. Place of big machine. *New Wave*, 10 May 1987; 2.

I go about from end to end in India, seeing new factories come up, great schemes take shape and great river valley projects develop, giving power and nourishing water to our fields. I see the Community Projects and National Extension Service spread in our rural areas with a speed which is remarkable and without precedent in history.

327. Nehru, Jawaharlal. Removal of inequalities. *New Wave*, 15 March 1987; 2.

Of course, in India we have not been very powerfully affected by the technological process. We have read about it, but we have no real sensation of it. In planning, however, we have to think in technological terms, because it is this growth of science and technology that has enabled man to produce wealth on a scale nobody could even dream of earlier. It is technology which has made other countries wealthy and prosperous and it is only through the growth of technology that we shall become a wealthy and prosperous nation.

328. Nehru, Jawaharlal. Changing India. *Foreign Afiairs*, 41(3) April 1963.

329. Nehru, Jawaharlal. *Mixed economy*. New Delhi, 1948.

330. Nehru, Jawaharlal. *Economic freedom for Asia*. Ootacamund, 1948.

331. Nehru, Jawaharlal. *Economic democracy*. New Delhi, 1952.

332. Nehru, Jawaharlal. *Progress by Consent*. New Delhi, Lok Sabha, 1954.

333. Nehru, Jawaharlal. *Flexible economic policy*. New Delhi, 1948.

334. Nehru, Jawaharlal. *Third plan and the national unity*. New Delhi, 12 September 1960.

335. Nehru, Jawaharlal. *Perspective planning*. New Delhi, Lok Sabha, 1960.

336. Nehru, Jawaharlal. *Concept of long-term planning*. New Delhi, N.D.C., 1956.

337. Nehru, Jawaharlal. *Changing India*. New York, Foreign Affairs, 1963.

338. Nehru and modern India: A panel discussion. *Akashvani*, 25 March 1973; 599-600.

339. Nehru for today. *Mainstream*, 24 May 1986; 32-33.

Religion comes into conflict with rationalism. The disciplines of religion and social usage fade away without giving place to other disciplines, moral or spiritual. Religion, as practised, either deals with matters rather unrelated to our normal lives and thus adopts an ivory tower attitude, or is allied to certain social usages which do not fit in with the present age. Rationalism, on the other hand, with all its virtues, somehow appears to deal with the surface of things, without uncovering the inner core. Science itself has arrived at a stage when vast new possibilities and mysteries loom ahead. Matter and energy and spirit seem to overlap.

340. Nehru's Concept of new India. *National Herald* (Lucknow), 27 May 1987.

Jawaharlal's message to people was, "we have to hurry for the time at our disposal is limited and the pace of the world grows even swifter."

341. Nehru's relevance. *Patriot*, 27 May 1979; 4.

342. Paranjape, H.K. *Jawaharlal Nehru and the Planning Commission*. New Delhi, 1964.

343. Paras Ram. Nehru and planning. *AICC Economic Review*, 27 May 1965.

344. Patel, I.G. Free enterprise in the Nehru era. *Amrita Bazar Patrika* (Sunday Magazine), 28 February 1988.

345. Patel, Rajni. Nehru's economic system. *Economic Times*, 15 November 1981; 5.

Nehru had succeeded in striking a balance between the industrialists, the politicians and the bureaucrats all through his regime. This balance is sadly lacking today, with the result that we have a political elite unabashedly steeped in corruption. No amount of evidence or open allegations seem to affect the public postures or moral pretences of the corrupt politicians in power.

346. Patra, Saral. Nehru's India. *Patriot*, 11 November 1979; 1.

347. Planning. In *QON*; 135-39.

348. Rao, V.K.R.V. Planner. In *Nehru legacy*. Bombay, Popular Prakashan, 1971; 39-51.

349. Rao, T.N. Nehru's grand design. *National Herald*, 27 May 1982.

350. Sarin, L.N. Planning. In *Jawaharlal Nehru*. Delhi, 1968; 43-53.

351. Satindra Singh. Nehru's legacy: Benign or baneful? *Economic Times*, 14 November 1979; 5.

352. Satnik, P.K. Time to recall Nehru's words. *National Herald*, 27 June 1984; 7.

Delivering the Azad Memorial lecture in 1959, Jawaharlal Nehru had said: "Tomorrow's India will be what we make by today's labours. We have started on the pilgrimage with strong purpose and good heart and we shall reach the end of the journey however long that might be." He went on to add "What I am concerned with is not merely our material progress but the quality and depth of our people." His theme was the synthesis of our tradition. He recalled how religion influenced India. At the same time he pointed out that we could not be untrue to science. What he wanted was a combination of science and technology on one side and the mind and spirit on the other. He wanted harmonious balance which could lead to all-round progress.

353. Sen, Mohit. Contribution and continuation. *Mainstream*, Nehru Special Number 1984; 25-29.

Nehru was certainly not a man without flaws. Nor is his contribution to world and Indian history unblemished. In the ultimate analysis, he contributed in great measure to the development of an independent capitalist India which put limits to his greatness. But it is also true that he furthered the national growth of India, strengthened world peace and anti-imperialism and established the alliance between the Soviet Union and India as the two foremost representatives of the socialist community and the zone of national liberation.

354. Sethi, J.D. Nehru's economic policies. *Indian Express*, 19 November 1982; 6.

355. Sharma, R.D. Making India of Nehru's dream. *Indian Nation* (Patna), 8 December 1985; 4.

India is the tenth industrial nation in the world, but over 40% of its people still live below the poverty line. India has built factories, roads, machines, computers but 70% of its population yet remain illiterate.

Despite large number of social welfare laws in our country the rich is getting richer and the poor poorer.

It is true that the complex socio-economic structure like ours cannot be changed overnight. Nevertheless the pace of progress has to be faster lest the people should lose patience in a peaceful democratic transformation of the present order.

What the country is witnessing today is a revolution of rising expectations. The poor and downtrodden sections of the society have begun to assert themselves. They are today more aware of their rights than ever before and they are rightly asking for a rightful place for themselves in society. In these circumstances things, for a while, might appear to be in a state of flux. We need not take an alarmist view of the situation simply because the Indian polity happens to be under strain in the face of ever rising aspirations. Herein actually lies the challenge which can be successfully met if we do not deviate from the path of Nehru.

It is high time to work for the causes that were dear to Nehru and live up to his great ideals of secularism, socialism, democracy and public service so as to make India of his dream.

356. Singh, T.N. Nehru and India's industrial revolution. In *FON*; 69-73.

357. Singh, T.N. Right approach to planning. *National Herald*, 16 September 1968.

358. Tarlok Singh. Jawaharlal Nehru and the Five Year Plans. In *NCV*; 127-360; *FON*; 50-68.

359. Tarlok Singh. Reassessing Nehru's perspective on planning. In *Jawaharlal Nehru and public administration*. New Delhi, IIPA, 1975; 23-36.

360. Terchek, Ronald J. Expanding equality of opportunity: The case of Nehru. In *SON*; 78-95.

361. Venkateswaran, R.J. *Impact of Jawaharlal Nehru on Indian economy*, Calcutta, 1962, 120 pp.

362. Verma, V.P. Political and economic ideas of Nehru. In *SON*; 136-46.

363. Vij, Brij Bhushan. Nehru—pioneering reforms. *National Herald*, 1 July 1984.

Two years before, Nehru became the President of Indian Science Congress Association, the Government were urged to standardise weights and measures on metric basis at its Bombay session—the Metric Committee of the Indian Science Congress, came into existence. Indian Decimal Society, also formed them, were to popularise the cause of metrication and decimalisation of currency. Later, a National Planning Committee was set up under the direct Chairmanship of Pt. Jawaharlal Nehru. It will only be right to imagine Nehru as the architect of Metric System in India for his dedication and vision of the envisaged changes, he planned for industrial change because by then it had become apparently clear that the British had to go and leave India's future in his hands.

Educational Advancement

364. Bhati, Shailesh H.D. Remembering Panditji, *Link*, 25 May 1986; 17-18.

Doon valley embodies Pandit Jawaharlal Nehru's sweet memories, and it was here in Dehradun that he delivered his first public speech in 1921. A major part of his prison life was spent in Dehradun Jail. It was here that he found a milieu favourable for writing letters, books and memoires.

Panditji was greatly attached to Doon Valley. Whenever he had leisure, he came here to refresh and reinvigorate himself.

365. Education. In *QON*; 112-17.

366. Gujral, M.L. Education. In *EFNIG*; 93-125.

367. Mathur, V.S. Education as Nehru viewed it. *National Herald* (Lucknow), 4 June 1987; 6.

Nehru's passion for children was almost proverbial. Through children he sought to nourish a brighter future for the people of free India. It was natural that he should have laid deep faith in the relevance of education as the basic support for the all round development of the child—the future citizen.

He believed that the people of a country are the masters of their destiny and that man is his continuing handiwork. And most certainly education comes very relevant to the process of human growth and development. Naturally he was ever anxious to put Indian education in the correct perspective, and aired his views frequently. Perhaps the current stress on human resource development is a fruition of his thoughts.

368. Nayar, K.S. Nehru's approach on education. *Madhya Pradesh Chronicle* (Bhopal), 7 January 1987; 4.

Pandit Jawaharlal Nehru was the confluence (sangamasthan) of East and West. That is why he was firm that English must have a second place in Indian education.

Nehru was a politician, statesman and educationist and he was the one who fixed the map of India on globe in all fields.

Once somebody asked Nehru to give a definition of the word "university". He said, humanity, tolerance, wisdom, progress, revolution in thinking and endless search of truth. Nehru wanted all these qualities in the product of an Indian University that was his dream of Indian education.

369. Singh, R.P. *Nehru on education.* New Delhi, Sterling, 1964.

Environment

370. Bhagat, O.P. Nehru and nature. *Hindustan Times*, 9 November 1980.

Nehru wrote his autobiography in prison. It was done during "a particularly distressful period of my existence". His aim was "to review past events in India, with which I had been connected, to enable myself to think clearly about them." Yet he puts in quite a bit of nature in its 600 pages. Scattered here and there, these passages are delightful like the sudden puffs of a cool, fragrant wind.

371. Mander, John. Indian autumn. *Encounter* (London), February 1963.

372. Mathai, M.O. Of animals and children, flowers and plants. In *MDN*; 9-16.

Apart from his attraction for mountains, love of animals and children as well as flowers, plants and trees was one of Nehru's pronounced qualities. His love of children was totally different from that of professional politicians of the West for whom patting and kissing children in public is a vote-catching gimmick. To all normal people children are a joy to watch and to play with. Nehru saw in their innocent faces and sparkling eyes the future of India. He was convinced that no amount of money spent on children and their mothers was too much, and that it was a sound investment for the future. He was deeply interested in any scheme designed to benefit children and women, more especially the provision of mid-day meal for the under-previleged school children.

Fascism

373. Fascism and Nazism. In *QON*; 103-7.

374. Nehru, Jawaharlal. *Fascism and empire.* In *Eighteen months in India.* Allahabad, 1938.

375. Nehru, Jawaharlal. Fascism and communism. In *REW*; 125-26.

376. Ravinder Kumar. Jawaharlal Nehru, the Indian National Congress and the Anti-fascist Struggle, 1939-45. *Indian Historical Review*, 11 (1-2) 1984-85; 97-110.

Feudalism

377. Mishra, Bibhuti. Nehru—the anti-feudal champion. In *Nehru's legacy.* New Delhi, 1966; 58-71.

Jawaharlal, with the blessings of Mahatma Gandhi, and amidst the acclaim of the nation, became the Indian head of the Interim Government, and on 15 August 1947, the Prime Minister of the Indian Union. The best and most human qualities of the Nehru leadership were amply demonstrated in those anxious days when he successfully ensured that Indian independence was not drowned in blood, and fratricidal conflict was brought to an end, despite the deliberately provoked communal riots all over the land and Pakistani armed invasion of Kashmir.

Films and Television

378. Abbas, K.A. Nehru film in foreign hands. *Blitz*, 30 August 1986; 24.

At any rate, Nehru must be saved from foreigners—the British at that ! Jawaharlal, by way of personal prejudices and preferences, may have selected a foreigner—but we must save his personality and politics from foreign influence and prejudices! There is only one—over-90-year-old-Britisher alive today who may treat a subject like Nehru with sympathy and compassion—Lord Fenner Brockway ! No other white man has the intellectual quality or ideological affinity to understand Nehru much less to interpret him to the world !

379. Singh, Shubhadarshani. Kenneth Griffith: In Search of Nehru. *Mid-Day* (New Delhi), 7 May 1987; 4.

In one of the many cool, high-ceilinged rooms of the old Doordarshan headquarters in New Delhi sits an old man looking vaguely like Pandit Jawaharlal Nehru. And the uncanniest part of this is that he is a film maker who is, in fact, making a TV film on Nehru. Kenneth Griffith, 66, has been assigned the task by none other than the Government of India. The filming on British locales is complete, only the Indian part remains. But even before he can see the final cut of his three-hour film, the accomplished British TV film maker is already fed up of the whole thing. "There are 650 million Indians I would love to meet out there," he grumbled, "but I am not supposed to meet them. And the only Indians I am supposed to meet—the bureaucrats—I don't want to."

Foreign Aid

380. Gujral, M.L. Foreign aid. In *EFNIG*; 219-34.

Foreign Relations

381. Abbas, K.A. Nehru, a citizen of the world. *Pioneer* (Lucknow), 3 December 1980; 8.

382. Bahuguna, H.N. Nehru—a world citizen. *Contemporary*, November 1974; 15.

383. Damodaran, A.K. Jawaharlal Nehru and the world order. *Mainstream*, 15 November 1986; 13-17.

Nehru had the priceless advantage of having formulated on his own, a few broad ideological guidelines to help him along uncharted paths: the essential principles of socialist planning, the need not merely not to forget but to stress the supreme importance of social justice in one's anxious search for political democracy and human rights; and the necessary collection of essential information and about our vast country with its enormous diversity, both horizontally in regional and linguistic terms and vertically, in widely separate levels of development—all these preoccupied his attention.

384. Roy. Choudhury, Prabir. Jawaharlal Nehru: The internationalist. *Indian Post* (Bombay), 14 November 1987; 7.

385. Doctor, Adi H. Nehru's foreign policy: A review. In *SON*; 147-59.

386. Harriman, Averell. Spoke for the world. *Blitz*, 27 May 1984; 19.

387. *Jawaharlal Nehru on International Cooperation*. Delhi, Publications Division, 1966, 127 pp.

388. Chalapathi Rau. On Foreign policy. In *Jawaharlal Nehru.* New Delhi, 1962; 15-20.

389. Khan, Abdul Majid. Foreign policy of Nehru. In *Jawaharlal Nehru and his ideas.* New Delhi, 1951; 98-102.

390. Krishan Kant. Decline of politics. *Mainstream*, Nehru Special Number, 1984, 13-14, 60-61.

Gandhi and Nehru were complementary to each other. Gandhi's identification with the masses was complete and he spoke a language, the idiom of which was understood by the people. Besides imparting a new value system to the freedom struggle, Gandhi was a great organiser and mobiliser of the people. Nehru would translate that idiom and the value system in modern language to facilitate modern minds to understand it. That is why Gandhi said that Nehru would speak his language when he was gone. Nehru was a propagator but not an organiser. Probably he realised that he could inspire political workers but not create them. So one of the wisest things that Nehru did was not to abide by the last advice of Gandhi of disbanding the Congress and confining it to constructive work.

391. Krishna Menon, V.K. Nehru and Internationalism. *Mainstream*, 13 November 1976; 7-9.

Panditji's internationalism, as we usually call it, has come about from his nationalism. That is, nationalism has come from his humanism and the unquenchable and insatiable thirst of the human soul for liberty, for expression and for being conscious of his fellow beings all around. Now it is not sufficient for us just to exhaust ourselves in these generalities.

In the early period of Indian independence, Panditji tried to draw the attention of his colleagues on the one hand, and the masses of the people, on the other, to the fact that India was a great country. That was the basis on which he proceeded. In fact all of you may remember his favourite phrase: "We may be this, we may be that, we may be other, but India counts," he used to say. Now from the earliest times, therefore, he impressed upon the people that while great as we were in the past and we hope we may be greater in the future, we could not exist in isolation. He tried to tell people that this isolation was neither good for us, nor good for the rest of the humanity without which we could not live. But at the same time he had no desire and did not encourage anybody to play, what we call, a role. He disliked the words "play a role" in international affairs, or to adopt what he said in one of his speeches, "a holier than thou" attitude.

So, going back to the early times he used to say, somewhere about the late twenties or early thirties, the struggle against British rule in this country to him was the struggle against imperialism. Now, if that was as widespread in our minds and as deep as it was in his, then we would understand those who are responsible for policy, our people as a whole and the rest of the world would understand our concern about what is broadly called colonialism. We would have a different view about the recent invasion of Congo by Belgian troops carried there by the United States. So, in the early days, he interested himself, long before colonialism had become a world issue. Colonialism at that time was very largely each nation trying to get something for itself. And, so, I believe, somewhere in 1928, he gathered himself to put it that way into the League against imperialism, although he found that the general circumstances for his work were not suitable. He made the Indian National Congress take an interest in it, and from that time onward you find, year after year, he inviting his colleagues, his colleagues cooperating with him in an attempt to portray India's struggle for liberation as part of one liberation.

392. Mahapatra, Ashok. Message of Jawaharlal Nehru. *Akashvani* (New Delhi), 31 May 1986; 1-2.

More than two decades after Jawaharlal Nehru's death, it is probably easier now to assess dispassionately his impress on the body politic of India and on the political aspiration and endeavour of all humankind. But the very attempt at objective analysis might distort the true image of Jawaharlal Nehru whose thoughts and strivings encompassed both the emotional and intellectual dimensions of man in their holistic indivisible unity. His achievements, therefore, although he functioned pre-eminently in the world of politics, belong to the collective conscience of man, and the common heritage of mankind.

393. Menon, K.P.S. Nehru's foreign policy. In *FON*; 21-27.

394. Misra, K.D. Liberal realism: Cornerstone of Nehru's foreign policy. *Socialist India*. Republic Day Number, 1973; 51-55.

395. Nag, Kalidas. Nehru the internationalist. In *NAG*; 119-27.

396. Nand Lal. Nehru's contribution to the theory of International Relations. In *SON*; 29-48.

397. Nehru, Jawaharlal. *India's foreign policy*. Delhi, 1961.

398. Nehru, Jawaharlal. Power vacuum theory. *New Wave*, 6 March 1988; 2.

Recently, two of the great men of the biggest and the most powerful nations in the world, the United States of America and the Soviet Union, made certain proposals. The President of the United States made some proposals which are called the Eisenhower Doctrine now. The Soviet Union made some independent proposals. I do not presume, at this stage, to discuss or criticize any of these proposals. I have no doubt that both were meant to advance the cause of security and peace. But what I ventured to suggest on another occasion was that any proposals that were made in an atmosphere of suspicion and fear would not take one far, even when they were good proposals because nobody accepted them as bonafide proposals.

399. Nehru, Jawaharlal. Testament of faith. In *Jawaharlal Nehru on International Cooperation*. Delhi, 1966; 72-76.

400. Nehru, Jawaharlal. *International Cooperation*. New Delhi, 1966.

401. Nehru's foreign policy acclaimed. *Hindustan Times*, 28 May 1987; 3.

402. Nehru's relevance to India and the World. *New Wave*, 1 June 1986; 3.

Nehru had worked among the poor peasants, and coming as he did from an affluent background, he understood the pangs of poverty that paralyse man's thinking and action in the right direction. He had lived in the company of the rich and knew their acquisitive meanness and preferred to keep them at an arm's length.

Aware of the complexity of the Indian and world reality he placed emphasis on planning which means planned resource mobilisation, well thought out investment priorities, allocation of resources to the areas critical to overall growth without allowing the nation to become once again dependent for food and other goods and services on foreign countries. In a nutshell, self-reliance which Mao confused with self-sufficiency. He was unsparing in his criticism of the advocates of "small is beautiful" or those who wanted to prevent India from becoming a modern industrial republic by showering praises on India's glorious past of self-sufficient village communities. Planning had no meaning without modern science and technology. He encouraged scientists and technicians to make India self-reliant in this vital area and imposed restrictions on import of technologies which could be produced in India, even if it meant the postponement of some secondary projects by a year or two. His doors were closed for power brokers and commission agents.

403. Panchsheel. In *QON*; 81-84.

404. Privat, Edmond. Great citizen of the world. In *NAG*; 42.

405. Range, Willand. *Jawaharlal Nehru's World View*. Athen; University of Georgia Press, 1961.

406. Sarin, L.N. Foreign Policy. In *Jawaharlal Nehru*. Delhi, 1968; 54-63.

407. Sethi, J.D. Nehru's foreign policy. *Tribune*, 18 November 1983; 4.

Despite India having signed more than 8,000 collaboration agreements and receiving more than Rs. 30,000 crore as foreign aid, its competitive position in the world has declined from 12th to 46th over the past 35 years.

Finally, Nehru was culturally a pro-British leader, although intellectually he claimed to be a semi-Marxist thinker. This contradiction has wrecked our education system and demoralised our intellectuals.

Even lavish invitations and glamorous fellowships have not attracted scholars to study his life and work. Why? The answer is that there is very little in the Nehru episode to study. A balanced and honest assessment of the Nehru legacy is necessary.

408. Shridharani, K. Nehru's international appeal. In *NAG*; 81-83.

409. Spear, Percival. Nehru. *Modern Asian Studies*, January 1967,

410. Suresh Ram. Nehru as World Citizen. *National Herald*, 27 May 1978; 5.

His whole life was a ceaseless voyage of quest and discovery, characterised by fearlessness to forge ahead, by courage to incur every risk for the cause and by longing to merge himself into the ocean of humanity. President Johnson of the United States spoke for the entire mankind when he made the following stirring observations on hearing of Jawaharlal's demise, "Perhaps more than any other world leader, Jawaharlal Nehru has given expression to man's yearning for peace. There can be no more fitting memorial to him than a world without war".

"World without war!" This unique tribute speaks volumes for Jawaharlal's remarkable role as world citizen and servant of humanity. If the people of this earth have to enjoy security and peace, if they have to move forward and make progress, if they have to blossom forth into a happy ever-growing family, there is only one way to make the world free of war, free of tension and conflict, free of fear and hatred. This is the path of Jawaharlal Nehru, as also his challenge and inspiration.

411. Vashisht, Subhadra. Nehru's Positive Neutralism. *National Herald*, 14 November 1985; 4.

Nehru's horse-sense in respect of world events, his concern, his interest, his mode of apprehension and methods of treatment and presentation were so perfect that foreign policy became his 'private monopoly'. His sensitive and almost unerring awareness of the world in its totality was such that none of his colleagues, however resistant to some of his ideas, ever challenged his authority in the sphere of foreign policy. He saw the connection of things which did not seem to be connected. Nehru's policy was realistic. Nehru knew that India's potential disqualified it for a satellite role. Nehru knew that given its size of population, strategic location and historic past, India could play a great role in international politics.

412. Vesey-Fetzgerald, S. Perfect Synthesis of East and West. In *NAG*; 97-100.

Africa

413. Dutt, V.P. Nehru's policy towards Africa. In *India's Foreign Policy*. New Delhi, 1984; 349-50.

414. Gupta, Aniruddha. Nehru and Africa. *JNU News* (New Delhi), April 1987; 9-11.

For Prime Minister Nehru the emergence of Africa from colonial bondage was part of the continuum of Asian-African resurgence. At a banquet in New Delhi held in honour of Kwame Nkrumah in December 1958. Nehru observed that the common background of colonial rule would "inevitably" bring the nations of Asia and Africa closer.

His deep sense of history helped him at once to grasp that Africa in the mid-fifties was "in a ferment" and undergoing profound changes. Ghana, he said had become "a kind of symbol to many other countries in Africa which sought their freedom. It was not merely that individual countries in Africa sought their freedom. It was something on a wider and bigger scale. Africa seemed to have moved very much into the centre of the picture, longing for freedom, not with too soft a voice but rather assertively and aggressively."

Asia

415. India and S.E. Asia: Nehru's solutions still valid. *National Herald*, 23 December 1972.

416. Yalman, A.E. Emancipation of Asia. In *NAG*; 13-14.

417. Khan, Rasheeduddin. Nehru and emergence of Asian identity. *Mainstream* Annual, 1987; 99-103.

418. Khan, Rasheeduddin. Nehru's Vision: Peace and Security in the Nuclear Age. *Secular Democracy*, November 1986; 11-14, 54.

Nehru's thinking and understanding is imprinted on many resolutions on international affairs adopted by the Indian National Congress. In fact, he was the conscience-keeper of the Congress on world affairs and on foreign policy matters. After 1927 he took keen interest not only in larger global concerns, but also in extending support and succour to other national and liberation movements, with the result that by the time India became independent, the major thrust and objectives of his foreign policy were already articulated in the resolutions and statements of the Indian National Congress. The anti-imperialist, anti-colonial, anti-fascist and anti-racist underpinnings were clear and forthright. So were the imperatives of solidarity with liberation struggles and friendship with socialist countries, particularly the Soviet Union, and of fraternal ties with Asian and African countries. What subsequently evolved as the principles of co-existence and postures of Non-alignment in a more specific international setting of the post-war bi-polar world were already in evidence in an embryonic form in the policy resolutions of the Congress, drafted with political acumen and foresight by Nehru.

Commonwealth

419. Commonwealth of Nations. In *QON*; 96-102.

420. Darbari, Raj and Janis. *Commonwealth and Nehru*. New Delhi, 1984; book review by Bhola Chatterjee in *The Telegraph* 8 July 1984.

Is the Commonwealth just a talking shop, an exclusive club that gives its members occasional opportunities to let off steam? A forum whose motto is "If you'll scratch my back, I'll scratch yours?" Of course not, the Darbari sisters say.

On the contrary, the authors emphasise, the Commonwealth may not be an ideal institution. It may not have been able, at every stage, to come up to the expectations of its constituents. But that is no reason why the Commonwealth should be flayed in season and out of season. Anyway, the authors argue, the Commonwealth is a useful organisation and it deserves every help and encouragement, so that it may continue to cater to the larger interests of not only its members but also the international community.

421. Nehru, Jawaharlal. Commonwealth and India. *United Asia* (Bombay), 13 (1961), 1964-66.

422. Nehru: Maker of the New Commonwealth. *Patriot*, 10 June 1987; 3.

423. Ramachandran, C.P. Commonwealth—an anachronism. *Link*, 20 November 1983; 12-13.

Czechoslovakia

424. Filip, Antorin. Nehru's first visit to Czechoslovakia. *Indian Nation*, 1 February 1987; 4.

As early as 1935 Jawaharlal Nehru was expected in Czechoslovakia but the visit did not take place due to illness, and subsequent death of his wife, Kamala Nehru. His visit realised in 1938 where the future of this last democratic state of Central Europe was immediately threatened with fascist aggression and the Western powers' policy of appeasement towards Hitler. By that time his name along with that of Gandhi and Indian National Congress, had won a permanent place in newspaper headlines. Right from the beginning of this century Czech press keenly followed the development of National movement of India against British imperialism. During the inter-war period (1918-1938), the knowledge of Indian culture and social upsurge made headway in several directions. Czechoslovak public showed strong sympathy towards India's fight for independence and its dramatic progress during the twenties and the thirties.

425. Krasa, M. Nehru in Czechoslovakia. *Tribune*, 10 November 1985; 4.

Nehru had been looking forward to visiting Czechoslovakia even before his departure from India and when Kamala's health imrpoved somewhat this visit seemed to be within reach. Indira, who at that time was in Switzerland preparing to enter Oxford, had seen a book of pictures of Prague and around the end of November she wrote to Lesny: "I had heard such a lot about Prague that I wanted to visit it and now, after looking at such beautiful pictures, the desire is greater than ever. I hope I shall accompany my father when he pays a visit to Prague this Christmas." Writing to Nehru shortly before Christmas, Professor Lesny repeated his invitation: "I am looking forward to meeting you with great joy and hope you will like Prague and my country and that this your visit will strengthen even more the already existing ties between our countries."

426. Krasa, M. Nehru's first visit to Czechoslovakia. *National Herald*, 22 June 1972; 5.

Nehru's friendly relationship to Czechoslovakia was by no means new; Indologist Vincenc Lesny had invited Nehru to come to visit Prague some years before, and Nehru had been unable to take advantage of the invitation. But this time, Jawaharlal Nehru's interest was not so much in his personal friends as in the political problems that had begun to pile up in this country, particularly since Hitler's annexation of Austria (Anschluss), forming a threat of international conflict.

Egypt

427. Heikal, M.H. Encounters with Nehru. *Secular Democracy* (New Delhi), 18 October-November 1987; 7-20.

428. Kamath, M.V. Nehru's influence on Nasser: Heikal's recollections. *Times of India*, 18 October 1973; 8.

Mr. Mohamed Hassanein Heikel, editor of *Al Ahram* has been described as "the most powerful journalist in the world, which may be poetic exaggeration, but there is no doubt that *Al Ahram* is the most influential journal in West Asia and Mr. Heikal, the personal confidant of President Nasser could not but have been a man of great influence and power in the region. Inevitably, his reminiscences have the stamp of authority about them, which is that gives them their special significance and fascination.

Some of the vignettes in this book have already been published in the *Sunday Telegraph* but Mr. Heikal's assessment of the relationship between President Nasser and Mr. Nehru is something new. "When Mr. Nasser and Mr. Nehru met for the first time in 1955", he writes, "they had a deep and instantaneous effect on one another. It was rather like a man looking across a crowded room and falling in love with a woman he has never seen before. The bond between the two men was as immediate and as strong as that."

429. Mathai, M.O. Gamel Adel Nasser. In *MDN*; 186-88.

Nasser was another man to whom Nehru did not take to spontaneously. But when Winston Churchill said at a meeting of the Commonwealth Prime Ministers' Conference in London that Nasser was an usurper who seized power through violence, Nehru defended Nasser by saying that such a development was inevitable under conditions that obtained in Egypt, to overthrow an oppressive and corrupt regime and that Nasser had the support of the Egyptian people.

After reading an auto-biographical book by Nasser, Nehru thought that Nasser was a light-weight and a rash and immature person. Nasser started with "positive neutrality" and ended up in non-alignment. He always treated Nehru with difference as an elder and his mentor in many ways.

430. Nehru, Tito, Nasser. *National Herald*, 14 March 1988; 6.

Europe, West

431. Ganesh Prasad. Nehru and the West. *Mainstream*, 15 November 1969; 11-12.

In the thirties and forties of this century, the awakened India looked at the West mainly through the eyes of Nehru. And for so many progressive colonials, including the septuagenarian Tagore, the West included Central Asia as well.

Those were the decades of the crisis of civilization. Naturally, disillusionment overpowered many progressive intellectuals. From the Asian or colonial end it was perhaps best expressed by Tagore in his death-bed message: "I had at one time believed that the springs of civilization would issue out of the heart of Europe. But today when I am about to quit the world, that faith has gone bankrupt altogether. As I look around, I see the crumbling ruins of a proud civilization strewn like a vast heap of futility."

432. India and Western Europe. *National Herald*, 19 October 1973.

Germany, East

433. Naqvi, Arif. Jawaharlal Nehru and the GDR. *National Herald*, 18 July 1984; 9.

Prof. Diethelm Weidemann, Director of the Department of Asian Studies of the Humboldt University, at a meeting, underlined the progressive elements of India's foreign policy and Nehru's anti-colonialist anti-racist, anti-fascist outlook, which was neither abstract nor confined to a limited geographical area. He felt strong affection for the people and this affection marked his strong commitment to the struggle for world peace at a time when new dangers were arising from the development of nuclear weapons in the world! Weidemann said.

Germany, West

434. Mathai, M.O. Kourad Adenauer. In *MDN*; 188-89.

India

435. Attar Chand. Nehru's India. *Patriot*, 21 August 1987.

436. Bhargava, G.S. Nehruism in foreign affairs. *New Socialist*, November 1959; 11-15.

437. Brecher, Michael. Nehru. In *India and world politics*, London, 1968; 289-91.

Panditji (Nehru) was not a superman; he was not a god or anything like that; he was a human being like all of us and very much of a full-blooded individual. He was impulsive; he came into Government very much as an amateur, and the first day that he went to Parliament he was the Leader of the House. Though I have been close to him in many ways, I have lived abroad for many years. I think that the wisest thing for me to do is to keep my mouth shut. That is how I feel. I am sorry that I cannot be more helpful, but what can I do?

438. Datta-Gupta, Shyamal. Nehru and India's foreign policy. *Madhya Pradesh Chronicle*, 14 November 1987.

439. Durga Das. India and the big powers. In *India*. London, 1969; 318-326.

The five years between the first and second general elections saw marked activity on the international front. The Big Powers made moves and counter-moves to woo (or, whenever necessary, to browbeat) India. A succession of dignitaries visited India. Some came to understand how this country, without military or industrial strength, had come to acquire a powerful voice in world affairs. Others came to seek Nehru's views and to check their own assessment of events. Nehru, for his part, forged ahead with his policy of non-alignment. He actively sought the friendship of China and Russia and played a leading role in bringing Afro-Asian nations together at Bandung.

440. Dutt, V.P. *India's foreign policy*. New Delhi, 1984, 447 pp.

441. Dutt, V.P. Jawaharlal Nehru and India's foreign policy-II, *Socialist India*, 15 November 1975; 33-36.

The policy of non-alignment, opposition to colonialism and the criticism of Western powers did not prevent Jawaharlal from maintaining a measure of continuity in the external relations of India. He believed it to be the demand of realism not to bring about a total rupture with past links. Criticism from the Left did not deter him from continuing the existing close links with the West. He did not deny the point made by many critics that India had more economic and other ties with the United Kingdom and the United States in the early fifties. But he defended this as "a situation which we had inherited". And he was clear that "unless we develop new bonds, we shall have to continue as we are doing".

442. India and the World. In *NFC*; 45-51.

443. India and World Affairs. In *QON*; 161-69.

444. Jayaramu, P.S. India's national security and foreign policy during the Nehru Era. *IDSA Journal*, July-September 1981; 62-72.

An attempt is made in this article to identify the major issues which posed threats to India's national security during the Nehru Era and examine the pattern of the leadership's responses to these threats. It is contended in this article that the leadership was able to perceive the threats to national security—and in advancing this view we reject the thesis that India's threat perception under Nehru was wrong—and generally pursued a diplomatic and foreign policy response to meet these threats. If Nehru's foreign policy and strategic posture was based on peace and conflict resolution and not on deterrence, a shift which began to manifest itself in the aftermath of the India-China conflict of 1962 such a peace posture was the inevitable outcome of Nehru's thinking on world affairs and his broad goals of Asian solidarity, area of peace and world order. The techniques that Nehru believed in, and followed, were negotiation, mediation and even friendly compromises and not those rooted in wars and military methods. Any attempt to analyse India's foreign policy under Nehru should be made keeping in mind the above mentioned perspective as, otherwise, the result often is an incorrect evaluation and unfair conclusions.

445. Kamensky, Anna. Meeting of East and West. In *NAG*; 10-12.

446. Kapoor, Yashpal. Nehru's door were open to all. *National Herald*, 14 November 1983; 4.

There would be an unending list of people, very ordinary people who could reach Jawaharlal Nehru even after he became the first Prime Minister of free India. I narrate here only two instances:—

(1) Once a young matriculate from Allahabad came to Teen Murti House. He had come to seek financial assistance for further studies in college. Just at the moment, the PM's car entered through the gate of Teen Murti House: he was coming home for lunch. I took the young man to the side door from where JN used to enter the building to go up to his rooms. He got out of the car, looked at the boy and me and asked, Kutch kahena hai? I introduced the boy and informed him of the purpose for which he had come. Panditji advised, "B.A. pas karne ke bad, kya karoga isse behetar hai koi technical course kar lo." Then he instructed me to get for him admission in an industrial training institute and sanctioned the expenses for it.

(2) It was after 9 p.m. that I was leaving Teen Murti House on my motorcycle. As I came to the gate I saw a tall young man in dust-covered khaki dress talking to the guard. I stopped. The guard told me that this young man had been insisting on seeing Panditji and Indiraji now. "Look at him, this man in dirty clothes calls himself Sunil Dutt." I saw it was really Sunil Dutt. He told me that he had driven straight from the Chambal Valley after shooting *Mujhe Jene Do*, and wanted to see Panditji and Indiraji. I rode him inside on my pillion, took him upstairs and just at that moment Panditji and Indiraji were coming out of the dining room after their dinner. I introduced Sunil Dutt to them. They gladly received him and started looking after him as though he were a child. Have you had your dinner? Would you like to have some hot coffee first? You have travelled such a long distance.

447. Nehru, Jawaharlal. *India and the World.* London, 1956.

448. Nehru, Jawaharlal. India looks at the World. In *Unity of India*, London, 1941; 335-42.

449. Nehru, Jawaharlal Neighbours all. In *Jawaharlal Nehru on International Cooperation*, Delhi, 1966; 55-58.

450. Nehru, Jawaharlal. *India's foreign policy*, New Delhi, 1962.

451. Pethick-Lawrence, Lord. India's place in the world. In *NAG*; 13-14.

452. Prasad, Bimala. India's foreign policy: The Nehru legacy. In *Great Power Relations, World Order and the Third World.* Ed. by M.S. Rajan and Shivaji Ganguli. New Delhi, 1981.

453. Weidemann, D. Formation of Nehru's Basic position in the question of an Indian foreign policy, 919-27. In *SON*; 160-78.

Japan

454. Mathai, M.O. Unusual hotel in picturesque surroundings. In *MDN*; 193-97.

In the autumn of 1957 Prime Minister Nehru paid a goodwill visit to Japan. Some years earlier President Rajendra Prasad had made an official tour of that country.

The Japanese were aware of the fact that before and during World War II, Nehru was an uncompromising and outspoken opponent of Japanese imperialism and militarism; but they also knew that Nehru made a distinction between the fascist government of Japan and the Japanese people.

Three gestures of Nehru in the post-war period, while Japan was treated as an international outcaste by most nations, touched the Japanese people. They were :

(1) India's refusal to take war reparations from Japan.

(2) The speed with which India concluded the Treaty of Peace and Amity. India was the first country to do so, formally terminating the state of war.

(3) Sending an elephant to Tokyo for the Japanese children. This perhaps moved the Japanese people much more than anything else.

Wherever we went, the Japanese people referred to these gestures with gratitude and warmth of feeling.

Nepal

455. Dutt, V.P. Nehru on Indo-Nepal relations. In *India's foreign policy*, New Delhi, 1984; 185-86.

Non-alignment

456. Bandyopadhyaya, J. Nehru and non-alignment. *Socialist India*, Independence Day Number, 1976; 81-88.

The strategic geopolitical location of India between the east and west has also a great significance for her role in international relations, and Nehru was one of the first to perceive this aspect as well. In his own words: " . . India becomes a kind of meeting ground for various trends and forces and a meeting between what might roughly be called the East and the West." The geographical insularity caused by the Himalayas and the Indian Ocean, which has made India very different from most of the European countries, for example, from the geo-political point of view, also enabled her to stay away, to a certain extent, from the political and ideological crusades of the mid-twentieth century.

457. Bandyopadhyaya, J. Nehru and non-alignment. In *Indian foreign policy*, by B.R. Nanda. Honolulu, 1976.

458. Bhatia, S.S. Nehru, *Link*. 3 June 1984.

Jawaharlal Nehru was an internationalist par excellence. His faith in humanism and preference for idea of one-world was not just a sentimental ideal. It was the centre of his search, struggle and activities. He devoted his whole life for the cause of human emancipation and world peace.

In the dark days of cold war Nehru promoted and nursed the idea of non-alignment which he believed would greatly contribute to world peace. He explained, "If by any chance we align ourselves with one power group we may perhaps from one point of view do some good, but I have not the shadow of a doubt that from a larger point of view, not only of India but of world peace, it will do definite harm. Because then we lose that tremendous vantage ground that we have of using such influence as we possess—and that influence is going to grow from year to year—in the cause of world peace."

Today non-aligned movement (NAM) carries in its fold over 101 countries of the world. NAM has become a very important and effective contributing factor for world peace. It is a living tribute to the practical vision and genius of Jawaharlal Nehru—one of its founding fathers.

459. Damodaran, A.K. Nehru and non-alignment. *Mainstream*, 28 May 1983; 13-17.

It is very rare in history that there is almost total identification between a political figure and a certain policy. The idea of non-alignment from power blocs, as distinct from the earlier concept of neutrality or the later pejorative phrase "neutralism", is associated both in its origin and in its evolution with Jawaharlal Nehru along with three or four leaders. Tito, Nasser and Nkrumah are the men who share with Nehru the credit for anticipating the needs of the newly independent countries in a world dominated by very powerful systems.

460. Gandhi, Indira. Chairperson speaks. *National Herald*, 14 November 1983; 5.

Unity is the best homage we can pay to the far-sighted founders of our Movement: Jawaharlal Nehru and Ahmed Soekarno of reawakened Asia, Gamel Abdel Nasser of the resurgent Arab world, Josip Broz Tito from independent Europe, Kwame Nkrumah from Africa astir. Indomitable fighters—all their message was one of struggle and sacrifice. They dared and suffered, they won and built. They inspired people. Only so can freedom be attained and strengthened.

The non-aligned movement is not a mere or casual collection of individual states. It is a vital historical process. It is a co-mingling of many historical, spiritual and cultural streams. It is the expression of the aspiration of the long-deprived and the newly free. It is an assertion of humankind's will to survive despite oppression, despite the growing arms race and ideological divisions. My father placed events within a broad conceptual framework. Our Movement has a framework, it has developed principles. More important, it is not dogmatic but dynamic. It is a major Movement attempting basic changes. By asserting the right of self-determination, our Movement enfranchised more than half the world which was under colonial subjugation. We continue to fight for the rest. We challenge the doctrine and practice of racism. We now strive to enforce the right to economic equality. The sights of our Movement are set not merely on short-term and limited benefits but on broader principles to transform the political and economic organization of the world. Non-alignment embodies the courage and strength of self-reliance. Alignment denotes dependence. That is why something akin to the non-aligned outlook is spreading noticeably even among peoples of aligned countries.

461. Gaur, V.P. Nehru's contribution to World civilisation: A study of the meaning and role of non-alignment. In *SON*; 179-96.

462. Jawaharlal Nehru. *Indian and Foreign Review*, 15 November 1986; 4 5, 22.

Once Gandhi had made the nationalist movement socially heterogeneous by mobilising the peasantry. Nehru, in a sense, took over and retained the interest and sustained the political activity of the kisans (farmers) by providing the Congress with an economic programme.

463. Goyal, D.R. Nehru's vision and strategy. *National Herald*, 14 November 1983; 5.

Contribution of free India to the contemporary world scene is of such a magnitude that no one ever grudges the place of honour it occupies in the comity of nation today. It was not just coincidence that at a time when nuclear holocaust stares humanity in the face the world looks to India with hope and the Non-Alignment Movement chooses to place on Prime Minister Indira Gandhi responsibility of leadership.

464. Jawaharlal Nehru and Non-alignment. *Socialist India*, 13 November 1976; 6-8.

The policy of non-alignment was the natural outcome of such thinking. For it meant, first and foremost, a declaration of independence in international affairs and a determination to follow one's own path, which made non-alignment so attractive to one nation after another as it emerged into freedom in course of the decolonisation process set in motion by the achievement of Indian independence.

465. Karanjia, R.K. National and International Co-existence. In *Mind of Mr.Nehru*, London, 1960, 81-94.

466. Kaul, T.N. Architect of modern India and non-alignment. *Patriot*, 14 November 1978; 2.

467. Misra, Panchanan. Nehru and non-alignment. *Young India* (New Delhi), 11 November 1971; 5-6.

Non-alignment did not envisage neutrality as practised by Austria and Switzerland, but active involvement, specially where problems of peace and freedom were concerned. The basic tasks facing India's non-alignment were, therefore, to support freedom struggle specially of the Afro-Asian peoples, "to strive for peace so that a new war did not destroy all chances of her development, to support the United Nations, which, according to Nehru, reflected the "profound strivings of peoples and nations to banish war and force for ever from mutual relations".

468. Nehru and non-alignment. *Indian and Foreign Review,* March 1983; 4-5.

469. Nehru creator of Non-alignment Movement. *Indian Express,* 18 November 1980.

470. Nehru gave thrust and vision to NAM. *Patriot,* 16 November 1986; 5.

Not only did Jawaharlal Nehru impart to the non-aligned movement its initial thrust and stability, he also had the depth of vision to comprehend the potential threat of thermonuclear war at a time when the world was still experimenting with creation of new weapons of mass destruction.

Pakistan

471. Chalapathi Rau, M. Friends of Pakistan. In *Jawaharlal Nehru,* New Delhi, 1962,; 21-25.

472. Khan, Abdul Majid. Pakistan. In *Jawaharlal Nehru and his ideas,* New Delhi, 1951,; 61-62.

473. Nehru, Jawaharlal. Military aid to Pakistan. *New Wave,* (New Delhi), 6 March 1988; 2.

I should like to refer to the proposed US aid to Pakistan. Recently the House has seen that there has been a pact between Turkey and Pakistan and it is said that this is likely to be followed by some kind of arrangement between the United States and Pakistan for military aid.

I spoke about last, before the House adjourned, and expressed our concern about it. That concern was not so much due to any ill feeling against Pakistan, and certainly not due to any ill feeling against America. But I felt then, and I have felt strongly ever since, that this step is a wrong step and step which adds to the tensions and fears of the world. It adds to the feeling of insecurity in Asia.

474. Nehru, Jawaharlal. U.S. military aid to Pakistan. In *Kashmir*, New Delhi, 1956; 37-39.

475. Nehru, Jawaharlal. *Pakistan seeks to profit from Chinese aggression*, New Delhi, 1963.

476. Nehru, Jawaharlal. With Pakistan. In *Jawaharlal Nehru on International Cooperation*, Delhi, 1966; 59-64.

477. Nehru, Jawaharlal. Military aid to Pakistan. *New Wave*, 15 December 1987; 2.

478. Nehru on amity with Pakistan. *Patriot*, 2 July 1972; 1-2.

Jawaharlal Nehru's first reaction to the Mountbatten plan for the partition of India was strongly hostile. When Mountbatten in May 1947 showed the plan in confidence to him at "The Retreat" in Simla where Nehru was staying as his private guest, Nehru the very next day wrote a letter which the Viceroy described as "a bombshell of the first order". In that letter, Nehru warned Mountbatten about the proposals for the transfer of power to India as they had been cleared from London: "Instead of producing any sense of certainty, security and stability, they would encourage disruptive tendencies everywhere and chaos and weakness."

People's Republic of China

479. Dasgupta, D. *With Nehru in China*. Calcutta, 1955.

480. Durga Das. China betrays Nehru. In *India*. London, 1969; 359-68.

Nehru decided to cultivate Peking after the revolution in 1949 not in a spirit of romanticism but because he realised India's security demanded this, although Peking had branded his Government a "running dog of U.S. imperialism." Peking responded eagerly; it wanted an influential friend who would provide a bridge to the non-Communist world.

Proof of this is an incident which took place when the Nepalese Prime Minister, Tanka Prasad Acharya, visited Peking. At a reception in his honour, he raised the slogan of Nepal-China friendship. Mao, who was present, quickly corrected him, 'Say it was Nepal-China-India friendship'. Acharya's mission to cultivate Peking at the expense of Kathmandu's ties with New Delhi did not pay off.

481. Jasjit Singh. India-China dispute: Nehru's approach—most rational. *Mainstream*, 14 November 1987; 9-10, 31.

It is not surprising that nothing constructive has emerged from the several rounds of border talks during the 1980s either and China still does not appear to have made clear the basis or principles on which a settlement may be possible. A closer reading of the facts would only reveal Nehru's perceptiveness and vision in dealing with the issues involved. It is still the most rational basis for an approach to the problem. Any realistic approach to the resolution of the Sino-Indian border/territorial problem must take into account an objective assessment of the merits of the case, the established international principles in resolving such issues and China's reluctance to confirm to them only in relation to India and China's incentives if any in settling the problem. In working towards an equitable and enduring settlement of the Sino-Indian border problem, it is not necessary to remain captive to history. But an understanding of the history of the principles involved, the facts and veracity of respective claims is vital to the success of any fresh initiative, whether at official or political level.

482. Jetly, Nancy. India-China relations, 1947-77. *Radiant*, (New Delhi), 1979; 294-95.

The Sino-Indian Agreement of 1954, embodying the endorsement of Panchsheel by both nations, ushered in a period of pronounced goodwill and co-operation. Nehru believed that nationalism played a far more important part in China than communism, which in turn would facilitate co-existence with it, despite ideological differences. Particularly after Geneva and Bandung, China appeared more and more as a nation devoted to the cause of peace. The fact that it endorsed the five principles of co-existence with many other Asian countries besides India and publicly declared its intention to resolve all differences with its neighbours by peaceful means has created an atmosphere of goodwill for China in Asia as a whole. It was presumed that Peking being busy with its own problems of reconstruction and economic development, did not pose any threat to Indian interests. Besides, Nehru welcomed the emergence of a strong China as it fitted well with his theme of Asian resurgence and its rightful place in world politics. Indeed, he thought, it would in no small measure be affected by how China and India behaved towards each other.

483. Kaul, B.M. *Untold Story*. Bombay, Jaico, 1970.

484. Kohli, Manorama. Nehru's World-view and China Policy. *China Report* (New Delhi), November-December 1985, 497-502.

Nehru's world-view was an amalgam of several experiences and influences. They include his education and upbringing at home, his training at Harrow and Cambridge, the popular currents of thought of his times and his political associations, by far the most powerful of which was with Mahatma Gandhi. Although he has been described as a curious mixture of East and West, politically speaking it was his experience of the Indian struggle for independence, the motivations and urges behind it, and the ideals and goals of this struggle, which formed the dominant force in Nehru's political framework within which he cast policies and plans in the post-Independence era.

Philosophically speaking, Nehru was influenced in one way or another at one stage or another of his life, by all the three principal ideologies and movements of the twentieth century, *i.e.*, liberalism, socialism and Gandhism. Consequently, as described by one of his biographers, "Jawaharlal Nehru appeared a curious mixture of apparently contrasting process and approaches."

485. Nehru, Jawaharlal. *China, Spain and the War*. Allahabad, 1940.

486. Nehru, Jawaharlal. Why India supports China. *Advance*, 21 August 1931.

487. Nehru, Jawaharlal. With China. In *Jawaharlal Nehru on International Co-operation*, Delhi, 1966, 65-71.

488. *Prime Minister (Jawaharlal Nehru) on Sino-Indian relations.* 2 vols. New Delhi, 1961-1963.

489. *Prime Minister Jawaharlal Nehru in China.* New Delhi, PRC Embassy, 1955.

490. Revolution in Tibet and Nehru's philosophy. *China Reconstructs*, June 1959; 1-19.

Nehru did not explain what kind of society in Tibet he referred to as a "static, unchanging society fearful of what might be done to it in the name of reform". But this is precisely the starting point of the whole question. Our discussion must and can only begin here.

491. Vohra, Sahdev. India-China: Nehru and Aksai Chin. *Mainstream*, 10 June 1987; 13-15.

The occupation in the Sumdorong Valley (June 1986) by the Chinese has once again given a 'live' character to the Sino-Indian border issue.

The beginning of the dispute with the construction of the Sinkiang-Tibet road through Aksai Chin and how Nehru dealt with it, will furnish an insight into the attitude of the two countries to the border dispute. While Nehru based the claim of India on the Treaty of 1842 between Jammu and Kashmir in respect of Ladakh, and the Indo-Tibetan Treaty of 1914 in respect of alignment from Bhutan to Burma, the Chinese were looking for a new frontier which would suit their security need as they saw it. Nevertheless, it was Nehru who was flexible and accommodating to the Chinese demands in Aksai Chin, while the Chinese steadily advanced west of Aksai Chin to the present line of actual control. This is at variance with the view that it was Nehru's intransigence that led to the border war of 1962.

492. Yun-Shan, Tan. Nehru and China. In *NAG*; 76-79.

Saudi Arabia

493. Mathai, M.O. Saud King of Saudi Arabia. In *MDN*; 179-81.

The visit of the King of Saudi Arabia was unique in many ways. The guardian of the holies of holy places for the entire Muslim world had an opportunity to see Islamic institutions, shrines, Mughal art and architecture, and to meet prominent Muslims in India. He threw money recklessly on tips wherever he went. On the way from Kalka at once stopped the car, found out the owner of the hen, and gave him a kingly sum as compensation which was large enough to start a mini poultry farm.

South Africa

494. Reddy, E.S. Jawaharlal Nehru and South African struggle. *Mainstream*, 14 November 1987; 11-13.

Jawaharlal Nehru, however, became interested in the South African problem when he attended the Brussels Congress against Imperialism, February 10-15, 1927, as the representative of the Indian National Congress, and met the South African delegation which consisted of Josiah Gumede, President of ANC; J.A. Laguma, a coloured leader and a Communist and D. Colraine, a white trade union leader. The Congress provided an opportunity for the three South Africans to consult and agree on a strategy for a united and multi-racial struggle against racism. They jointly drafted the resolution on South Africa adopted by the Congress. Later that year, Nehru, Gumede and Laguma were guests at the Tenth Anniversary Celebrations of the October Revolution in Moscow.

Spain

495. Abbas, K.A. India, Nehru and Spain. *Mainstream* Annual, 1967; 79-80.

Nehru was not content with expressing India's sense of solidarity with Spain only through speeches and statements. Accompanied by Krishna Menon, he flew to Madrid and Barcelona and stayed there for several days, while the bombs burst around then to personally convey the comradely sentiments of the Indian people to the brave defenders of Spanish freedom. During his visit to Spain, Nehru shared the life of danger and tension behind the barricades and in the trenches, he met the gentle warriors of the international Brigade, and told them that if he was younger he would have wanted to be one of them. He met the great woman revolutionary 'La Passionara' and later shared a platform with her in Paris at a meeting to support the Republican cause.

496. Nehru, Jawaharlal. *China, Spain and the War*. Allahabad, 1940.

Sweden

497. Alm-Lindstrom, Ulla. Greeting from Sweden. In *NAG*; 51-52.

498. Reddy, E.S. Olof Palme and Jawaharlal Nehru. *Mainstream*, 7 March 1987; 10-30.

I knew Olof Palme for over two decades and he was always kind and generous to me—a Prime Minister to a mere international servant—only because he knew that I was trying sincerely to promote international action against apartheid. (I was a UN Assistant-General and a long-time head of the Centre against Apartheid.) I happened to meet him in Stockholm on October 31, 1984—the day of the assassination of Indira Gandhi and I could see not only his sense of personal loss, but his love and concern for India. I saw him last at the People's Parliament against Apartheid in Stockholm a week before his tragic assassination on February 28, 1986. He walked over to greet me and enquire about my work since retirement from the UN, instead of waiting for me to make a courtesy call on him and pay my respects.

Olof Palme always reminded me of Jawaharlal Nehru. They were both members of the "bourgeoisie", who embraced and espoused democratic socialism—with compassion for the oppressed people and respect for their struggles for justice as well as vision of a New World Order, devoid of exploitation and humiliation. They were uncompromising in their detestation of racism, fascism and imperialism, refusing to be confined by any attempts by the Western powers and vested interests to pressurise them.

For many years after the Second World War, India then a poor and weak country, played a far greater international role than its weight in power politics, because Pandit Nehru had a rapport with some of the best intellectuals of the world, espoused causes that are vital to human survival and progress and exercised a powerful influence on world public opinion.

After Nehru's death, Olof Palme, leader of a small country in the West, played a similar role. What Nehru achieved in developing the Non-Aligned Movement, encompassing the majority of humanity, Olof Palme extended within the privileged West so that peace and freedom, and rejection of war and the Cold War as the destiny of international life have now a wider constituency. The Six Nation Summit is one symbol of that broader unity in the cause of sanity.

United Nations

499. United Nations Organization. In *QON*; 89-95.

UNESCO

500. *Jawaharlal Nehru : A document prepared by the Indian National Commission for UNESCO*. New Delhi, Ministry of Education, 1966; 36 pp.

Union of Soviet Socialist Republics

501. Abbas, K.A. Jawaharlal Nehru: Friend of the Soviet Union. *Soviet Review*, 13 November 1975, 37-38.

There were so many facets of the remarkable and fascinating personality of Jawaharlal Nehru. He was a freedom fighter in the vanguard of the struggle for India's independence. He was a great internationalist whose efforts for world peace may be traced all the way from the Congress against imperialism in Brussels to the Bandung Conference. He was a writer of exquisite prose, a historian of rare perception, and a scholar and a nationalist of clear vision. And, he was also a steadfast friend of the Soviet Union.

502. Banerji, Anjan Kumar. *Nehru and Soviet Russia*, Calcutta, Benson's, 1965, 60 pp.

503. Tapan. Soviet regard for Nehru. *National Herald*, 16 November 1983; 4.

The Soviet people's deep respect and admiration for him is also reflected in the institution of an Annual Nehru Prize in the Soviet Union. The award is given to scientists, cultural and art workers for their contribution to the promotion of Soviet-Indian friendship and understanding.

504. Darbara Singh. Nehru's evaluation of October Revolution. *Patriot*, 14 November 1987.

505. Gafurov, B. Great son of India. *National Herald*, 14 November 1976; 6.

Nehru was the great protagonist of national integration through unity of all religions which is the tradition of Indian culture and the basis of our nationalism. Therefore, it is natural that he could not be reconciled to the Sanghites who consider India to be 'Hindu Rastra', and who refuse to recognise the Muslims as Indian nationals. According to them, "In India only the Hindus are nationalists, and any person till such time as he rejects Islam cannot regard himself as an Indian national."

506. Gafurov, B.G. Nehru: A tribute. In *Nehru and the modern world*, New Delhi, UNESCO, 1967; 53-58.

507. Ganpati, Rai. *Nehru Conquers Russia: A pilgrimage for Peace.* Ambala, 1965.

508. Gupta, K.L. "Soviet Land" salutes Jawaharlal Nehru's memory. *National Herald*, 14 November 1976; 8.

The name of Jawaharlal Nehru is dear to every patriotic Indian. It evokes the memories of a titan who led our country's freedom struggle, gave it a programme of social and economic advance, and brought it into the mainstream of the world-wide struggle against colonial and imperialist rule. We in India feel gratified when we see the people of friendly USSR honouring his memory as a savant of mankind, as a messenger of peace and, above all, as the pioneer and builder of friendship between our two great neighbouring countries. As a token of Soviet people's love and veneration for this great countryman of ours, the Soviet Land magazine has been giving awards, named after him, to eminent Indian literary luminaries who have trodden on the path blazoned by Nehru. The awards were instituted in 1964 soon after his death, as Vice-President B.D. Jatti said at the last year's award-giving ceremony, "as a significant token of Indo-Soviet friendship, and a symbol of the esteem in which the memory of Nehru is held by the Soviet people." Every year, on the occasion of his birth anniversary, the Soviet Land Nehru Awards are given to eminent Indian men and women of letters who, through the realm of literature, espouse the cause of friendship with Russia and of world peace—a cause Nehru upheld till the last days of his life. The Government of India has instituted similar prizes which are given annually to leading Soviet writers and artists for promoting the cause of Indo-Soviet friendship. The award committee has Prime Minister Alexei Kosygin as its patron.

509. Jawaharlal Nehru and the Soviet Union. *Socialist India*, 8 November 1975; 21-25.

Jawaharlal Nehru by right occupies a unique place in the political history of the 20th century India. "His contempoıaries and history remember him as a man with a profound philosophical intellect, a convinced humanist, a consistent opponent of social injustice, a resolute enemy of imperialism and democracy, a friend of the Soviet Union.

Nehru's life as a theorist and statesman, a life full of struggle and search, can only be seen in perspective and assessed in its entirety in the light of the revolutionary changes which have been the hallmark of our era that opened with the victorious Socialist Revolution of 1917 in Russia.

510. *Jawaharlal Nehru in the Soviet Union*, Moscow, 1956.

511. Mathai, M.O. Nikita Khrushchev. In *MDN*; 189-92.

Khrushchev had a weakness for cashewnuts, mangoes and cashewnuts were sent to him in Moscow every year by the Prime Minister as was done to some other foreign dignitaries.

Nehru's visit to the Soviet Union in 1955 and the visit of Khrushchev and Bulgarin to India well and truly laid the foundations for a fruitful relationship between the two countries. Khrushchev remained as one of the best friends of India ever since.

512. Mathai, M.O. Visit to the Soviet Union. In *MDN*; 25-37.

For purely personal reasons of my own, I did not accompany Nehru on his visit to the Soviet Union. In a sense I preferred a private visit to a conducted one. KPS arranged for me to visit several places in and around Moscow. I also visited Yesnaya Polyana (the place where Tolstoy lived), Kiec and Leningrad.

513. Menon, K.P.S. Jawaharlal Nehru and Soviet Union. *Patriot*, 14 November, 1980; 4. *The Assam Tribune*, 14 November 1980; 4.

514. Mezentseva, O. Soviet monograph on Jawaharlal Nehru's philosophical views. *Soviet Land* (New Delhi), March 1988; 31.

515. Nehru, Jawaharlal. Visit to Russia. *New Wave*, 6 December 1987; 2.

516. Nehru, Jawaharlal, *Soviet Russia*, Allahabad, 1928.

517. Nehru in the USSR. *Youth Review* (New Delhi), 4 June 1983; 3.

518. Nehru peak in USSR. *Socialist India*, 15 November 1975; 36.

519. Nehru's book (Glimpses of World History) in Russian. *National Herald*, 21 October 1975.

520. Nirvana, Arnravati Swami. Who preached Indo-Soviet friendship ? *Nagpur Times*, 1 January 1987; 4.

Our journalistic precepters deserve congratulations on enlightening us with the pleasant tidings that it was no less a person that Jawaharlal Nehru who had initiated Indo-Soviet friendship. We are indebted to their free democratic service. But as it would be rash for us to move in this world with the knowledge of one road only and we should learn to form independent judgement, we cannot but desenchant ourselves from such a semi-truth, biased and image-building news.

521. Shankar Narain. Revolution's impact on Nehru. *Madhya Pradesh Chronicle*, 18 November 1981; 6.

Nehru has been acclaimed both in India and USSR as the architect of Indo-Soviet friendship but the significant thing to note is that it is not based on transient considerations which grew up in the post-independence period but much earlier in Nehru's understanding of the world's development. The premises of his outlook are still valid today and that is why Indo-Soviet relations have grown from strength to strength.

522. Singh, G. Lenin, Gandhi and Nehru. *Mirror* (Bombay), November 1967; 16-19.

523. Vafa, A. Jawaharlal Nehru: Architect of Soviet-Indian friendship. *Soviet Land* (3), February 1979.

United Kingdom

524. Atlee, Eail. Jawaharlal Nehru. In *LON*; 19-24.

525. Curzon and Nehru. In *India* by Durga Das, London. Collins, 1969; 47-49.

Nehru, in theory, was not in sympathy with the princely states; he dubbed them anachronism. He presided over the first session of the Indian States People's Conference in disregard of Gandhi's practice of leaving the states severely alone. But what Sardar Patel accomplished, through the integration of these states into the Indian polity in consolidating the country's post-independence stability and strength, Nehru the theorist would probably have flinched from attempting himself.

Curzon has often been described as an arrogant imperialist, but he was an intellectual and worked steadfastly to lift India to the status of Britain's greatest partner in the Empire. This partnership concept assumed wider dimensions when, notwithstanding his dedication to the cause of complete independence, Nehru saw the wisdom of India's continuing as a partner in a Commonwealth to which he strove to impart a larger meaning.

It is thus one sees the two men of destiny side by side, regardless of the distance in time that separated them: each lonely in his individual splendour, each striving after greatness, each lifted up in spirit by praise and downcast by criticism and unkindness, his sensibilities sharpened by the rarefied height from which he gazed upon the world below.

Curzon left behind a lore, Nehru a legend.

526. Indo-British Relations. In *NFC*; 96-103.

527. Mathai, M.O. Aneurin Bevan. In *MDN*; 181-84.

In 1960, while I was no longer with the Prime Minister officially, Nehru was going to London for the Commonwealth Prime Ministers, Conference. Nye was ill then—a mere bundle of skin and bones of what was once a tall and impressive looking figure who used to create a flutter whenever he entered a room or an assembly of people. I suggested to Nehru that he might visit Nye at his farm. Nehru found the time to do this. He was overwhelmed by this gesture and the entire British press lauded Nehru for this. Nye died soon after in 1960 at the early age of 63. He belonged to the band of rare men of elemental force and grandeur who leave their footprints on the sands of time.

It was Aneurin Bevan who first drew Nehru's attention to Marshal Tito. After a visit to Yugoslavia, Bevan wrote to me a personal letter in the late forties in which he said that Tito was a considerable person and that he and Nehru should meet. I placed the letter before the Prime Minister who forwarded it to the External Affairs Ministry with a short note to indicate that he was in no particular hurry to meet him. After the arrest and imprisonment of Djilas by Tito, Bevan's enthusiasm for Tito dimmed. Before his arrest, Djilas was a right hand man to Tito, but was later to write the book "Land Without Justice".

528. Mathai, M.O. Harold Macmillan. In *MDN*; 186-88.

Macmillan was a noted liberal among the conservatives. While in India, Nehru, among other matters, discussed with Macmillan at length the liberation movements in Africa and the desirability of ensuring orderly change in the continent. Nehru said that he saw no advantage for the colonial powers in prolonging the agony, and added that, if the British took the initiative other colonial powers were bound to follow suit. This obviously had some effect, for, within a short time, Macmillan visited Africa and made the most celebrated speech of his career—"The Wind of Change in Africa".

529. Nehru, Jawaharlal. British foreign policy. *National Herald*, 10 January 1939.

530. Nehru, Jawaharlal. England's dilemma. In *China, Japan and the War*, Allahabad, 1940, 134-51.

United States of America

531. *America revisited*. New Delhi, USIS, 1962.

532. *As America remembers Jawaharlal Nehru*. New Delhi, USIS, 1964.

533. Banjani, H.C. *Jawaharlal's discovery of America*, Delhi, 1950.

534. Durga Das. Washington on Kashmir. In *India*, London, 1969; 420-23.

The U.S. attitude on Kashmir has been generally pro-Pakistan, although from time to time it has put forward different proposals for a solution, including handing over to the U.N., forming a condominion, or dividing it between India and Pakistan. To begin with, Washington took its cue from the British, but later it took the line recommended by the U.N.—appointed American mediator on Kashmir, Graham, and from Galbraith.

Two months after the war with Pakistan, Johnson's aide told our Ambassador to ask New Delhi to settle the Kashmir issue, but the aide was told firmly that Pakistan was out of court for resorting to arms. It was pointed out that India had withdrawn from the sitting of the Security Council, stating that Kashmir was a domestic issue. This withdrawal helped India's cause more than Menon's nine-hour oration on a previous occasion.

535. Kennedy, John F. Nehru. In *John F. Kennedy, January 20 to December 31, 1961*. Washington, U.S., Govt. Printing Office; 698-99.

536. Nehru, Jawaharlal. *Inside America*. New Delhi, National Book Stall, 1950, 226 pp.

537. Nehru, Jawaharlal. *Prime Minister Nehru's visit to USA*. New Delhi, November 1961.

538. Nixon, Richard. Nehru. In *Memories of Richard Nixon*. London, Sidgwick & Jackson, 1978, 131-32.

539. Parasuram, T.V. How US interpreted Nehru's visit to Red China. *Indian Nation*, 10 October 1987.

540. Roosevelt, E. *As He Saw It*. Bombay, Asia, 1947.

541. Schlesinger, Arthur M. Nehru and J.F. Kennedy, In *A thousand days*, London, 1965; 454-57.

542. Schlesinger, Arthur M. and L.B. Johnson. Nehru. In *A thousand days*. London, Andre Deutsch, 1965; 472.

543. United States of America. In *QON*; 207-13.

Yugoslavia

544. Mathai, M.O. Marshal Josif Broz Tito. In *MDN*; 184-86.

It was Aneurin Bevan who first drew Nehru's attention to Marshal Tito. After a visit to Yugoslavia, Bevan wrote to me a personal letter in the late forties in which he said that Tito was a considerable person and that he and Nehru should meet. I placed the letter before the Prime Minister who forwarded it to the External Affairs Ministry with a short note to indicate that he was in no particular hurry to meet him. After the arrest and imprisonment of Djilas by Tito; Bevan's enthusiasm for Tito dimmed. Before his arrest, Djilas was a right hand man to Tito, but was later to write the book "Land Without Justice".

545. Nehru, Tito, Nasser. *National Herald*, 14 March 1988; 6.

546. Tito—from Stalin to Nehru. *National Herald*, 20 March 1988; 7.

Yugoslavia emerged from the last World War a communist country headed by Marshal Josif Broz Tito backed by both the Soviet Union and the United Kingdom during years of partisan struggle against the Nazi occupation.

It was a model Soviet ally at first and made more rapid headway toward communisation than any other East European country.

But differences soon developed between Tito and Stalin heading the Soviet Government and the Communist Party over what are considered purely internal party matters.

Stalin, ever distrustful of foreign communists, is said to have tried to infiltrate the League of Communists of Yugoslavia and subordinate the party as well as its politics to dictation from Moscow.

Freedom Struggle

547. Butler, Lord. *Jawaharlal Nehru, the Struggle for independence.* Cambridge, 1966, 28 p.

548. Chattopadhyay, B., Nehru, the historical significance. *Link*, 20 November 1973; 7-11.

The Historiography of the national movement in India has yet to evolve any clearly set out analytical framework—Marxist or otherwise—capable of relating ideological phenomena to the relatation embedded in socio-economic formations. At the same time, the national movement, even the leadership of the Indian National Congress, has never been ideologically homogeneous, even before the numerous splits in recent years. In fact, in every major phase of the Indian National Congress great battles raged between the more radical elements and the conservative elements as new social forces swung into action on the national arena.

549. Chatopadhyay, Kamaladevi. Battle-scarred soldier. In *NAG*; 68-71.

550. Darbara Singh. Nehru: Some reminiscences. In *NP*; 188-90.

551. Durga Das. *India: From Curzon to Nehru & after*. London, Collins, 1970.

552. Elwin, Verrier. Ancient and modern man in India. *NAG*; 317-19.

553. India's freedom. In *NFC*; 104-13.

554. India's Freedom struggle. In *QON*; 51-56.

555. *Jawaharlal Nehru: Jewel of India*. Poona, December 1942, 156 pp.

556. Khilani, Niranjan M. India's freedom and the Second World War. In *India's road to Independence*, 1857-1947. New Delhi, Sterling, 1987, 103-6.

557. Mathai, M.O. Some Stalwarts. In *MDN*; 214-28.

558. Nehru, Jawaharlal. Discovering India: Freedom & licence. *New Wave*, 31 July 1987; 2.

559. Nehru, Jawaharlal. *Eighteen months in India*. Allahabad, Kitakistan, 1937.

560. Nehru, Jawaharlal. *Independence and after*. New Delhi, 1950.

561. Nehru, Jawaharlal. Independent approach. *New Wave*, 19 April 1987; 2.

We feel, in so far as international policy is concerned, that right or wrong counts. But it is not the rightness of a proposition that makes it listened to but rather the person or the country which says so and the strength behind that country. The international policy of a country depends ultimately on the domestic state of affairs in that country; the two have to be in line and they cannot be isolated from each other.

562. Nehru, Jawaharlal. *India on the march.* Lahore, 1937.

563. Nehru, Jawaharlal. *India's freedom.* London. Unwin Books, 1962. (First published as *India and the World*, 1936).

564. Nehru, Jawaharlal. *India's quest.* Bombay, Asia, 1963.

565. Nehru, Jawaharlal. Tryst with destiny. In *India's freedom*, London, 1962; 94-95.

Long years ago we made a tryst with destiny, and now the time comes when we shall redeem onr pledge, not wholly or in full measure, but very substantially. At the stroke of the midnight hour, when the world sleeps, India will awake to life and freedom. A moment comes, which comes but rarely in history, when we step out from the old to the new, when an age ends, and when the soul of a nation, long suppressed, finds utterance. It is fitting that at this solemn moment we take the pledge of dedication to the service of India and her people and to the still larger cause of humanity.

566. Nehru, Jawaharlal. *Where are We ?* Allahabad, 1939.

567. Nehru, Jawaharlal. Whither India? In *India's freedom.* London, 1962; 20-33.

Never in the long range of history has the world been in such a state of flux as it is today. Never has there been so much anxious questioning, so much doubt and bewilderment, so much examining of old institutions, existing ills, and suggested remedies. There is a continuous process of change and revolution going on all over the world, and everywhere anxious statesmen are almost at their wits' end and grope about in the dark. It is obvious that we are a part of this great world problem, and must be affected by world events And yet, judging from the attention paid to these events in India, one would not think so. Major events are recorded in the news columns of papers, but little attempt is made to see behind and beneath them, to understand the forces that are shaking and reforming the world before our eyes, to comprehend the essential nature of social, economic, and political reality.

568. Nehru, Jawaharlal. *World struggle and India.* Calcutta, 1938.

569. Nehru, Jawaharlal. Indian struggle for freedom. In *REW*; 113-20.

570. Patil, V.T. Assessment of Nehru's contribution to the freedom struggle. In *SON*; 401-6.

571. Patil, V.T. *Nehru and the freedom movement.* New Delhi, Sterling, 1977, 235 pp.

572. Patil, V.T. Nehru's theory of the Indian national movement. In *SON*; 23-28.

573. Ram Gopal. *Trials of Jawaharlal Nehru.* Bombay, 1962.

574. Rama Rao, K. Paper of liberation. *National Herald*, 14 November 1987; 7.

575. Shiva Rao, B. *India's freedom movement.* New Delhi, 1972.

576. Smith, J.H. I met Cripps in Nehru's home. *Christian Century*, **59**, August 1942.

577. Tandon, P.D. *Nehru, your neighbour.* Calcutta, 1946.

578. Tondon, P.D. Nehru—Apoignant memory. *National Herald*, 23 May 1968.

Jawaharlal Nehru had watched the mighty river Ganga in its various moods. Whenever he was near the great river he looked at it with eyes full of awe and amazement, and seemed to be deriving great strength from it. He has written most eloquently about it. I saw him many a time on its bank gazing at it in reverence and wonder. One evening as he stood up in the car and had a panoramic view of it he was muttering something to himself.

579. Tandon, P.D. Nehru's moments of anguish. *Tribune*, 27 May 1977; 5.

As the fascinating figure of Jawaharlal Nehru recedes more and more into the clouds of time, his image becomes brighter and more stable in the hearts of his people whom he served with a jolt the unique man that was Nehru. His feelings and emotions had a nobility about them. He loved life, lived it well and knew it in its proper perspective.

Gadgil, N.V.

580. Mathai, M.O. N.V. Gadgil. In *MDN*; 251-52.

Before the Indus Water Treaty was signed by India and Pakistan, the sharing of waters flowing from India through Pakistan was beset by constant disputes. While the subject of irrigation and power was with Gadgil, he took delight in playing monkey tricks. He was a man who had no capacity to see beyond his nose. He was woefully lacking in statesmanship. On one occasion he exceeded all limits by drastically reducing supply of water to Pakistan. When there were protests, there were immediate denials. Finally flew foreign observers and foreign journalists over vast areas of parched earth in west Punjab. Tell-tale photographs were published in newspapers in Pakistan and abroad. India was put in an akward position. Nehru was deeply upset. He summoned a meeting of representatives of the Punjab government and senior civil, engineering and technical officers of Gadgil's ministry. Gadgil himself was present. Nehru asked for explanations. No valid explanation was forthcoming. Gadgil made a feeble attempt to defend the indefensible. Nehru shouted at him and asked him to resign. This was the only time that Nehru asked a cabinet colleague to resign in the presence of officials and other subordinates. Nehru did not follow up and press for the resignation. However, "Irrigation and Power" was taken away from Gadgil to constitute a separate ministry.

After the 1956/57 general elections Nehru refused to take Gadgil into the government. Subsequently Gadgil was sent as a governor which he gave up in disgust after a brief experience.

Gandhi, Indira

581. Chalapathi Rau, M. Nehru and Indira: A study in style. *Socialist India* Repulic Day Number, 1976.

As in literature, so in life, there is, I suppose, a difference between possessing style and possessing a style. Shakespeare has style; Milton has a style. Jawaharlal Nehru, even with the climaxes and curves of his career, had style; his long term of Prime Ministership and the profusion of his output or the evenness of his approach and temper, in spite of occasional explosions, moulded it. Indira Gandhi has shown that she possesses a style of her own.

582. Durga Das. Father and daughter: After Nehru, Who? In *India.* London, 1969; 368-69.

Nehru doted on his sister Vijayalakshmi Pandit, whom he affectionately called Nan. She mothered him, and was his friend and companion in the lonely years of his widowerhood. This relationship suffered, however, when M.O. Mathai came on the scene as his personal assistant after Nehru became Prime Minister. This aide had the knack of gauging Nehru's feeling and wishes, and he strove to fulfil them. He thus gained his confidence and began gradually to influence Nehru's thoughts and decisions without appearing to do so. One of his qualities which impressed Nehru greatly was his deftness in drafting letters and notes; and in looking after Nehru's personal finances.

583. Gorev, Alexander. Indira Gandhi: Her dreams and achievements. *Soviet Land* (New Delhi) (22) November 1986; 33-36.

Nehru shared the political views with his daughter. The situation in the world was deteriorating further. A global crisis was imminent into which all the imperialist powers would be drawn, while many small and dependent states would become their victims. What place in all this had been reserved by England for India?

Jawaharlal Nehru had a long talk with Lord Linlithgow, the Viceroy of India, who was then in London.

The English Lord asked Nehru whether the Indians would agree to the status of a dominion.

As Indira learnt, her father disappointed the Viceroy by telling him in plain terms that India could not become a self-governing state until it achieved complete economic independence and the right to determine the structure of its economy without considering the City of London. And if under certain circumstances India would agree to the status of a dominion, the Congress Party would regard it only as the first step towards true independence.

Jawaharlal Nehru said that as a patriot of India he could think only of the increase of the power of his land, but as a man who was sincerely interested in stable peace upon the earth and in international co-operation, particularly in the establishment of friendly relations between India and Great Britain at a time when they were threatened by a new world war, he called upon the British government to take a just and correct step in respect of India and grant it its independence.

It is to be regretted that the talk disappointed both its participants. Taking leave of Indira's father, Linlithgow, said: "We are divided by a wide abyss. . . .".

Nehru was indignant. He called Chamberlain "a boy who ran errands for Hitler". The same day Indira's father gave an interview to a correspondent of *the Daily Worker*. He said that peace at any cost, at the cost of blood and other people's sufferings, at the cost of abuse of democracy, of breaking up friendly relations between countries, was not peace, but a continuation of the policy of conflicts and blackmail, a continuation of the domination of violence, and in the end,—war.

584. Martyshin, O.V. Heart of national history. *New Wave*, 29 December 1985; 9.

After the Salt Satyagraha, the Left moved to the fore. In the mid-1930s, it really united the nation, representing all classes and political trends. The Socialist Party, set up in 1934 within the Congress and Communists who joined it, made up the Congress Left Wing alongside the followers of Jawaharlal Nehru, a person enjoying immense authority not only with the Left but in the Congress as a whole.

The Left wanted a stepped-up non-cooperation and argued that workers' and peasants' organisations were to be drawn into the Congress. It saw the working people's activities in defence of their class demands as part and parcel of the national effort. In his Presidential address to the 1936 session of the Congress in Lucknow, Nehru called on the Indian National Congress to solidarise with world progressives, demanded an agrarian reform, and opposed the current relapses into parliamentarianism. As Nehru saw it, bourgeois mentality determined the policies of the Congress top far more than the interests of the bulk of the Indian population did. Gandhi defended the unity of all trends on one basic condition: that the old social strategies of "pure" anti-imperialist struggle be kept intact. The exacerbated social tensions and the momentum gained by the workers' and peasants' movement made Gandhi ever more cautious in applying satyagraha, lest it went out of his control to stimulate the independent revolutionary activities of the people. From taking part in legislature elections, the Congress evolved to accepting posts in provincial governments—a step that Gandhi saw as a chance to prevent not only revolutionary violence but civil disobedience in an unheard-of scope.

585. Misra, K.P. Nehru, Indira, Rajiv: Their roles. *World Focus*, (88), April 1987; 26-28.

586. Nambiar, K.K.G. Nehru and Indira—A study in contrast. *Sunday Standard* (New Delhi), 13 November 1977.

Nehruwas both sensitive and scrupulous in safeguarding them—in letter as well as in spirit. But Mrs. Gandhi had no hesitation in inflicting mortal wounds on our infant democracy with her periodic "amendments" to the Constitution. With every amendment, which was designed to strengthen her political power, a substantial part of the fundamental rights was taken away.

Nehru was a firm believer in an independent and fearless judiciary for that alone could prevent a government from depriving citizens of their constitutional rights. But Mrs. Gandhi looked upon independence and fearlessness of the judiciary as a challenge to her power and supremacy. So she went about frightening and demoralising the judiciary. Independent and fearless judges were superseded and persons who would not prove incovenient to the government were appointed as judges. Worse still, Mrs. Gandhi wanted "committed" judges-committed to her peculiar political style. Indeed, she will go down in history as one who eminently succeeded in eroding the independence of our judiciary.

587. PM promoting Nehru's ideals. *Tribune*, 5 May 1983; 2.

588. Sarin, L.N. Nehru's daughter. In *Jawaharlal Nehru*. Delhi, 1968; 82-86.

589. Tandon, P.D. Jawaharlal Nehru as friend and father. *Patriot*, 14 November 1985; 4.

Nehru played many roles in life and whatever he touched, he adorned. As a writer, he acquired world recognition. As a statesman he was highly respected. He was a patriot of the "purest ray serene". As an agitator for India's freedom, he was unparalleled. As a father, too, he gave an excellent account of himself.

He was a remarkable man in many ways. His nobility was never in doubt. His integrity was always beyond question. He was one of the finest men of our age.

Gandhi, M.K.

590. Agarwal, S.N. Gandhi's great heir. In *NAG*; 4-5.

591. Brockway, Fenner. Gandhi and Nehru. In *NAG*; 117-18.

592. Chalapathi Rau, M. *Gandhi and Nehru.* Calcutta, Allied, 1967, 152 pp.

There was no one who could pay an adequate tribute to Jawaharlal Nehru, when he died, the kind of tribute, moving and truthful and memorable, which he paid to men of history and to his great contemporaries; and he was like Gandhi, his own best commentator and no comment could add anything to what he said. There have been other great men in Indian history, even in this century, other men more intellectual, more spiritual, more courageous, or more energetic, and he commemorated them all. But for nobility of nature, for modernity of outlook, for a combination of physical and mental endurance, for harmonizing the temper of science with the spirit of art, for chivalry and humanity, for consistency of vision, he was the greatest of them all. It was the combinaton of many qualities in such a degree that made him the finest possible instrument of historical forces.

593. Damodaran, A.K. Of Gandhi, Nehru and Hew India. *Mainstream*, 13 August 1985; 7-9.

To my generation Attenborough's Gandhi was a return to one's youth, to the aims and the ambitions which we used to console ourselves with during a period when freedom and independence were receding mirages. The film took us back to 1942 and that year—the movement, the excitement, the failure and the sad aftermath—was something significant in the lives of most of us who were young and happy to be foolish in those distant days. Some of us gave everything for it and paid a price; there were others like myself whose commitment was less total and by an 'ironic' twist of fate, whose awards were near total.

To look for the real Jawaharlal Nehru or the real Vallabhbhai Patel in such a picture is asking for the wrong thing. We are not being given an encapsulated history of the times, but a deliberately distorted picture of India in a transitional period seen through one man's actions. Even this would be too much, too detailed; some events only of this one man's life have to be selected, many attractive alternatives rejected, many great moments passed over in silence.

Thirty-six years after the achievement of Independence, the people of India have reasons for restrained satisfaction; disappointments and frustrations are also there but even in our more self-critical moments, we should not forget that many of our present discontents are due as much to global developments over which we have no control as to our own shortcomings. Not surprisingly, it has been a mixed story of achievement and failure.

The men who dreamt dreams about Independent India, its economic organisation, were great men who dared to have these dreams about the future of the nation at a time when the prospects of realisation seemed remote indeed. Gandhi and Nehru have left behind them in immortal prose several descriptions of their picture of what free India should be like. It seems therefore appropriate to go back to some words of Gandhi which impressed Nehru very much. "I shall work for an India in which the poorest shall feel that it is their country, in whose making they have an effective voice, an India in which there shall be no high class and low class of people, an India in which all communities shall live in perfect harmony. . . There can be no room in such an India for the curse of untouchability. Women will enjoy the same rights as men. . . This is the India of my dreams."

It was more than 70 years ago, on a lonely sea voyage between India and South Africa, that Mahatma Gandhi worked out his picture of a self-governing India, an India which would return to its traditions, reject much that was attractive in the modern world and bring happiness to the Daridranarayans—the poorest of the poor. Gandhiji's seminal book 'Hind Swaraj' shown the reach, the power of imagination, the creative originality as well as the limitations of our great leader. On his part, Nehru, during the years of his association with Gandhiji learnt to adjust his own equally uncompromising scientific and humanistic vision to Gandhi's spiritual philosophy.

594. Das, D.D. Relevance of Gandhi-Nehru approach. *Mainstream*, 12 November 1983; 47-49.

Nehru was among Gandhiji's first converts when the Mahatma gave the revolutionary call to the masses for a countrywide hartal in April 1919 hurling defiance at the British Raj. Gandhiji did it initially, not through the Congress but by forming a Satyagraha Society. . . . Nehru was aglow with inspiration. Gandhiji's emergence lifted him up from tame, uninspiring liberal politics of the Congress which he found suffocating and lifeless. In Nehru's own words, "Gandhiji was like a powerful current of fresh air that made us stretch ourselves and take deep breath, like a beam of light that pierced the darkness and removed the scales from our eyes, like a whirlwind that upset many things but most of all the working of people's minds. Get off the backs of these peasants and workers, he told us, all of you who live by their exploitation; get rid of the system that produces this poverty and misery". (*Towards Freedom*, p. 48).

595. Dutt, R.C. Gandhi-Nehru values ignored. *New Wave*, 22 November 1987; 5-12.

596. Gandhi, M.K. Jewel of India—Gandhi on Nehru. *National Herald*, 13 November 1977; *Harijan*, 25 April 1936.

One could not but have been struck forcibly with two outstanding traits in the character of our beloved leader Pandit Jawaharlal Nehru, as one saw him at work during the past hectic weeks in Allahabad and Lucknow. Preoccupation, without rest or respite, with the problem of the poverty, the unemployment, the degradation and the subjection of the vast mass of our countrymen, and a tender regard for the poor and the down-trodden. Often, in the midst of his heavy preoccupation I have seen him giving a tender and patient hearing to miserable-looking waifs and strays who came to the doors of Anand Bhavan and who required perhaps nothing so much as a sweet word.

597. Gandhi, Nehru and the Congress, *National Herald*, 29 May 1977; 5.

It was Nehru who laid the foundations of secularism, democracy, and socialism, and non-violence, drawing upon the ideas of Gandhi and upon the heritage of the future with both clarity and consistency of vision. He clearly showed how democracy was inevitable in this country and how socialism was also inevitable in this country, and how both could go together. There could be no socialism without democracy and no democratic process and the socialist process could be reconciled at every step. The Indian people cannot afford to forget Gandhi. They cannot afford to forget Nehru also. Gandhi and Nehru cannot be separated.

598. Gandhi, Rajmohan. Nehru, Patel and Indira. *Nagpur Times*, 20 October 1983; 4.

Politics may be called the art of acquiring and retaining power, and administration the skill of using power. A demanding mistress, democracy wants those that seek her favours to be adept at both.

Very few are. Of these Jawaharlal was undoubtedly one. His political acumen was sharper than it appeared to be; and what seemed a Hamlet-like vacillation was often, in his case, only a decision to wait for a more opportune time.

599. Gandhi's influence on Nehru. *National Herald*, 15 October 1977.

Every great man, howsoever great he is, is the product of his age, and Jawaharlal Nehru was the product of the Gandhi age. If he had been born in the days of the American Revolution, he would have been a Jefferson drafting the Declaration of Independence or one of Jefferson's close colleagues. During the French Revolution, he would have been a leading Girondist or Jacobin, a Danton or a Robespierre. At the time of the Russian Revolution, he would have been Lenin or one of his close associates. He was one of the finest instruments of historical forces and did not claim to be anything more. He was not any one's caricature.

600. Haksar, P.N. Restoring Gandhi-Nehru Nexus. *Hindu*, 10 November 1987; 8.

601. Husain, S.A. *Way of Gandhi and Nehru*. London, 1961.

602. Jain, Girilal. Gandhi and Nehru. *Times of India*, 14 November 1979; 6.

Unable to grapple with the present, old men often relive their past. Mr. Charan Singh and Mr. Raj Narain are doing precisely that. Or else they would not be blaming Mr. Nehru for the country's ills more than 15 years after his death. It would have been a different matter if it enhanced their electoral prospects. But it does not. On the contrary, it annoys and alienates their Congress (U) ally and gives Mrs. Gandhi an additional stick to beat them with.

Like other old men, the two Lok Dal leaders are quite selective about the past. Mr. Charan Singh would not like to recall that in Mr. Nehru's life-time, he voiced differences of opinion with the deceased leader only on the issue of co-operative farming which the latter never seriously tried to push through and that he held various ministerial offices in subsequent Congress governments in U.P. and neither would like to admit that in that period the differences between them were far sharper than those of either of them with Mr. Nehru. For, while, broadly speaking, Mr. Charan Singh was even then a spokesman of the peasant lobby (in ideological terms a rightwinger), Mr. Raj Narain was an ardent follower of Dr. Ram Manohar Lohia who poured venom on the late prime minister because he was convinced that the latter was not socialist enough in his action.

603. Jain, Girilal. Gandhi and Nehru: Two different moral universes. *Times of India*, 15 November 1979; 8.

604. Jha, Akhileshwar. Was Nehru un-Gandhian? *Hindustan Times*, 14 November 1980; 9.

Most of us have come to take an antagonism between Gandhi and Nehru for granted. Gandhi, we believe, was for village-based politics and economics, traditional rural culture, and a life-style based on voluntary negation. Nehru, we think, was in favour of things that contravened Gandhian tenets. He stood for modern urban civilisation, modern economic and political systems, and scientific and technological revolutions, all of which—so we readily argue—are antithetical to Gandhian thought.

605. Moraes, Frank. Gandhi and Nehru. In *Nehru: Sunlight and shadow*. Bombay, 1964; 1-14.

606. Nehru, Jawaharlal. Light has gone out. In *India's spokesman.* Ed. by. C.D. Narasimhaiah. Madras; 1960; 285-86.

607. Nehru, Jawaharlal. Mahatma Gandhi. In *India's freedom.* London, 1962; 66-68.

It should be remembered that the nationalist movement in India, like all nationalist movements, was essentially a bourgeois movement. It represented the natural historical stage of development, and to consider it or to criticize it as a working-class movement is wrong. Gandhi represented that movement and the Indian masses in relation to that movement to a supreme degree, and he became the voice of the Indian people to that extent. He functioned inevitably within the orbit of nationalist ideology, but the dominating passion that consumed him was a desire to raise the masses. In this respect he was always ahead of the nationalist movement, and he gradually made it, within the limits of its own ideology, turn in this direction. Economic events in India and the world powerfully pushed Indian nationalism towards vital social changes, and today it hovers, somewhat undecided, on the brink of a new social ideology.

608. Patil, V.T. Gandhi and Nehru. In *SON*; 240-54.

609. Patil, V.T. Nehru and Gandhi. In *Nehru and the Freedom movement*, Delhi, 1977; 225-67.

610. P.N. Haksar on Nehru's validity: Gandhi-Nehru vision, *New Wave*, 15 June 1986; 4.

Nehru's and by implication Gandhi's legecy was that in India religion would have its own sphere but it would not be mixed up with the affairs of the state. In politics, calculations based on caste and religion are destructive of the building of a modern nation-state.

611. Radha Krishnan, S. Gandhi and Nehru. In *On Nehru.* New Delhi, 1965; 52-54.

612. Snow, Edgar. Great Sovl's heir. In *NAG*; 88-92.

613. Vakeel, Naval B. Gandhi and Nehru. *Deccan Chronicle*, 21 January 1980.

The lesser men who criticise Nehru, his policy and work do so out of an inferiority complex or political reasons. So to denigrate Nehru, to tarnish his image, to under-rate his contribution and to undo his measures is not only setting the clock back but also rank ingratitude to a leader who was a titan among his contemporaries and who lived and died for his beloved country. . . .

Gandhi, Rajiv

614. Mathai, M.O. Rajiv and Sanjay. *MDN*; 61-67.

While Rajiv and Sanjay were little childern, I told Indira of the danger of the kids being spoilt by staying in a big house with numerous servants and other facilities, and the likelihood of their growing up with wrong ideas and values and taking many things for granted. However, she could do little about it. The children grew up as rather self-centred boys with little thought or consideration for others. They grew up in an atmosphere which instilled in them the wrong idea that the rest of the world was made for them. To say "thank you" did not come naturally to them. They developed no family feelings or family ties.

615. Misra, K.P. Nehru, Indira, Rajiv: Their Roles. *World Focus* (88) April 1987; 26-28.

616. Rahul Singh. Jawaharlal and Rajiv. *Sunday Observer*, 15 November 1987.

Rajiv Gandhi clearly looked up to his grandfather rather than his mother for inspiration. He wanted a clearer polity, more savoury and go-ahead characters around him and when he talked about leading the nation into the 21st century it was not mere rhetoric. But there was the question of financing the Congress party and elections. This seems to have been his undoing.

Gandhi, Sanjay

617. Mathai, M.O. Rajiv and Sanjay. *MDN*; 61-67.

Health Services

618. Gujral, M.L. Health. *EFNIG*; 126-30.

Hindu Mahasabha

619. Nehru, Jawaharlal. Hindu Mahasabha and Communalism. *REW*; 43-44.

Hinduism

620. Altekar. A.S. Hinduism—Asiatic structure or a dynamic force. *NAG*; 421-25.

History and Heritage

621. Khullar, K.K. Nehru—The historian. *Patriot*, 27 May 1973.

622. Kidwai, Anser. Nehru: Positive heritage. *National Herald*, 24 May 1984; 7.

The triumphs of Nehru as the national hero are rooted in his capacity to withstand the challenges in a spirit of tolerance and magnanimity. At this juncture of the challenges to our values of social cohesion and political integrity, the imperative is to revive the old spirit and to fight ideas with ideas: regionalism, communalism and casteism cannot stand up to the test of national resurgence. And the light that went out on May 27, 1964, continues in fact to shed its luminous halo to guide us through the present ordeals in the face of internal and external threats.

623. Moddie, A.D. Pointers from the Past. *Imprint* (Bombay), July 1987; 26-29.

Browsing through my old editions of *Encounter*. I came across John Mander's article 'Indian Autumn' (*Encounter*, February, 1963) about India in 1962, and it stirred a comparative interest on India now—25 year later. The article is especially topical now with news of fresh Chinese mobilisation in Tibet, and the fluid political situation in India. One remembers November 1962, Nehru, Krishna Menon, the 'Himalayan Blunder', the ineffective non-aligned movement, our turning to the US for help in the first major crisis after Independence, and the revival of periodic speculation about India's survival by our politicians, now conveniently called 'destabilisation' by our ruling politicians when their position is threatened.

Mander described NEFA, 1962, not 'as a check but a rout', which the Indian public knew, despite official hide-outs to the contrary. They also got to know about the quiet connivance of Nehru government earlier to the occupation of Aksai Chin by the Chinese since 1957 just as they have a pretty shrewd idea of the allegations behind Fairfax, the German submarines, and the Bofors affairs now, despite less than credible explanations and more. The common sense of the people is more than a match for the public relations and devious ways of authority, Mander then said, "India's democracy, whatever its faults, has proved itself a good deal more robust than the other fair-weather democracies of the Afro-Asian world." India has since confirmed this repeatedly, despite internal and external 'hands', in 1967, 1971, 1977, 1980, 1984, and now again in 1987. Some brave and honest sections of the Indian press have been as much the custodians of our nascent democracy, as the higher judiciary and the electoral system.

But, he goes on to say, "India is a one-man democracy", with Jawaharlal Nehru as that man and "the most enlightened despot in the world". Authority in India was almost synonymous with Nehru. It was so later too, with his daughter Indira Gandhi after 1969, and partly for hereditary reasons and no alternative in the wings. It seems to be the case with Rajiv Gandhi also, at least when the chips are down. His authority and credibility are, however, eroding much faster than his mother's and grandfather's. Mander was right when he observed: "A striking feature of the political scene is the difference in quality between the leadership of a party and its rank and file." Now that gap has narrowed. There is not much to choose between the leaders and the led. There is all-round mediocrity, and worse, in our politics. He thought the keenest apologist of the ruling party would not claim that most Congress Parliamentarians 'are more than a bunch of ignorant, yes-saying back-woodsmen'. Today no one damages the dignity of legislatures more than the ranting, desk-thumping, debateless legislators themselves.

624. Mota, H.N. Nehru page in history. *National Herald*, 30 December 1983.

The passion for freedom welled up in Jawaharlal's heart while he was a student in England. His feelings were aroused by the Indian political situation which was in a state of upheaval in 1907 and 1908. By the time he was called to the Bar in 1912, Jawaharlal had developed a keen interest in world affairs. But he was pretty well conscious of the fact, as revealed in his *Discovery of India*, that "internationalism can indeed only develop in a free country." Shortly after returning from England, he decided to take active part in the freedom movement which was symbolised and spearheaded by the Indian National Congress. Soon after coming into contact with Gandhiji in 1916, Jawaharlal was irresistibly drawn towards the Mahatma whose remarkable success in the non-violent struggle at Champaran on behalf of the tenants of the planters brought about a revolutionary change in his outlook insofar as the methodology of leading the unarmed freedom-fighters was concerned.

625. Murrav, Gilbert. Historic figure of stormy age. In *NAG*; 8-9.

626. Nagaraj, Ranga N. Nehru's perspective on history. *Akashvani*, 16-31 May 1984; 4-5.

Jawaharlal was a luminous celebrity and a multifaced personality. He was an aristocrat by birth, and an advocate by profession, a peripatetic by accident and a rationalist by disposition, a statesman by destiny and an undisputed architect of modern India. He was by inclination a lover of literature and the quality of his writings clearly indicates that he was essentially a literary soul that was lost to the world of politics.

627. Nehru, Jawaharlal. *Letters from a father to his daughter*. Oxford, 1931.

628. Nehru, Jawaharlal. *Bunch of old letters*. Bombay, Asia, 1958.

629. Nehru, Jawaharlal. Our common heritage. *New Wave*, 10 May 1987; 2.

While all people agree about the unity of India, there are many people and even some parties that act in a way which can only result in breaking the unity of India. Why they do so I do not know. While, on the one hand, we the people of India, are bound together by strong bonds of culture, common objectives, friendship, affection, on the other, unfortunately, there are inherent in India separatist and disruptive tendencies which raise head whenever some new question arises.

630. Nehru, Jawaharlal. *Discovery of India*. Bombay, Asia, 1945.

631. Nehru, Jawaharlal. *Glimpses of world history.* Bombay, Asia, 1934.

632. Nehru, Jawaharlal. *Letters from a father to his daughter.* Bombay, 1931.

633. Nehru, Jawaharlal. *India rediscovered.* London, 1961.

634. Nehru, Jawaharlal. *Nehru on world history.* London, Bodley Head, 1960.

635. Padover, Saul K. Nehru's philosophy of history. *Socialist India*, 8 November 1975; 23-24.

The many years that Jawaharlal Nehru spent in jail for his leadership in the struggle for India's freedom served him as a post-graduate course of education in history, literature and philosophy. Behind prison bars, Nehru enriched and deepened his mind. This aspect of his career began at the age of thirty-two, when, he said, "I started my pilgrimages to prison." There were eight subsequent imprisonments, so that he finally concluded ironically that his only career was the "popular and widely practised profession of jail--going in India".

636. Panikkar, K.M. Nehru as historian. *NAG*; 47-50.

637. Tandon, P.D. Instrument of history. *National Herald*, 13 November 1977.

638. Tandon, P.D. Instrument of history. *National Herald*, 14 November 1980; 11.

Whenever I write about Nehru a procession of memories passes my mind and I am reminded of his unparalleled magnificence as a man. His human failings did not detract from his greatness, but added to his charm and glory. One day in the large lecture theatre of the Allahabad University a Professor of History in the presence of Nehru said that the members of the Congress Working Committee did not know history and had no sense of history. This put Nehru on his mettle. He that day chose to address the audience in English and held it spell-bound. Out rolled the English language as to the manner born.

639. Wintringham, Tom. Better history and better English. *NAG*; 29-31.

Hossain, Syud

640. Mathai, M.O. Dr Syud Hossain. *MDN*; 53-55.

Humanism

641. Aiyar, S.P. Mind and Work of Jawaharlal Nehru. *Radical Humanist*, New Delhi, 3 March 1966.

642. Attar Chand, Nehru—the great visionary. *National Herald*, 15 August 1987.

643. Chakravarty, Nikhil. Nehru, the supreme humanist. *Newstime* (Weekend), 15 November 1987; 2.

644. Gafurov. Nehru a great humanist. *Patriot*, 14 November 1976.

For a figure and thinker of such a mould as Nehru's, it was quite natural to appeal to the principles inherent in the progressive tradition of Indian social thought; they were naturally entrenched in the face of the struggle with mediaeval bigotry and colonialist oppression, of the awakening of national consciousness, political activeness of various social strata, of the quests for ways of achieving India's further development and under the impact of the world revolutionary process and of the successes scored by the socialist states.

645. Heard, Gerald. Nehru's significance for mankind. *NAG*; 36-39.

646. Jawaharlal: Humanity's heritage. *New Wave*, 30 May 1982; 1.

647. Karan Singh. Jawaharlal Nehru as a humanist. *Akashvani*, New Delhi, 7 January 1979; 34-35.

Jawaharlal's was a many-faceted personality: thinker, writer, statesman; endowed at once with the scientific temper and the capacity to dream of the future; active participant in the rough and tumble of daily politics and yet a visionary who could comprehend the grand sweep of human history; passionate lover of India, yet untrammeled by narrow nationalism and able to encompass the entire human race—Jawaharlal was a truly unique figure of this century. All the major elements of his world view can be seen to flow from his deep humanism. "The modern mind", he writes, "is practical and pragmatic, ethical and social, altruistic and humanitarian . . . Humanity is its God and social service its religion".

648. Malkani, N.R. In the footsteps of the master. *NAG*; 33-35.

649. Mammen, P.M. Content analysis and a case study in Nehru's value-profile. *SON*; 347-66.

650. Mohindra, P.D. Focus on the Nehru ethos. *Tribune*, 5 January 1981; 12.

651. Mookerjee, G.K. *Nehru the humanist*. New Delhi, Trimurti, 1973.

652. Munshi, K.M. Dedication to vision of ideal. *NAG*; 149-51.

653. Nanporia, N.J. When Nehru snorted. *Amrita Bazar Patrika*, 17 March 1988; 6.

It has been mentioned often in the past but deserves to be said again and again, that Jawaharlal Nehru was a man of exquisite courtesy. Courtesy is being polite with style, and style is what he had. Often, and not surprisingly, he would be late by a minute or so for an interview. Yet he never failed to apologise, not piling on the gentlemanly act but putting it right with a few well-chosen words. Then in my experience, there was another aspect of him that deserves to be recorded and remembered. In fiction and life one hears of people "snorting" without ever encountering the real thing. But Nehru had mastered the snort as no one else had.

654. Narasimhaiah, C.D. *Human idiom: three lectures on Jawaharlal Nehru*. Bombay, Blackie, 1967, 76 pp.

655. Sargent, John. Great Humanist. *NAG*; 80.

656. Shorte, Bani. *Nehru—A voice for mankind?* New York, 1970.

Idealism

657. Novek, Ondrej. Role of tradition in Nehru's thought. *Socialist India*, 8 November 1975; 20-31.

658. Radhakrishnan, S. His [ideals. *On Nehru*, New Delhi, 1965; 22-29.

659. Radhakrishnan, S. Clean advocate of great Ideals. *NAG*; 93-96.

660. Reddy, Raghunatha. Nehru's ideas. *National Herald*, 14 November 1968.

661. Santhanam, K. Nehru—the Statesman and Idealist. *FON*; 80-85.

662. Sarin, L.N. Personal equation. *Jawaharlal Nehru*, Delhi, 1968, 93-98.

663. Wilson, Harold. Man of unbending faith. *Blitz*, 26 May 1984; 19.

Ideology

664. Khan, Abdul Majid. Ideology of Nehru. *Jawaharlal Nehru and his ideas*, New Delhi, 1951; 41-47.

665. Litman, A.D. Ideological legacy of Gandhi and Nehru. *Democratic World*, 22 December 1985. *New Wave*, 29 December 1985; 8-9.

The century-long path travelled by the Indian National Congress (INC) also marks a definite historical stage in the movment of the Indian people itself from colonial enslavement to national liberation, from backwardness and poverty to a cultural revival and social progress.

The second half of this path is directly connected with the activity of the two most outstanding INC leaders—Mahatma Gandhi and Jawaharlal Nehru, who exerted an enormous, perhaps even the decisive influence on the political character, the ideological credo and the organisational principles of this party.

666. Pathak, Avijit. Politics, ideology and alternatives. *Patriot*, 15 August 1987.

However, not many would like to believe that with Nehru began our fall. Doubtless, Nehru was a leader of a different kind. Moreover, Gandhi's faith in him was supreme. Yet, astonishingly enough, Nehru spoke the language of a new generation for which the Gandhian negation of the West looked ridiculous. Gandhi spoke of oceanic circles, village swaraj, simple and solidly integrated communities with manageable technology. Whereas Nehru—an admirer of Darwin and Marx—knew that a twentieth century civilisation was fast becoming uniform, that isolated experiments could not succeed and that India, in order to survive, must welcome the next stage of societal evolution.

So with Nehru began the process of political modernisation. Nehru's intention was as noble as that of Gandhi. But because of his extraordinary urge to catch up with the West, Nehru could not visualise the incompatibility between the institutions he welcomed and the expectations of the people.

Imperialism

667. Imperialsm. In *NFC*; 15-23.

668. Jawaharlal on the Brussels International Congress against Imperialism, 1927. *Socialist India*, Republic Day Number, 1973; 57-64.

669. *Jawaharlal Nehru: Active fighter against imperialism.* New Delhi, Soviet Review, 1969.

670. Katragadda, G. Impact of Brussels meet on Nehru. *Patriot*, 27 May 1979; 2.

671. Khan, Abdul Majid. Imperialism, democracy and war. *Jawaharlal Nehru and his ideas*, New Delhi, 1951; 46-47.

Indian National Congress

672. Attar Chand. What weakened the Congress. *Current* (New Delhi), 22 August 1987.

673. Chalapathi Rau, M. Nehru and Syndicate of 1951. *Young Indian*, 11 November 1971; 4.

Nehru expounded to me his philosophy of withdrawal. Gandhi had always withdrawn wherever he was not wanted or could not carry other Congress leaders with him. "The more you withdraw from positions, the more you may be wanted", he said. He had other thoughts, too, of his closeness to the people and the distance of his critics from the people.

674. Chicherov, Alexander. *Jawaharlal Nehru and Indian National Congress.* New Delhi, Allied, 1985, 117 pp.

675. Durga Das. *Kamraj Plan in India.* London, 1969; 372-73.

The Kamaraj Plan cleared the line of succession for India by eliminating Morarji Desai, who after Pant's death was "number two" in the Government. I, therefore, sought Kamaraj's own explanation of the plan named after him. What Kamaraj told me confirmed the information gathered by me from other members of the Congress High Command. This is what he said; "The D M.K. had won only fifteen seats in the Madras Legislative Assembly in 1957, while it won fifty in 1962 and about twenty-seven per cent of the votes cast. This was a danger signal and Kamaraj decided to devote himself fully to countering the D.M.K. and strengthening the Congress organisation in Madras. He suggested to Nehru that he resign the Chief Ministership for this purpose. The Prime Minister asked Kamaraj to let him think over the matter. This was soon after the 1962 elections."

Then came the Chinese attack and the defeat of the Congress in three by-elections to Parliament which were won by Kripalani standing as an independent, the Samyukta Socialist leader Ram Manohar Lohia and the Swatantra spokesman Minoo Masani respectively. At the time, Biju Patnaik, Chief Minister of Orissa, met Kamaraj and said he would like to join the Central Cabinet and strengthen it. Others too should do the same, he said. Kamaraj told him it was more important to strengthen the party organisation by resigning office and working among the people. Patnaik fell in line with this view and expressed readiness to give up the Chief Ministership of Orissa. Nehru was in Kashmir and Patnaik went there and discussed the matter with him.

Nehru came to Hyderabad for a week and sent for Kamaraj and asked him for details of his proposal. Kamaraj replied that it was meant only for Madras, but Nehru said it should be applied to other states where the Congress was not strong. He gave the impression that he was worried by the by-election results and the effect on public opinion of the Chinese invasion and the controversy over Menon. Subramaniam was with Nehru and Sanjiva Reddy was also in Hyderabad. After consultations, it was agreed that attention should be paid to organisational work. Nehru suggested that Kamaraj raise the issue in the Working Committee which was to meet shortly. He did not know what was in Nehru's mind but did as he was bid.

There was general agreement on it in the Committee. Nehru said the principle should apply to leaders in the states as well as at the Centre. He christened it the Kamaraj Plan and had it endorsed by the A.I.C.C. It was decided that all Ministers at the Centre and the Chief Ministers should place their resignation in Nehru's hands and he would decide who should work for the organisation. Kamaraj's own idea was that it would be enough if as a symbol of the new resolve two Chief Ministers and one or two central Ministers vacated office and took up organisational work. Until then, he did not suspect that Nehru had a deeper motive. But he realised this when Nehru said he had decided to relieve several Chief Ministers and top leaders, including Morarji Desai.

676. Durry, Kaokab. King emperor. *The Times of India*, 29 January 1987; 8.

Whatever we may say of politicians, we must credit them with supersensory perception of power and its extent. And if in Mr. Girilal Jain's words, senior Congress leaders have proved that "there is no limit beyond which they will not bend," they have admirable reasons to do so. The issue simply is whether the Prime Minister is accountable to the party or not? The answer to this depends on how you look at the complex relationship between the government and Congress party organisation. The question, therefore, is whether the party should be considered supreme or the government? It may be recalled that when Acharya Kriplani was the President of the Congress he had clashad with Jawaharlal Nehru on this very issue. Panditji, despite being a firm believer in democratic functioning, did not agree to subordinate the government to the party. Acharya Kriplani, therofore, had to go. Then followed the conflict between Mr. Nehru and Mr. Purushottamdas Tandon. The issue that provoked the disagreement can be stated in Mr. Tandon's own words: "His (Pandit Nehru's) demand has been that the whole working committee should be dissolved and a new working committee constituted. This demand is neither constitutional nor proper." "I cannot accept the resignation of Jawaharlal Nehru because at present he is the symbol of our nation. At the same time, from the point of view of the Constitution and propriety, I cannot fulfil his desire. Out of this dilemma I see no other way but to place my resignation before you and (request you) to relieve me of the Presidentship" (Aloud and Silent: Congreess Presidents by A.M. Zaidi, pp. 216-217).

Finally, there was a clash between Mr. Kamraj and Mrs. Gandhi. At that time, Mr. Kamraj was a mighty figure and Mrs. Gandhi had still to make the grade. That she did so eventually was entirely because of the inexorable accumulation of political power by the Prime Minister. This is inherent in the system. So why blame Congress leaders? After all they know where the power lies. They would certainly not be wanting in willingness to take it in their own hands if they could.

677. Indian National Congress. *NFC*; 120-24.

678. Khan, Rasheeduddin. Congress culture and heritage of Nehru. *Mainstream*, 28 December 1985; 23-26, 35-36.

679. Pande, M.K. Nehru on the role of the Congess. *Socialist India*, 11 November 1972; 12.

Nehru always exhorted Congressmen to participate in the implementation of National Schemes by taking part in such activities. In his opinion this would identify them not only with the masses but also contribute to the national cause. For "if they shirked this work they will isolate themselves from the masses and will weaken themselves and the Congsess."

680. Pavadya, Balaram Singh. Nehru, the Indian National Congress and India's Membership in the Commonwealth. *SON*; 367-86.

681. Sarin, L.N. Congress without Nehru. *Jawaharlal Nehru*. Delhi, 1988; 87-92.

Intellectual

682. Anand, Mulk Raj. Jawaharlal Nehru as an intellectual. *National Herald*, 29 November 1987.

683. Anand, Mulk Raj. Nehru' as an intellectual. *Socialist India*, 28 November 1970; 16-17.

Besides Jawaharlal Nehru's own position as the leader of the Indian people rather than merely as a leader of one party, made for a certain amount of reconciliation among the classes and the masses, all engaged in an economy which cannot, from its inner compulsions, be a laissez faire capitalist economy of the 19th century British kind or of the 20th century American kind, but a dynamic egalitarian economy, if the people of India as a whole are to build India together and to survive on any plane of human existence. Actually, this dominantly socialist economy, with its large capitalist sector, may be forced by the interplay of rapid industrialisatio n towards integral socialism sonner or later.

684. Anand, Mulkraj. Nehru as an Intellectual-II. *Socialist India*, 21 November 1979; 20-21.

I do not think he has stated this doctrine consciously anywhere, or differentiated his particular kind of humanism from the Christian and other humanisms, espoused in our time by several philosophers like Maritain, Berdayev, Santayana or Sartre. For while the average European thınker has been on the defensive against the disintegration of European society, through the pull of the unbridled cash-nexus competition, insecurity, lack of faith, aggrandisement and other traits of the armament death-culture, Jawaharlal Nehru had to bring forth more positive sympathies.

685. Mashruwala, K.G. Intellect, faith and action. *NAG*; 136-37.

Iqbal, Mohammed

686. Iqbal told Nehru: "your are a patriot, Jinnah is a politician". *Organiser*, 15 August 1983; 10.

According to Tariq Ali, who has little hope of survival of Pakistan, "the support for Muslim separatism was the strongest where the competition between the Hindu and Muslim middle classes (for jobs) was the most severe." And that was the root cause of Pakistan. But it is significant that Iqbal came out with his idea of Pakistan at the Muslim League session in December, 1930 exactly one year after the Lahore session of the Indian National Congress where complete Independence was adopted as the goal of the Congress. It was a command performance indeed.

687. Mahmood, H. Nehru and Iqbal. *Statesman*, 23 April 1978.

Jawaharlal became a critic of Europe and European polity much later, and as a consequence of many things, including his plunge into the freedom struggle, study of Iqbal and his European tour during the illness of Kamala. And thus the two wayfarers, following different paths, converged on one, to proclaim the humanism of the East. I do not know if Iqbal had Nehru in mind (though my suspicion is great) when he said, "In the West intellect is the source of life, in the East love is the basis of life; arise and lay the foundation of a new world by wedding intellect with love."

688. Nehru, Jawaharlal. Reply to Sir Mohammad Iqbal. *REW*; 60-69.

Iyengar, Srinivasan

689. Mathai, M.O. Srinivasan Iyengar, 1874-1941. *MDN*; 224-28.

Seshadri Srinivasa Iyengar, an outstanding Madras lawyer, was at one time the most important Congressman in the south. He belonged to the galaxy of eminent men and women in the Congress: Motilal Nehru, C.R. Das, Vithalbhai Patel, and Sarojini Naidu. In 1926 he was elected Dupty Leader of the Swaraj party in the Central Legislation of the Indian National Congress in 1926. S. Satyamurthi and K. Kamaraj were his early disciples.

690. Sastri, K.A. Nilkanta. *Great Liberal: Speeches and Writings of Sir P.S. Sivaswami Aiyar*. Madras, Allied, 1965; 478-80.

The address delivered by Pandit Jawaharlal Nehru as President of the Lucknow Session of the Congress is a momentous pronouncement which deserves to be deeply pondered not merely by the members of the Congress Party, but by all politicians and publicists, by the people and the Government. The speech is remarkable not merely for frankness and courage, but also for the clarity with which it expounds the political and social ideals of the President and the policy which he desires the country to pursue. His speech is further remarkable for its directness in brushing aside all issues which he considers to be of secondary importance and focussing attention on the two issues which, in his opinion, are fundamental. Political independence and socialism, or rather communism, are the two vital issues which count.

Jagjivan Ram

691. Jagjivan Ram. Jagjivan salutes Jawaharlal. *Blitz*, 26 May 1964; 21.

Jawaharlal Nehru was the most powerful Prime Minister, not only in India but anywhere in the world, being the undisputed leader, I would rather say, the darling of the nation.

He was free to function in any way he liked, but he scrupulously avoided doing anything which in the slightest measure infringed the norms of democracy.

Jan Sangh

692. Jan Sangh estimate of Jawaharlal Nehru. *Socialist Congressman* (New Delhi), 15 April 1969; 62.

Nehru was the great protagonist of national integration through unity of all religions which is the tradition of Indian culture and the basis of our nationalism. Therefore, it is natural that he could not be reconciled to the Sanghites who consider India to be 'Hindu Rashtra', and who refuse to recognise the Muslims as Indian nationals. According to them, "In India only the Hindus are nationalists, and any person till such time as he rejects Islam can not regard himself as an Indian national."

Journalism

693. Anjanevulu, D. Nehru—the writer and journalist. *Indian and Foreign Review*, 15 November 1986; 9-11.

The literary maxim, 'the style is the man', is nowhere more true than in Nehru the writer. In his hectic life as the nation's leader and Prime Minister, Nehru must have addressed countless public meetings and there were memorable occasions when he rose to loftly heights of impassioned eloquence. His famous outpouring at Mahatma's funeral, "The light has gone out of the world", lingers as a powerful, moving piece. But more than in his public speeches, it was in his writing, that he was in his element—sensitive, accurate and brilliantly communicative.

694. Ranganathan, A. Nehru as a journalist. *Akashvani*, 16-31 May 1984; 5-6.

It is difficult to classify Jawaharlal Nehru a statesman who wrote and made history, a writer who restated modern India's intellectual attitudes in the wake of such publications as *An Autobiography*, *Glimpses of World History* and *The Discovery of India* and a journalist who dramatized the history of his times. He wrote with elegance, wit and discernment. And in the ultimate analysis, Pandit Nehru brought to journalism as well as occasional writing an inclusive vision that was based on his continuing access to history-in-the-making.

695. Subha Rao, N.V. Nehru the writer. *Swarajya* (Madras), 18 January 1978; 4-6.

Among Nehru's innumerable books *Glimpses of World History*, *An Autobiography* and *Discovery of India* gained the acclamation of the intelligentsia throughout the globe. His other writings like *World Struggle and India*, *India's Freedom*, *Before and After Independence* were widely read and appreciated for their specialised subjects with minute details and technique of presentation. His other speeches and letters collected and brought out in a number of volumes, too, are of everlasting value.

Khan, Abdul Gaffar Khan

696. Mathai, M.O. Khan Abdul Gaffar Khan. *MDN*; 214-16.

It is obvious that he was so obssessed with "absolute" non-violence that he did not want to put that precious commodity to test. It is also quite likely that he had a more realistic sense of Muslim public opinion in the North-West Frontier at that time than Nehru and others.

It has been said that the meek shall inherit the earth. This did not happen in the case of Khan Abdul Gaffar Khan maybe because he clung to an abstraction and failed to act. This reminds me of the story of a man who had read in the scriptures "throw your bread upon the waters, and it shall return to you ten-fold." He acted on it and later told a cynical priest "I put a loaf in a water-proof polythene bag and threw it on the waters. I had taken the precaution of attaching a string to it in case the almighty forgot his promise. I spent the whole night on the river bank. By the morning nothing happened; so I drew it back and went home disappointed." The priest told him wryly, "If you had not used the polythene bag, water would have soaked into the bread which would then have weighed ten times!"

Fate and circumstances made this great and good man Khan Abdul Gaffar Khan a tragic figure of the sub-continent who spent most of his life, after partition, in prison or in exile. A worse fate befell that fine jovial man with a cherubic face: Khan Abdul Samad Khan known as the Baluchi Gandhi who was brutally murdered.

Khan Abdul Gaffar Khan deserves the veneration and salutes of the Indian people, but conferring on him the Nehru award for international understanding was a thoroughly misplaced gesture. Between Khan Abdul Gaffar Khan and "international understanding" there was nothing common.

Kripalani, J.B.

697. Mathai, M.O. Acharya J.B. Kripalani. *MDN*; 216-19.

Of the many types of Congressmen the Gandhian era threw up, Acharya Kripalani was unique. The prefix "Acharya" does not mean that he is a Brahmin. It stuck to him because he was a teacher. All Sindhis whose names end with "ani" are Kshatriyas. The Sindhi Kshatriyas are successful businessmen; but dada Kripalani, who richly deserves the prefix "Acharya", remained a delightfully unbusinesslike and disorganized person. In the simplicity of personal life he stuck to the severest of Gandhian standards. He was one up on Gandhi in the practice of Brahmacharya. Gandhi adopted Brahmacharya after producing several children. Kripalani was a Brahmachari throughout. To many, who were not in tune with Gandhian ways, Kripalani's marriage was a joke. A prominent Congressman once told me that he never understood the meaning of platonic love until he came to know of the relationship between Kripalani and his wife Sucheta.

Labour

698. Nehru, Jawaharlal. Labour and Congress. *Recent essays and writings*, Allahabad, 1934; 127-29.

During the great social and economic crisis that the world is passing through today, labour has a very special duty before it. For, inevitably, the burden of ideological leadership must remain with labour. In India, the national struggle covers and hides social differences. That is natural. But world events themselves are today forcing the pace and making even national movements more and more economic and social movements. All over the world there is a great struggle between the forces of labour and the forces of entrenched vested interest. The stakes are high and therefore we cannot afford either in our national struggle or in our social struggle to compromise with petty changes. If we are to profit by the world situation, we must make up our minds to struggle for a complete and fundamental change of regime. Nothing else should satisfy us, nothing else can solve our problems.

India is today in a somewhat confused state of mind. She finds that her old nationalist ideology does not fit in with the existing circumstances in the world. So she struggles to adopt a new way of thinking and this attempt to change over from the old to the new is a painful and confusing one. But the attempt must be proceeded with, for only thus by adopting a progressive ideology of social revolution can India take an effective part in the freedom struggle as well as in the world struggle.

699. Nehru, Jawaharlal. Trade Union Congress. *REW*; 130-32.

700. Saxena, Kiran. Jawaharlal Nehru and the Indian Working class. *Secular Democracy* (New Delhi), (1) 1977; 23-26.

Nehru's wavering attitude towards Marxism and Socialism is reflected in his relationship with the working class movement. The working class movement in India, in spite of its militancy and its capacity to wage unceasing struggles, could not organise itself until the end of the First World War. A glance would show that the Indian working class from its very inception has played a very important role in the Indian national movement as well as for the cause of social and economic justice. It has a glorious record of struggles. The industrial workers during the decades preceding the First World War were increasingly displaying solidarity in action and growing class consciousness.

Language

701. Duggal, K.S. Listening to Nehru. *Century* (New Delhi), 3 February 1968; 7-8.

Nehru was a distinguished writer in his own right. Along with success as a political leader, to him came spontaneous recognition as a man of letters. He was happy to be associated with arts and artists. He loved creative activity. But he loved people more. He loved the people, who were backward, ignorant and illiterate. Writing of any kind, much less sophisticated writing, had little use for them, the teeming millions he was pledged to serve. He, therefore, decided in favour of spoken word and developed it as an art-form in the tradition of mighty preceptors such as Buddha, Christ and, in recent times, Gandhi.

702. Hindi Backlash and Nehru's Promise. *Mainstream*, 22 November 1966; 22-23.

While the Centre's solicitude for Urdu and Sindhi should hardly be surprising on the eve of a crucial general election, it underlines, nevertheless, the certain failure of the Government's language policy under the impact of the Hindi backlash.

The interaction of pressure politics on the language policy has led to certain distortions giving a new edge to the controversy. The long-term implications of the controversy are serious. A promise that Nehru made to the non-Hindi people, on the continued use of English as an associate language for official purposes, remains to be fulfilled though two Prime Ministers have changed since the promise was made.

Last Journey

703. Gupta, K.P. *Nehru, last jourrney*. Lucknow, India Publications, 1964.

Leadership

704. Aga Khan. Leader, thinker and practical dreamer. *NAG*; 85.

705. Attar Chand. No strong personality to save the nation. *Sunday Mid-Day* (Bombay), 9 August 1987.

706. Bhalerao, C.N. Nehru's contribution in nation-building. *National Herald*, 27 May 1983; 5.

Jawaharlal Nehru was intellectually reared in the Western tradition. His father gave him almost an exclusively European training. In 1905, Jawaharlal Nehru went to England where he studied at Harrow and Trinity College, Cambridge, and took his natural sciences tripos with second class honours from Cambridge University in 1910. He also joined the Inner Temple in London and was called to the Bar in 1912. Though a product of English education, it is a paradox that the man with this background should have become the heir to Mahatma Gandhi and the greatest nation-builder of his country. The same Jawaharlal wrote in his will that a handful of his ashes after cremation should be thrown into the Ganges and the major portion scattered over the fields where the peasants of India toil so that they might mingle with the dust and soil of India and become an indistinguishable part of her.

707. Brecher, Michael. *Political leadership in India*. New Delhi, Vikas, 1969; 32-33.

Among the Opposition leaders only one articulated a view and this was positive: "A substantial asset, to which she brings certain qualities, modernism, liberalism, and grace." Most pointed were the comments of Indian Journalists. One was complimentary: "She counters the pervasive image of the corrupt, disagreeable Congress politician," but even she did "not necessarily win votes." Another remarked, "Nehru's mantle was partial compensation for her inadequacies as speaker, thinker, and administrator." But the most critical remark of all 80 respondents came from still another Journalist: "If anything, the link had the reverse effect—a serious reflection on the nation that among 500 million people we need a woman to rule, 500 million eunuchs ruled by one woman."

708. Kher, B.G. Personality which compels attention. *NAG*; 86-87.

709. Mahtab, Hare Krishna. Great man of the century. *National Herald*, 14 November 1983; 6.

710. Martyshin, O.V. Leadership of Jawaharlal Nehru. *Nagpur Times*, 28 December 1985; 4.

In December 1946, addressing the Constituent Assembly in connection with the resolution on objectives which he had tabled, Nehru said that he himself favoured socialism and hoped that India would follow that road and build some type of a socialist state. Nehru pursued a well-balanced line of using every opportunity for development and simultaneously promoting state control, of inducing the private sector to serve the interests of the nation.

711. Mathur, Girish. Quality of Nehru's stewardship. *Daily*, 27 May 1983; 8-9.

Most writers on Jawaharlal Nehru who take up centrist of leftist positions, including his biographer Dr. S. Gopal and the Marxist historian Prof. Bipan Chandra, have been less than fair to him in attributing the gap between profession and performance during his stewardship of the country to either his failure to develop a coherent outlook and strategy like Lenin and Mao or his class background.

712. Mathur, Girish. Way out of leadership crisis. *Link*, 15 August 1987; 19-22.

Jawaharlal Nehru was great enough to be brutally self-critical when he was at the height of his popularity. But he was not a demagogue. He was more of a pedagogue. His appeal was couched in rational terms and in historical perspectives. The ethusiasm he roused was not blind passion. He urged people to stand up against injustice, not the unjust; against oppression, ignorance, obscurantism and lethargy of the system, not against the individuals who presided over the system. He sought to carry the people with him by educating them and not by rousing their fury.

713. Mohan Kumaramangalam, S. Panditji—As I know him. *Mainstream*, 15 November 1969; 13-15.

The crisis in the Congress is not an accident born out of a quarrel between two different groups lusting after power. The crisis is only another reflection of what took place even in Nehru's life time; first, at the time of the election of Purushottamdas Tandon as President of the Congress; secondly, when in the late fifties Panditji seriously thought of resigning because of his dissatisfaction at the slow progress of India's development; and finally, in the last phase of his life when, after Bhubaneshwar, the Kamaraj Plan was put into action to clear the decks for a more radical and decisive policy in the economic sphere.

714. Munshi, Lilavati. Not only maker, but doer. *NAG*; 143-44.

715. Nunn, William. Outstanding in leadership. *NAG*; 45-46.

716. Sarin, L.N. Leadership. *Jawaharlal Nehru*, Delhi, 1968; 70-81.

717. Schlessinger, Arthur M. *Thousand days.* London, Andre Deutsch, 1965, 918 pp.

718. Sharda Prasad, H.Y. Qualities of Leadership. *Mainstream*, 14 March 1987; 7-8, 31.

As a nation we have become too dependent on great men. There are leaders whom the faith of their followers drives to reckless deeds. There are others who regard it as a trust which should be deserved. One of the most moving passages in Jawaharlal Nehru's autobiography is his discovery of rural India:

"They (the peasants) showered their affection on us and looked on us with loving and hopeful eyes, as if we were the bearers of good tidings, the guides who were to lead them to the promised land. Looking at them and their misery and overflowing gratitude, I was filled with shame and sorrow, shame at my own easy-going and comfortable life and our petty politics of the city which ignored this vast multitude of semi-naked sons and daughters of India, sorrow at the degradation and overwhelming poverty of India. A new picture of India seemed to rise before me, naked, starving, crushed, and utterly miserable. And their faith in us, casual visitors from the distant city, embarrassed me and filled me with a new responsibility that frightened me".

To the end of his days, Jawaharlal Nehru's endeavour was to justify this faith. He wanted not to fail the poor millions of this land.

719. Singh, Akhileshwar. *Political leadership of Jawaharlal Nehru.* New Delhi, Deep & Deep Publications.

720. Sivaprakasam, N. Paradox of Nehru's many-faceted personality. *Socialist India*, 13 November 1976; 22-24.

An aristocrat by birth, an autocrat by temperament, a democrat by action, a socialist by conviction and spiritualist by tradition—Jawaharlal Nehru presents the picture of a perfect paradox. Yet, it is this apparent paradox that casts an eerie spell over the exquisite mosaic of Nehru's many-splendoured life. He has confounded alike his contemporaries and his caricaturists.

721. Sodhbans, P.S. Dynamic personality. *NAG*; 152-54.

722. Spender, Stephen. Only cultivated statesman. *NAG*; 145.

723. Suri, Surinder. Political leader par excellence. *New Socialist*, November 1959; 7-10.

Legacy

726. Abbas, K.A. Fascinating personality. *National Herald*, 14 November 1981; 15.

727. Abbas, K.A. Relevance of Jawaharlal. *Patriot*, 14 November 1980; 45.

728. Ahmed, S.I. Nehru: A tribute. *Indian Nation*, 27 May 1987; 4.

Nehru was unequivocally a whole man—a man with convictions and principles of the knowledge and experience probably of his writings and speeches are not mere decorations or skilful arrangements of dead flowers but works of passion, things of beauty which induce in us a sense of the significance, meaningfulness of life, evoke in us 'ideas' of the larger beauty, justice and charity of the universe and remind us all the time of our duty to share in the general movement and push it along.

729. Asaf Ali, Aruna. Nehru legacy. *Link*, 15 August 1964.

730. Attar Chand. Buried legacy. *Newstime*, 31 July 1987.

731. Attar Chand. Nehru a part of our future. *Clarity*, 16 August 1987.

732. Attar Chand. Nehru's contribution. *Mid-Day*, 13 August 1978.

733. Attar Chand. Nehru's relevance. *Patriot*, 1 August 1987.

734. Brahm Dev. Last farewell. *Newstime*, 27 May 1984; 7.

To Nehru, the call of the Himalayas was irresistible. It is perhaps because of this that he had a liking for Dehra Dun, which is situated at the foot of the Himalayas. During his visit to Dehra Dun in 1963, I was all set to click the shutter of my Hasselblad camera as he got out of the Dakota. But Nehru was a problem for photographers.

735. Chakraverti, P.R. Nehru legacy—royal status. *Pioneer*, 7 December 1983.

Pandit Nehru had sought to analyse his own philosophy of life, confronted with the cross currents of political aspirations of his country people, participating in the freedom movements led by

Mahatma Gandhi. It was a searching quest and conscious appraisal of the rapidly changing facts of history.

736. Chalapathi Rau, M. Place in history. *Jawaharlal Nehru.* New Delhi; 1962; 26-30.

737. Chitta Ranjan, C.N. Significance of Nehru today. *Mainstream,* 15 November 1969; 6-8.

It has to be recognized that the largest contribution in terms of producing massive popular awareness of the need for, and the inevitability of, a democratic socialist order in India was made by Jawaharlal Nehru who even in the twenties emerged as the most striking spokesman of the aspirations of the common people. He was not alone in believing, even in those times, that independence would have no meaning for the masses if it did not constitute a firm step towards the establishment of a just social order based on secularism and equality. The Communists, whose ideals even the Mahatma accepted but whose methods were rejected by Jawaharlal among others, were already actively on the scene mobilizing the working class wherever possible, despite their inability to comprehend fully the potentialities of the national liberation movement guided and inspired by Gandhiji.

738. Das, Tapan. Legacy of Jawaharlal Nehru and its relevance today. *Soviet Review* (New Delhi), 22 November 1979; 41-47.

739. Dasgupta, Subhayu. Is the light of Asia fading? *Amrita Bazar Patrika*, 13 November 1983.

It was Winston Churchill who greeted Nehru in the following words: "I hope you will think of the phrase 'The light of Asia'. It seems to me that you might be able to do what no other human being could in giving India the lead, at least in the realm of thought, throughout Asia, with the freedom and dignity of the individual as the ideal rather than the communist party drill book" (Churchill to Nehru 21 February 1955). Churchill referred again to this phrase in his letter of 30 June 1955 (Gopala: Jawaharlal Nehru: A Biography).

740. Deva, Narendra. Favourite of fortune. *NAG*; 107-112.

741. Dinesh Singh. Reminiscences and notes. *Nehru legacy.* New Delhi 1966; 48-57.

Jawaharlal knew that non-alignment was based on peaceful co-existence. Unless countries had the assurance that there would be no interference in their domestic affairs and that their territorial integrity would be preserved, they would not be able to remain non-aligned and would gradually move towards foreign assistance to preserve their independence. He, therefore, advocated the abandonment of the use of force to settle disputes between countries.

742. Dubey, Suman. Twenty years after: A troubled legacy. *India Today*, 15 June 1984; 80-89.

743. Dutta, Pratap C. Procession of men. *Patriot*, 14 November 1981; 2.

744. Emerging World. *Souvenir volume*. Bombay, Asia, 1964.

745. Fight over Nehruism. *Tribune* (Chandigarh), 3 November 1979; 4.

"Nehruism" was unacceptable to Dr. Lohia mainly because of the former Prime Minister's refusal to reject Western values. No one could in fairness accuse Jawaharlal Nehru of being "un-Indian". In fact, he knew more about Indian history and culture than the vast majority of his critics. Nevertheless, some of the critics such as Dr. Lohia on the one hand and Babu Purushottam Das Tandon on the other, not to mention extremists among the Hindu community, regarded him as an alien uprooted from his national moorings. This was either a tragic misunderstanding of what Nehru stood for or a deliberate and calculated attempt to misrepresent him for political reasons. Mr. Charan Singh and Mr. Raj Narain now appear to have picked up the theme where Dr. Lohia and other opponents of the Nehru approach left off. It must be admitted too, that the present day supporters of Nehru are at least partly responsible for exposing him to attack by projecting his views as something akin to a religion. Blind adulation often leads to unexpected reactions.

746. Gandhi, Indira. Jawaharlal Nehru. *Socialist India*, 18 November 1972; 11-12.

While he was a teacher, he was also a student. He believed that one never ends learning and the day one thinks one knows everything there is to know, that day one closes one's mind, that day one is not really alive. So he was a student, constantly learning, constantly absorbing new knowledge and factors, not merely from those whom one would have thought more learned—because amongst his friends he counted some of the topmost scientists, writers and artists of the world—but he learnt even from the tribal areas, even from our villagers.

747. Gandhi, Indira. Jawaharlal Nehru. *National Herald*, 14 November 1972; 5.

He was real teacher. Most of what I know came from him. But the people of India, those of you who ever heard him speak, must have noticed that his speeches were not to make points, they were not rhetoric and fine words, but were an effort to teach the people, to teach whichever audience he was addressing, something which would last with them and which would make a difference to them for the rest of their lives. Even when he spoke in tribal areas and to rural people, he spoke about the discoveries of science, about the trends of history, about the forces that were at work in our world.

748. Gilding the rose. *New Wave*, 4 January 1987; 3.

Nehru was a many-splendoured personality. His contribution to India, which he loved, and to the world, which he cherished, has been so varied and vast that it would require a great deal of imagination and thought to make his birth centenary worthy of him.

He had so many faces to his personality that one of his admirers, once described him as "a procession of men". He was an anti-imperialist, a socialist, founder of the public sector, architect of non-alignment and panchsheel, a liberal, a visionary, a committed democrat, promoter of secularism and an agnostic. It is hardly possible to define the man, the politician and the statesman in words or images. And yet, he found himself "out of place everywhere, at home nowhere."

749. He continues to inspire. *National Herald*, 14 November 1981; 15.

750. India today and Nehru. *National Herald*, 15 November 1978; 5.

751. Jain, Girilal. Relevance of Mr. Nehru. *Times of India*, 27 May 1970.

752. Jaswant Singh. India: 20 Years after Nehru. *Mainstream*, Nehru Number 1984; 13-14, 63.

This Nehruism is perhaps best illustrated by two quotes from Nehru himself. Speaking to the Constituent Assembly, on March 9, 1949, he characteristically injected the personal and said that "he left a secret emotion at being privileged to participate in the services of India at this tremendous stage of her journey". This same Nehru, about six years later, while writing to Sheikh Mohd. Abdullah gave voice to his fears, "We, who are in charge of heavy responsibilities have to deal with all kinds of forces at work and often they take their own shape. We see in the world today great statesmen, who imagine they are controlling the destinies of a nation, being pushed hither and thither by forces beyond their control. The most that one can do is to endeavour to function, according to one's judgement in the allotted sphere".

753. Joshi, Navin Chandra. Foresight of Nehru. *Deccan Chronicle*, 18 November 1987.

754. Kamaraj, K. Nation's leader and his legacy. *Nehru Legacy*. New Delhi, 1966; 1-13.

I have been asked what made Jawaharlal the leader of the Congress—which qualities of his, and through what contributions he made. I do not think the question can be answered briefly. That is why I have attempted in a general way to explain the role of Jawaharlal in the early years of struggle under Gandhiji's leadership. The qualities which really endeared him to the rank and file of the Congress all over the country, and made him a hero in the eyes of the nation's youth, were his sincerity, his dedication to the great cause, his impatience with the slowness of the then leadership to react to the vast changes taking place all over the world, his readiness to make any sacrifice, and his fearless and persistent efforts to convert the conservative sections of the Congress leadership to his own way of thinking.

755. Kamaraj, K. Path Nehru showed us. *Towards Socialism*, New Delhi, 1966;41-44.

756. Khusro, A.M. Jawaharlal Nehru's legacy-I. *National Herald*, 27 May 1983; 5.

It was precisely owing to the prevalence of a tolerant culture that democracy had found favourable ground to take roots here, and Gandhi and Nehru had nurtured the plant of democracy and nationalism for a life-time. But typified by the dastardly and fatal attack on Gandhiji, the emergence of intolerant and undemocratic ideas and actions had become a source of great worry to Nehru after him.

757. Khusro, A.M. Nehru's legacy-II. *National Herald*, 28 May 1983; 5.

I think Panditji would have viewed the great rural programmes with immense satisfaction even as Gandhiji would have. But large as these programmes are—IRDP more than Rs. 4,000 crores, NREP approaching Rs. 2,000 crores etc. these have to be monitored very carefully in order to avoid wastage, corruption and favouritism. These programmes essentially involve the identification of the poorest among the poor, identification of viable economic activity in rural areas, marrying the individual or families with the activity and activating them so that they generate real output and create assets. Preliminary investigation already reveals that sometimes the really downtrodden families are being neglected; the scheduled castes and the minorities are not getting their proper share, the activities are not always viable, the training and marketing infrastructure and other capital requirements of the programme are inadequately provided and a good deal of leakage might be existing.

758. Legacy and a pledge. *National Herald*, 4 November 1987; 6.

759. Lest we forget. *National Herald*, 27 May 1978; 6.

760. Mathur, Girish. Nehru's vision overrides disruption. *Link*, 27 May 1984; 15-20.

The two decades since Jawaharlal Nehru passed away have been marked by a continuing turmoil in the country. Goals seem to have been lost sight of, and norms have broken down in almost every sphere of national life. Our society seems to be suffering from anomie, our policy from disorientation, our economy from lack of direction. Despite attainments in science and technology, uor education seem to be breeding new obscurantisms, and there has even been some retreat from secularism. Premonitions have been voiced about the country sliding fast towards disintegration.

761. Mehra, Mannwhan. Legacy of Jawaharlal Nehru. *Hindustan Times*, 13 January 1986; 9.

Jawaharlal Nehru brought to bear his democratic concepts of freedom, justice, equality, fairplay, human dignity and fraternity on international relations. He laid down the guidelines of India's foreign policy, which declared friendship with all States, advocated self-determination for all peoples, and the elimination of war. For the implementation of his foreign policy and achieving the right international order, Nehruji evolved the strategy of non-alignment. He developed the concept of non-alignment and peaceful co-existence based on the rich traditions of the Indian ethos. The philosophy of non-alignment was his brain child, and he was the chief architect of the non-aligned movement. Along with Nasser and Tito, he made a clarion call to the newly independent nations to join the non-aligned movement in order to save the world from the scourge of war, and to build the defence of peace in the minds of men.

762. Menon, K.P.S. If Nehru were alive today. *Indian Express* (*Sunday Standard*), 26 May 1974.

If Nehru were alive today he would have been 85. He could easily have lived up to that age, and beyond, because unlike many politicians who are too busy and distracted to pay attention even to their health Nehru kept himself in perfect trim. He was fond of exercise such as yoga and riding and this kept his body as youthful as his mind.

763. Menon, M.S.N. World vision of Jawaharlal. *Mainstream*, 29 May 1971; 29-31.

For Jawaharlal, history is not a meaningless succession of events, but a great striving of the human spirit to reach some common goal. The striving is of the individual as also of the collective. Each civilisation, he says, like the individual, must find out by trial and error, through suffering and experience, a path for itself. He was, therefore, against notions of a common culture and a common way of life for the world. A civilisation is the unique product of the objective inner experience of a people, which can be ignored only at its peril.

764. Misra, Shripat. Remembering Nehru and fulfilling his dreams. *Blitz*, 26 May 1984; 20.

765. Nanda, B.R. Nehru: A retrospect. *Nehru and the Modern World*, New Delhi, UNESCO, 1967; 564.

766. Natwar Singh, K., ed. *Legacy of Nehru-A memorial tribute.* New York, 1965.

767. Nehru's vision of India. *New Wave*, 31 May 1987; 2.

Proud of the love he universally enjoyed, Jawaharlal had inscribed in his heart a lofty quotation from Lenin with which he ended his *Discovery of India*.

'Man's dearest possession is life and since it is given to him once, he must so live as not to be seared with the shame of a cowardly and trivial past, so live as not to be tortured for years without purpose, so live that dying he can say: all my life and my strength was given to the first cause in the world, the liberation of mankind."

768. Raghavan, A. Emergence of new right demolishes Nehru's vision—Whither India? *Blitz*, 15 August 1987; 21.

Let us get back to the mind of Mr. Nehru. "The pace of the Congress could be slowed down or accelerated but I don't think that it would be possible to take a whole people backwards."

What is the assurance? "The best insurance against any throw-back is the hope level of our people. It might be possible to frustrate this by making the people lose hope and faith. . . it is difficult to say whether our people or any people are strong or mature enough to resist fascist or communal trends and pressures."

Here, one discerns clearly that Nehru had self-doubt.

He was hoping that once the "Second and Third plans go into action, we shall be breaking through the static barrier of inertia, poverty and under-development and taking off, that is, our economy will work on its own steam power. With this development backed by the will of the people, the effectiveness of which is secured through parliamentary democracy, it should not be difficult to maintain the continuity".

As for the Congress, "there might have been setbacks. The progress might have been slowed down here and there, now and then, but on the whole it is the basic socialistic current that has carried the party forward."

Here is plenty for Congressmen to mull over when they celebrate the fortieth year of Independence. The socialistic trend, emphasised over and over again by Nehru, has imperceptibly been changing since the Emergency and perceptibly in the eighties.

The unstated aim of building a happy and prosperous India for 100 million people out of its 800 million has thrown up a new class. You can see them everywhere: in Parliament, in state legislatures, in five-star hotels, on aeroplanes, in the media and now in automobiles fitted with radio telephones.

This class is neo-Swatantra, which is an anti-thesis to everything that the Congress stood for, Nehru stood for, Praful Kidwai of the Times of India calls it the "New Right". This class is making mincemeat of Nehru's vision of an independent economy draped in a vibrant parliamentary democracy.

769. Ramachandran, C.P. Legacy of Nehru. *Hindustan Times*, 27 May 1980; 9.

There were two Jawaharlal Nehrus. One was the romantic, the idealist who saw a harmony in the universe, who found meaning in continuity and tradition—above all, one who believed in the essential goodness of man. This was the Nehru who loved poetry and flowers, thrilled to see the woods and took delight in art and music. There was another Nehru, That was the man who wanted to hang black-marketeers on the nearest lamp-post, burn city slums to ashes, shatter the feudal and religious shackles that held the people in ignorance and superstition. This was the Nehru who railed at the waste of money over marriages and funerals, who flew into a rage at the pomp and ostentatiousness of the wealthy. These two Nehrus were at war till the very end.

770. Ramachandran, T.R. Remembering Nehru. *Daily*, 26 May 1986; 9.

Nehru was a gentleman-statesman of a category entirely different from the one that includes today's politicians. He was the author of the policy of non-alignment and dynamic neutrality. This is still the sheet-anchor of our foreign policy. He was the champion of parliamentary democracy and untiringly worked for communal harmony, secularism and the rights of the individual. Undoubtedly, he laid the foundation for the modern India.

771. Rao, V.K.R.V. *Nehru Legacy*, Bombay, 1971.

772. Relevance of Nehru. *National Herald*, 27 May 1987; 5.

773. Remembering Nehru. *Nagpur Times*, 15 November 1983; 4.

774. Remembering an extraordinary man. *Tribune* (Chandigarh), 24 May 1987; 4.

Jawaharlal Nehru, whose death anniversary falls on May 27, was, to the people of India, not "the lotus-eater of Kashmir" as described by D.F. Karaka but "an extraordinary man" of Sydney Smith's conception. "The meaning of an extraordinary man", said Smith, "is that he is eight men in one man, that he has as much wit as if he had no wit, that his conduct is as judicious as if he were the dullest of human beings and his imagination as brilliant as if he were irretrievably ruined."

775. Remembering Nehru. *National Herald*, 27 May 1987; 6.

Communalists have to be put down with all our might, but it is not only a law and order problem. People's hearts and minds have to be cleansed before the evil of communalism can be buried once and for all. For this the citizens of this great country must take a pledge to beat back the forces of communalism from wherever they spring. That will be the finest tribute to Jawaharlal Nehru and what can be a better occasion for the pledge to be taken than the death anniversary of the man who was always prepared to shed the last drop of his blood in defence of secularism.

776. Remembering Nehru. *Patriot*, 14 November 1976; 4.

777. Russell, Bertrand. Legacy of Nehru. *Illustrated Weekly of India*, 27 May 1984; 44-45.

Nehru was a man of rare dedication who devoted himself to his country from the time of his earliest years. It is not often appreciated that through the long greater part of his life, he had to live under the shadow of potential imprisonment or brutality. Westerners are not sufficiently aware that Nehru spent 14 years in prison because of his passionate belief in the emancipation of his country from the indignity of foreign subjection and of poverty, ignorance and disease. Fourteen years is an inconceivable time to be separated from one's own lands to secure release by abandoning the milder manner. During the years that I was President of the India League in London, I knew of the invaluable leadership and direction which Jawaharlal Nehru gave to India.

778. Sneider, Daniel. Nehru and his legacy. *New Wave*, 27 November 1977; 4.

Jawaharlal Nehru is alive today. He is alive in his writings, in his ideas and commitments and alive in the concrete legacy he has left behind in modern India today. But if we are to remember Nehru, as I do, then we must revive his most passionate commitment, his belief in the power of man's creative abilities, in science and technology and their role in the transformation of India and the world.

779. Survival of Nehru. *National Herald*, 27 May 1974; 5.

It is amazing how for ten years since his death Jawaharlal Nehru has survived much detraction and denigration and remains as relevant as ever. The detractors and denigrators are comparatively unknown and it remains to be seen how long they will survive, apart from their relevance or irrelevance. The latest, according to reports, is Dr. Sen, Director of the Institute of Historical Studies, Calcutta, which is publishing a Dictionary of National Biography, about which much is not known. If the auspices have something to do with the director and the results of research, they must be known so that the historicity of the material used in history-writing can be assented. Dr. Sen has chosen a strange way of denigrating Nehru. He holds a press conference and circulates an "editorial addendum". Mr. Jain should protest against this insult to himself added to the injury done to Nehru.

780. Two decades after Nehru. *Sunday Statesman*, 27 May 1984; 6.

781. Two decades of void. *Sunday Tribune* (Chandigarh), 27 May 1984; 4.

Today the nation will mourn (as indeed it has been doing this day for two decades) the death of Jawaharlal Nehru. Everybody who is somebody will mouth pontifical platitudes, exhorting the people to follow the path shown by India's first Prime Minister. If few turn up to hear them and fewer still register what is said, it is because of the widespread feeling that his professed followers are not worthy of much respect. But, to salve our collective conscience for having betrayed his ideals, we will today describe him as the "architect of modern India" and stop at that. That is just as well, for otherwise we would have to admit that each one of us is busy taking down the edifice brick by brick. Almost every ideal cherished by India's first Prime Minister is being systematically repudiated in action both by the leaders and the people of our country.

782. Under Nehru's mantle: The past and the future. *Daily*, 4 November 1984; 15-16.

This holds good in relation to the economy and its intertwining with science and rapidly advancing technology, the state in which she inherited them and as she left them for the present and future generations. It also holds true of other realms—defence and securing the nation's territorial integrity. Pursuit of a domestic political conception based on the Nehruite vision of Indian unity amidst linguistic diversity, and above all, the further elaboration of the Nehru's foreign policy of non-alignment in a manner as to make it the shield for India's economic prosperity and security.

In so far as the nation's economic physiognomy is concerned, the strident changes of Indira period encompassed the rise of India's nuclear capability and the soaring of its genius as a power in outer space and in the frozen land of Antarctica. Allied to this is the rapid advance in industry and agriculture registered in this country under the aegis of Indira Gandhi.

783. Venkataraman, R. Nehru's legacy and human emancipation, *Mainstream*, Nehru Birthday Number 1984; 7-8.

784. Vepa. Jawaharlal Nehru 20 years after. *Newstime*, 27 May 1984; 7.

Few of the present generation can realize the fascination Jawaharlal held for us. It was more than his magnetic personality.

There was something in the man—sensitive, understanding, human that attracted youth.

He was a complex and sensitive person. As Cameron, the perceptive news correspondent, wrote in 1959, "Nehru is too many men within himself: an Indian who became a European, an individualist who must identify himself with the world's most enormous proletariat, a Brahmin who became a socialist, an intellectual nationalist leading a land of monstrous mediaevalism."

785. Why Nehru continues to be relevant. *Free Press Journal*, 10 November 1979; 6.

786. Why Nehru is relevant. *Patriot*, 14 November 1986; 4.

Literature

787. Chakraborty, A.K. *Jawaharlal Nehru's writings : A literary supplement*, Calcutta, 1981.

788. Chhibber, V.H. *Jawaharlal Nehru—A man of letters.* New Delhi, Vikas, 1970.

789. Gopal, ed. *Jawaharlal Nehru: An anthology*. Delhi, 1980, 662 pp.

Jawaharlal Nehru was one of the most articulate of modern statesmen. He wrote a great deal and spoke very much more. All figures in public life have, of course, by necessity, to convey their ideas in order to persuade those whom they aspire to lead, and in this respect Nehru was not unique. The speeches and writings of Lenin, Gandhi, Mao and Churchill all run into many volumes. But what makes Nehru different from the rest was the variety of his interests and his love of words. He was, to use his own phrase, a 'dabbler in many things'. Committed to politics, which expanded from an intense commitment to the freedom and modernization of his own country to an acceptance of the imperative of world peace, Nehru was never just a professional politician. It was not only during the long years in prison that he found time to take an interest in nature and wild life, drama and poetry, history, science and almost everything else. Even as Prime Minister, while providing the initiative in every sphere of policy, nothing outside the official range was too trivial to escape his attention. Be it the crisis of war or the menace of nuclear weapons, the treatment of monkeys in aircraft or the establishment of an orchidarium in a remote part of India—whatever the subject, Nehru treated it with equal zest and with the same amount of concern.

790. Gopal, S. (*ed.*). *Selected Works of Jawaharlal Nehru*, 4 vols. New Delhi, 1987. Book Review by Shyam Ratna Gupta. *Hindustan Times*, 24 May 1987.

But for the two great Indian leaders, Jawaharlal Nehru and Vallabhbhai Patel, who with a unique singleness of purpose, grappled with the complex, inter-related issues of that time we might have well-nigh nullified our freedom. Though they often differed, both threatening to resign on matters of principle, they worked together to bring sanity and good sense to those on the verge of *revanchist dementia.*

791. Goyal, S.R. Nehru's view of history: *SON*; 310-21.

792. Kabir, Humayun. Nehru as a man of letters. *FON*; 5-14.

793. Kabir, Humayun. Nehru the writer. *NAG*; 53-57.

794. Moraes, Frank. Jawaharlal the artist. *FON*; 74-79.

795. Nehru, Jawaharlal. *Selected Works of Jawaharlal Nehru*, 5 vols. New Delhi, Nehru Memorial Fund, 1987. Book review by K. Natwar Singh. *Times of India*, 5 April 1987.

What is voluminous is not generally luminous. But Jawaharlal Nehru could make even a routine and official note both lively and arresting. No cliches, no officialese, no bureaucratese. Nehru was a prolific writer; his range was wide; he had a great fluency with his pen. He could also dictate a six-page letter on a complex and important subject to a head of state without much effort while paying due respect to grammar and syntax.

796. Nehru, Jawaharlal. *Jawaharlal Nehru's Speeches*, 4 vols, 1946-63, New Delhi, 1965.

797. Nehru Studies. *National Herald*, 27 August 1972; 5.

There could be no end to study of Jawaharlal Nehru, who remains as relevant as ever, though the new forum need not have used his name at this stage. The Nehru Memorial Trust, the Jawaharlal Nehru University and other bodies are broad-based and have the support of disinterestedness and scholarship. The Congress is carrying forward Nehru's policies and there could be no better trustee of the Nehru tradition than Indira Gandhi. Not many of the leaders of the new forum have been known to be close followers of Nehru.

798. On re-reading Nehru. *Socialist India*, 11 November 1972; 11-31.

799. Patil, V.T. (ed.). *Studies on Nehru*, New Delhi, Sterling, 1987; 412 pp. Book Review by M.V. Kamath in *Pioneer*, 26 July 1987.

It may be considered somewhat unfair to judge a book on not what it contains, but for what it does not. And yet a book on Nehru which claims to study him, cannot possibly be considered complete if it studiously ignores certain aspects of his life which many of his biographers refuse to touch upon as, for example, his relations with women.

800. Sen, N.B. (ed). *Glorious thoughts of Nehru.* New Delhi, 1964.

801. Tewari, S.M. Nehru's philosophy of literature. *Akashvani*, 16-31 May 1984; 2-4.

Much has been written, and more will be written, indeed much more can be written on Nehru who was a multi-splendoured personality: a man of many moods and memories, contrasts and even contrary qualities. He has been deservedly depicted and dealt with as a freedom-fighter, political leader, politician, statesman, democrat, angry aristocrat, writer, thinker, philosopher, artist in public life, revolutionary, liberator of humanity, king with the common touch, historian, maker of history, nation-builder, architect of modern India, man of peace, originator of the Non-aligned Movement, enunciator of the Panchsheel or the Five Principles of Political Conduct, sceptic, socialist, secularist, humanist, nationalist, internationalist etc.

802. Velupillai, C. V. Nehru. *Socialist India*, 19 June 1971.

The wisdom—
The many petalled suns,
The ages built

On Himalaya's face
Its love-seeds strewn
In fields and forest groves
Matured the waters
That Ganga is . . .

All these gathered
In a solitary rose
He carried
On his breast . . .

His breath drilled
Into flame,
Led us discover
The glory smouldering
Within our hearts ashes.

Management

803. Ali, Arshi Salim. Nehru's style of functioning. *Northern India Patrika* (Allahabad), 10 June 1987; 6.

Had Mr. Nehru been alive today the smile on his face would surely have changed into a pensive and grim expression.

Punjab would never have been the hot bed that it is today, He would have convinced the rebellious Punjabis that they were as important to India as any other people. His fatherly affection together with the sterness would have convinced them that they were being misguided.

Assam would never have felt neglected and the great Jawaharlal would have taught them that none is a foreigner and that anyone living in any part of India is an Indian.

804. Nehru, Jawaharlal. Government and the people. *New Wave*, 29 March 1987; 2.

Democracy is a means to an end. What is the end we aim at? I do not know if everybody will agree with me, but I would say the end is the good life for the individual. What form it should take can be argued about, but the good life certainly must imply a certain satisfaction of the essential economic needs, which will release him from continuous oppression, and which will give him a chance to develop his creative faculties,

Marxism

805. Karanjia, R.K. Marxism in the modern world. In *Mind of Mr. Nehru*, London, 1960; 26-36.

806. Sen, Mohit. Nehru and Marxism : A Rejoinder. *Mainstream*, 24 June 1967; 29-31.

At best, Nehru could have developed into what Marxists now-a-days call, a revolutionary democrat. But there were objective factors militating against this: the greater strength of the capitalist class in India as compared to other colonial and semi-colonial countries and a stronger, even if immature, working class than, say, Egypt or Algeria possessed. The petty-bourgeois intellectual in India, even if he has more scope of independent action than in developed capitalist countries, has lesser possibilities of maintaining an independent identity than in any other newly-independent states. The compulsions of choice are far stronger and, in many ways, more cruel. Nehru, in the end, chose the national bourgeoisie and sought to act as a link between it and the masses, particularly the middle strata in town and village. He accomplished much for the nation but, in a very profound sense, betrayed himself.

Mass Media

807. Bhargav, M.L. Pandit Nehru and the press *Link*, 24 May 1987; 9-11.

If Pandit Motilal Nehru had his way, his son Jawaharlal would have, after taking his degree at the Cambridge, appeared in the Civil Service like most of the talented youngmen. But it is difficult to say if he would have fitted in there or followed the footsteps of Surendra Nath Banerjee or Aurobindo Ghose. But talented as Pandit Nehru was, even the Bar did not attract much of his attention, and a few years after his arrival in India, the Press Act and the Press enchanted him most.

808. Bhatia, Prem. Nehru as a reporter knew him. *Mid-Day* (New Delhi), 14 November 1986; 7.

On the whole, however, Nehru knew that a free press (by which he swore) was an unavoidable nuisance in a liberal democracy. The frequency and regularity of his full-scale press conferences was evidence enough of that attitude. He always came prepared with the answers to likely questions and seemed to like the cut and thrust of argument even though some of us irritated at times.

809. Chalapathi Rau, M. Nehru and the press. *Nehru Legacy*, New Delhi, 1966; 72-81.

Jawaharlal not only tolerated criticism but appreciated it, if the level was high; what upset him were malice, lack of dignity, or ignorance of history. But he upheld the principle of a free press even when he did not respect sections of the press for not being equal to the high standards he expected of them.

Jawaharlal addressed editors' gatherings several times and spoke with greater understanding of the problems of the press than they did. They talked of growth, but growth in what direction? What about the social responsibilities of the press.

810. Chaturvedi, J.P. Nehru from the press gallery. *NP*; 10-14.

811. Joshi, P.C. Communication challenge in India: Some reflections. *Mainstream*, 26 March 1988; 5-10.

812. Mehra, Anil. Nehru and the press. *National Herald*, 25 May 1984; 5.

To every professional journalist his sources of information are scared, but we believe that they are also responsible citizens who know their duties. Here it would be apt to quote Nehru on the aim and purpose of a news-paper. Writing about the starting of National Herald in September 1938, he said our aims should be "not to suppress or distort news in the mistaken belief that it might injure our cause. We cannot serve our cause by untruth, we cannot serve the public by withholding news and thus preventing it from forming right judgement, we cannot advance democracy by methods dear to the fascists, we cannot be true to the spirit and ideals of journalism itself by suppression or distortion of news". If we stick to these objectives and ideals there should be no need for us to disclose the sources of our information.

813. Nehru, Jawaharlal. Tasks for the press. *New Wave*, 5 April 1987; 2.

We criticize and condemn communalism because it is the very opposite of the conception of broad tolerance and of India's emotional unity. Another phase of communalism is casteism. I do not think we have given sufficiently intensive thought to the removal of this scourge and curse of casteism. We have taken it for granted and sometimes I fear we have even encouraged caste for fear of losing the votes of one caste or another. So far as I am concerned I am prepared to lose every election in India but to give no qurater to communalism or casteism.

814. Nehru, Jawaharlal. Functions of newspapers. *New Wave*, 19 July 1987; 2.

What does a democratic government want from a newspaper? I think normally a government likes or should like criticism from a newspaper. It does not matter how hard the criticism is, provided it is free from malice and ill-will. Criticism is a necessary thing. Criticism, to be worth-while, must have depth.

A government would like the newspapers to help, apart from discussing major issues, in bringing before the public the activities of the nation, like the five year plans and in maintaining an atmosphere favourable to the advance of the country and to the consideration of the big problems before it. It is really a test of newspaper how far it can think of big things or how far it is led away by petty things. It is as well a test of the people at large. We would naturally like the newspapers to help generally the good causes in the country and to discourage the evil and the wrong tendencies.

815. Newspapers. *QON*; 214-18.

816. Ranganathan, A. Jawaharlal Nehru as a Journalist *New Wave*, 13 November 1983; 2.

Matthai, John

817. Mathai, M.O. Dr. John Matthai, *MDN*; 248-250.

Military Affairs

818. Mathai, M.O. Nehru Clan and a Brigadier. *MDN*; 78-83.

When Nehru became the Prime Minister, relatives were all over "Jawahar Bhai" and "Indu". Nehru was too big a man to nurse petty grievances, but Indira could not shed her coldness and kept her distance. Members of the Nehru clan began to treat the Prime Minister's House, the official residence in New Delhi, as a convenient Rest House. Sometimes they came in numbers and quarrelled with the staff for cars to roam about. Each one thought that he or she should have a separate car. I had to tell the Prime Minister that these people were not entitled to government transport and, in any event, there were not many cars available. He asked me to tell the staff to let them know that they had to hire taxis. The Prime Minister, of course, paid for their food expenses personally which itself was a burden enough.

Minority Question

819. Communalism and the minority problem. *NFC*; 72-85.

820. Gittler, Joseph B. Understanding minority group. *UMG*; 126-37.

821. Khan, Abdul Majid. Minority problem. *Jawaharlal Nehru and his ideas*. New Delhi, 1951; 59-61.

822. Sait, Azeez. We won't pay for Nehru's blunders. *Current* (Bombay), 23 July 1983; 14.

Museum

823. Jagmohan. Teen Murti: Past, present, future. *Blitz*, 26 May 1984; 16-17.

Teen Murti House also was the home where he recieved Kings and Queens, Prime Ministers and Foreign Ministers, philosophers and writers. It was at Teen Murti that he evolved the philosophy of Non-alignment to stem the onrush of the power politics of the super-powers. And it was at Teen Murti that he drafted his celebrated speeches in favour of peace and co-existence and against neo-imperialism, and fascism. In other way too, these two homes were different. Nehru was a lonelier man at Teen Murti House than in Allahabad. His father and mother, his wife, Kamala, his mentor Gandhiji and several comrades in the national struggle were all gone. He was almost like an orphan. And he had many problems to solve—communal riots, influx of refugees, integration of the princely States—but he carried the burden on his slender shoulders.

824. Maxism, V.S. Nehru memorial. *Indian and Foiregn Review*, 15 November 1986; 14-15, 23.

Behind the Teen Murti House in New Delhi where Jawaharlal Nehru lived as Prime Minister from 1948 until his death in 1964, on a polished stone under the spreading foliage of an ancient tree is inscribed an excerpt from his "Will and Testament": "If any people chose to think of me, then I should like them to say 'this was a man who with all his mind and heart loved India and the Indian people and they in turn were indulgent to him and gave him of their love most abundantly and extravagantly'."

825. Mathai, M.O. Meaning of humiliation and insult. *MDN*; 176-78.

Morarji was able to live in a large house in New Delhi after he ceased to be a minister because of a new rule introduced on the directive of Prime Minister Nehru issued at my instance. That rule conferred on MPs who have been cabinet ministers, governors, and heads of Indian diplomatic missions abroad, as well as leaders of opposition groups in both Houses of Parliament entitlement to independent bungalows.

826. Murali, G. In memory of Nehru. *Patriot Magazine*, 26 May 1974.

827. Narender Kumar. Historial house. *National Herald*, 14 November 1980; 13.

828. Pande, N.D. Nehru Memorial Fund: Library and Multi-purpose Centre. *Socialist India*, November 1975; 6-8.

Soon after Jawaharlal Nehru died in May, 1964, the Government of India decided to convert the Teen Murti House, where he had lived for nearly sixteen years, into a museum and library dedicated to his memory.

Jawaharlal Memorial Museum, which was inaugurated by the then President, S. Radhakrishnan on November 14, 1964,is today the most popular museum in the capital. People from all over India visit the museum to see the place where stayed their beloved leader. The living rooms at the Teen Murti House are preserved as they were on May 27, 1964 when Jawaharlal Nehru died. Foreign tourists also visit the museum in large numbers to pay their homage to the great humanitarian and world statesman that Nehru was.

829. Year of good work. *Mainstream*, 24 June 1967; 32-33.

Muslim League

830. Khan, Abdul Majid. Muslim League and Independence. *Jawaharlal Nehru and his ideas*. New Delhi, 1951; 57-59.

Muslims

831. Puntambekar, S.V. Future of Muslims in India. *NAG*; 413-15.

Naidu, Sarojini

832. Das, J.L. Jawaharlal Nehru and Sarojini Naidu. *Contemporary* (New Delhi), August 1979; 18-19.

833. Nehru, Jawaharlal. Sarojini Naidu. In *India's Spokesman*. Ed. by C.D. Narasimah. Madras, 1960; 278-84.

Narayan, J.P.

834. Nehru, Jawaharlal. *Jayaprakash Talks*. Bombay, *PSP*, 1953.

National Integration

835. Ahmed, S.I. Hindu-Muslim Unity: Maulana Azad Nehru Still Hold Good. *Indian Nation*, 19 February 1987; 4.

Most of us are narrow-minded and not very wise. Can we presume to imagine that we know the whole truth and to force this down the throat of our neighbour ? It may be we are right. It may be that our neighbour is also right. If you see a flower on a tree, you do not call it the tree. If another person sees the leaf only and yet another the trunk, each has seen part of the tree only. How foolish it would be for each one of them to say that the tree was the flower only or the leaf or the trunk and to fight over this. (*Glimpses of World History* : Jawaharlal Nehru).

836. Attar Chand. Will his dream come true? *Daily*, 8 August 1987.

837. Gandhi, Kishore. Nehru: Years of integrity. *Pioneer*, 14 November 1987.

838. Katju, K.N. Symbol of our unity. *NAG*; 128-29.

839. Nehru, Jawaharlal. *Unity of India*. London, 1948.

840. Nehru, Jawaharlal. *One nation, one heart*. New Delhi, 1963.

841. Nehru, Jawaharlal. Emotional Integration. *New Wave*, 22 February 1987; 2

Always when I come to South India, the question arises in what language I should speak. I am afraid I do not know your language, Kannada. Otherwise, I would most certainly speak it here, because my object is to be understood, not to propagate any particular language in which I can make you understand best of all.

Unfortunately, I can speak with some fluency only in two languages, Hindi and English. Normally, of course, I speak in Hindi. I have no idea how many of you here understand Hindi and how many of you understand English. So I am in a quandary. Perhaps, it might be best for me to be bilingual on this occasion, and speak a little in English and a little in Hindi. Anyhow, I should like your help in this matter. Will those of you, who understand English, please raise your hands?

842. Saiyidain, K.G. Nehru and Integration. *Mainstream*, 29 May 1971; 19-20, 39.

When India was confronted with the task of defining her political future and hammering out a new Constitution, it deliberately decided, after prolonged discussion, to establish a secular, democratic, socialistic State. It was obviously open to us theoretically to adopt a Constitution based on the religion of the majority community. But we wisely decided not to do so. In a multi-religious society, which aims at assuring to every citizen equality of rights and opportunities, freedom in the matter of faith and worship and full participation in national life, there is, in reality, no other reasonable alternative. In any other kind of set-up there is the danger that every one may not enjoy full and responsible citizenship but there may be, in effect, many second or third class citizens on the basis of their religious affiliations or other differences. Even in a democracy, based on secularism, this danger cannot always be eliminated. All citizens may, *de jure*, be equal but not so in fact. In a Constitution, designed on a non-secular basis, the risk is much greater.

843. Sangam Lal. Nehru's perception of national unity. *Hindustan Times*, 15 November 1985; 17.

Nehru rightly believed that the British rule in India was greatly responsible for giving rise to fissiparous tendencies in India. According to him the process of synthesis, an old feature of the Indian society, was stopped by the British to serve their own interests. The feudal elements were encouraged by them which resulted in the coming into existence of a large number of princely states in India which were "astonishing anachronisms" in the age of revolutionary change.

844. Unity of India. In *NFC*; 86-95.

Nationalism

845. Birendra Prasad. *Indian Nationalism and Asia, 1900-1947*. Delhi, B.R. Publishing Corporation, 1979; 206-9.

Though the Asian Relations Conference was convened from March 23 to April 2, 1947 the idea of convening such a Conference had been in the air immediately after the termination of the Second World War. Nehru played a dominant role in convening this Conference but even he admitted that it so happened that "we in India convened this Conference but the idea of such a conference arose simultaneously in many minds and in many countries of Asia". The authentic report of the Conference made it clear that it was difficult to trace from the available records who first gave public expression to the general desire among Asian peoples to meet and confer together.

846. Gandhi, Mahatma. *Jawaharlal Nehru*, Allahabad, 1929, 159 pp.

Therefore you cannot ignore the political structure of the country, nor can you watch passively the national struggle that is going on around you. Nationalism to-day in India is fighting imperialism and although its outlook may be narrow and limited it is at least trying to overcome the greatest opponent of labour. Labour must therefore side with nationalism in this great fight but it must at the same time make perfectly clear what it stands for, and it should try to win the nationalist to adopt its own wider ideal.

What is this ideal that you should have? It will not profit you much if there is a change in your masters and your miseries continue. You will not rejoice if a handful of Indians become high officers of the state or draw biggest dividends, and your breaks down through incessant toil and starvation and the lamp of your soul goes out. You want a living wage and not a dying wage. You want to prevent the exploitation of man and to ensure equal opportunities and fair conditions of living for all. It is certain that this cannot be done under the existing system.

Today modern industry is a battlefield and woe to those who are conquered. In the battle of capitalists whoever may win, the worker always suffers. To this greatest of monsters—capitalist industry—is offered as an unceasing sacrifice the blood of the workers, but its appetite is insatiable. How can this monster be subdued and brought into the service of humanity? In the past, and even now largely, the employer was all-powerful. Then came the stage of labour organization and gradually we find in many countries two powerful groups—capital and labour—facing each other, and waiting for opportunities to do each other injury. This was an inevitable development but it is obviously no solution of the problem. That solution can only come by the removal of all causes which create poverty and inequality. It can only come when the sources of wealth are owned by the community and not by individuals.

Therefore our ideal must be of a socialistic order of society in which the interests of the workers are supreme; indeed, in which everyone is a worker and no one is a drone or a parasite.

Today you have an immediate problem facing you and you may want me to say something about it on this occasion. Some of you have already decided on your line of action. Others have not done so.

847. Ganesh Prasad. Nehru and Nationalism. *Mainstream*, 29 May 1971; 22-25.

The historic Independence Pledge shows how the awakened patriot of the thirties looked at Mother India. Under the British rule she was a victim of a "four-fold disaster". She was ruined "economically, politically, culturally and spiritually".

They sincerely believed that it was "a crime against man and God" to submit to such inhuman rule. They "solemnly" resolved to struggle in a non-violent way against foreign rule and for national independence. Nehru fully shared their feeling, conviction and determination. In fact, the Pledge clearly bore his literary touch. He along with them, dreamt of a free Mother India of Tagore's poetic dream. So inspiring were the poet's lines that he ended with them the last letter to Indira on the history of mankind.

848. Gayon, Naba K. Jawaharlal Nehru the national idea. *Patriot*, 9 November 1980.

849. Nehru, Jawaharlal. How deep is our nationalism. *New Wave*, 20 March 1982; 2.

850. Nehru, Jawaharlal. Nationalism and mass struggle in India. *Labour Monthly*, 20 August 1938.

851. Patil, V.T. Nationalism, freedom and socialism. *Nehru and the freedom movement*. New Delhi, Sterling, 1977; 44-111.

852. Venkatasubbaiah, P. Nehru's nationalism and internationalism. *Indian Nation*, 14 November 1986; 4.

Pandit Jawaharlal Nehru did lay firm foundations to the Independent India, and it was he who gave a new direction and dimension to rebuilding India on planned and scientific lines. A man of immense sacrifices and love for the country and the people, Nehruji correctly comprehended the needs of modern India and laid, with great vision, a base for national amity. He was a nationalist to the core with an international understanding.

Nazism

853. Fascism and Nazism. *QON*; 103-107.

Nehru, Kamala

854. Kalaan, Promila. Kamala and Nehru. *Patriot*, 27 May 1973.

855. Kalhan, Promila. *Kamala Nehru—An intimate biography*. New Delhi, Vikas, 1973, 145 pp.

856. Subramaniam, Meenakshi. Kamala Nehru—Gentle yet great. *National Herald*, 28 February 1985; 12.

857. Tandon, P.D. Kamala Nehru—A song of silent service. *Northern India Patrika*, 2 August 1987.

Nehru, Motilal

858. Nanda, B.R. *Motilal and Jawaharlal.* London, 1962.

859. Nehru, Jawaharlal. My Father. *Motilal Nehru*, Ed. L.R. Nair, Delhi, 1961; 19-29.

Nehru Awardees

860. Dr. Salk. *National Herald*, 10 January 1987; 6.

Scientists can become citizens of the world but science never considers and cannot consider the world as a whole. Any science proceeds by abstracting a part of the universe to be considered by and for itself. This fragmentation carries with it the secret of the scientific triumph. Dr. Salk's special field is molecular biology, the study of the molecular structure and function of human organism. He has been striving to discover how diseases start at the level of the individual cell, and that helped him to develop the vaccine against polio. He is hopeful of discovering a vaccine against cancer. At the Salk his team of scientists some of whom are Nobel Laureates conduct basic research not only in such areas as the nature of the cell but the mysteries of the human race and the process of ageing. In a way, man is discovering himself.

861. Humanist's Vision. *Indian Express*, 10 January 1977; 6.

There could not have been a happier choice for this year's Jawaharlal Nehru Award for International Understanding than Dr. Jonas Salk, inventor of the polio vaccine, which has been a boon to millions of children the world over. Although as a scientist Dr Salk has his high place among the outstanding scientists of our time, he must be honoured more as a great humanist who regards himself not as a member of one nation or community but as a member of the human family.

862. Nehru Award for Dr. Jonas Salk. *Statesman*, 15 August 1977.

863. Nehru Award for Tucci (Dr. Guiseppe). *National Herald*, 14 November 1976.

Dr. Gulseppe Tucci of Italy has been given the Jawaharlal Nehru Award for International Understanding for 1976 in recognition of his contribution towards promoting understanding of the philosophy and culture of Asia, and especially of India.

864. Nehru award presented (to Olof Palme). *Indian and Foreign Review*, 28 February 1987.

The 1985 Jawaharlal Nehru Award for International Understanding was conferred posthumously on the late Swedish Prime Minister, Mr Olof Palme, on January 27. Mrs. Lisbeth Palme received the award on behalf of her late husband from the President, Mr. Zail Singh, at a solemn function in Vigyan Bhawan, New Delhi.

865. Nehru Award for Nelson Mandela Presented. *Indian and Foreign Review*, 1 December 1980.

Mr. Nelson Mandela, the South African freedom fighter, who has been languishing in jail for the last 16 years, was conferred the 1979 Jawaharlal Nehru Award for international understanding in New Delhi on 14 November. Mr. Oliver Tambo, President of the African National Congress, received the award and a citation from the President, Mr. Sanjiva Reddy, on behalf of Mr. Mandela.

Speaking after presenting the award, President Reddy said that in honouring Mr. Mandela, "We are honouring a great tradition in the world started by Mahatma Gandhi in South Africa, the tradition of sacrificial struggle against oppression and injustice, the tradition to uphold human dignity, freedom, truth and justice". In conferring this Award, the President said "We pay our warmest tributes to Mr. Nelson Mandela for his dedication and unwavering commitment to the struggle for justice, human and political rights in South Africa. The conferment of the Award is also a reiteration of India's unflinching support to the African people in fight against apartheid and racialism. They should be honoured with an Award instituted in the name of a great emancipator of mankind who relentlessly strove for the freedom and dignity not only of his countrymen but for all the oppressed people of the world. Jawaharlal Nehru, in whose memory this Award has been instituted, was himself a valiant fighter for freedom and was irrevocably opposed to colonial domination, racial exploitation, hatred and fanaticism. Mr. Mandela is fighting for similar ideals".

In a brief speech the Prime Minister, Mrs. Indira Gandhi, said "Wherever people care for freedom and human dignity, Nelson Mandela's name is known and respected. But he himself is today being denied both freedom and dignity in his own home. He is confined to Robben Island, locked in a cell, facing the loneliness and frustration, missing his loved ones and above all impatient at not being able to get on with the fight outside. Yet wherever he is there too is the struggle".

Mrs. Gandhi said: "The white man's burden has too long been carried on the shoulders of the black and the brown. A struggle for freedom can be suppressed, its soldiers killed, imprisoned, humiliated, but the idea of freedom cannot be stamped out; some spark will persist to burst into flame somewhere some time to light the way and illumine hearts and ultimately lead to success. Neither colour nor caste nor sex makes one person superior or inferior. No matter what laws South Africa devises for itself, history cannot be denied nor will the onward march of the future be halted. Apartheid cannot survive."

Receiving the award on behalf of Mr. Mandela, Mr. Oliver Tambo said that it was an honour not only for Mandela but for the entire people of Africa. The unique significance of the 1979 Jawaharlal Nehru Award is that it has identified in Mr. Mandela "the indomitable spirit of a people, the supreme justice for their cause and their absolute determination to win final victory". Mr. Tambo declared that Mr. Mandela and the African National Congress would remain worthy of the great recognition for ever.

866. Nehru Award given to Olof Palme. *Tribune*, 28 January 1987; 16.

President, Giani Zail Singh (on January 27, 1987) conferred the Jawaharlal Nehru Award for international understanding for 1985 on the late Swedish Premier, Mr Olof Palme, describing him as a "messiah of peace" and "relentless crusader for disarmament".

The award, which carries an amount of Rs. 15 lakh in cash and a citation, was received by Mrs. Lisbeth Palme on behalf of her husband.

867. Nehru Award for Senghor, Kreisky, *Tribune*, 29 May 1984.

868. Radhakrishnan, Dr. Salk—Biologist who is a humanist. *Indian Express*, 10 January 1977; 6.

It is natural for people to acclaim Dr. Jonas Salk as the great inventor of the vaccine that has miraculously helped to curb the dread of polio. But the very concern for the welfare of mankind which made Dr. Salk give up a very successful medical practice for research on the anti-polio vaccine, is not so well-known facet of this eminent biologist.

869. Scientist as well as a philosopher. *Indian Express*, 9 January 1977.

Dr. Jonas Edward Salk, inventor of the polio vaccine, is as much a philosopher as a scientist and for him the two seem inseparable.

You have to understand the biological nature of man to be able to deal with his lethal as well as his constructive attitudes.

870. Nehru Literacy Award for Mrs. Durgabai Deshmukh. *National Herald*, 15 March 1973.

President, V.V. Giri, presented the Nehru Literacy Award for 1971 to Mrs. Durgabai Deshmukh. The presentation was made at the Gandhi Peace Foundation.

In his speech Mr. Giri said: "We should plan to wipe out illiteracy within a decade or so and we must draw up a concrete plan for this purpose."

Nehru Forum

871. Nehru Forum being revived. *Statesmen* (New Delhi), 25 July 1987; 1, 7.

Now, suddenly has emerged on the scene again the Congress Socialist Forum with the former actors of the stage, and this time Mr. V.N. Gadgil raising of the eye brows by the rank and file in the party, who are wondering whether the restarting of the Forum was at all necessary. The party rank and file think that the Congress (I) today is facing a threat from Mr. V.P. Singh. The Socialist Forum seem to have taken up cudgels of this fight against Mr. Singh. This is the role the Forum seems to have given to itself. The foundation-document of the Forum says: "It is not accidental that a thin upper crust of our society is lured by consumerist outlook of the decadent sections of the West has misused the Prime Minister's desire to speed up the pace of scientific and technological upgradation. This section of our society is also in the forerank of the battalion that is trying to demolish the Indian National Congress by turning the focus from genuine issues to non-issues like corruption which is a natural concomitant of an acquisitive society of self-promoters."

Non-Violence

872. Non-Violence. *QON*; 68-74.

Nuclear Power

873. Elias, K.R. Nehru and India. *Deccan Chronicle*, 20 December 1981; 4.

874. Jawaharlal Nehru's ideas as guide to action—Nuclear power. *Patriot*, May 1976; 4.

I have no doubt that the attention which we have paid to atomic energy has been right and very worth while. It is worth while from the point of view of the practical advantages which are beginning to come to us and which will come to us in greater measure. It is worth while from an even deeper point of view because a new age began with the bursting of the atom bomb at Hiroshima and with atomic power coming into use. Ever since then, the development of atomic energy has made considerable progress, both for destruction and for construction. Atomic power is a real symbol of the modern world which, Janus-like, faces two ways, the way of vast destruction and annihilation and the way of great speed in construction and progress.

So far as we are concerned, we are determined not to go in for making atomic bombs and the like. But we are equally determined not to be left behind in the advance in the use of this new power. It is true that in the ultimate analysis a country which has atomic power fully developed can use it for good or evil purposes. And no declaration which I can make today will necessarily bind people in future, but I do hope that we shall create an atmosphere in this country which will bind every Government in future not to use this power for evil purposes.

875. Mehta, G.L. Atomic pile of energy and vigour. *NAG*; 101-106.

Oil Politics

876. Mathai, M.O. How oily was oil? *MDN*; 100-117.

The Indian Oil Corporation Limited has grown in size with the current annual sales of about Rs. 3,000 crores but the profitability is low and the cumulative reserves and surplus are negligible as compared with public sector enterprises in other countries and with the oil prices having increased five-fold from 1972 to date. The private sector companies, both refining and marketing, have been nationalized and even today they continue to operate in the manner as before. There is no move to nationalize their distribution system and economize whereas, on the other hand, the refiners' process margin recently has been increased from Rs. 17 to Rs. 50 per ton.

Experts are concerned that the delay on part of the government to undertake a gas fractionation plant at the Uran terminal will result in enormous national loss. In June 1977 the ONGC had indicated to the World Bank that engineering consultants for the terminal at Uran had been selected whereas in reality no consultants had been appointed even as late as the end of October 1978.

The process I helped to initiate with Mr. Sahni early in 1956 to eliminate exploitation by foreign oil companies was, ironically enough, completed by the oil-producing Arabs, Iranians and others successfully exploiting the exploiters. This exploitation of the exploiters has also landed innocent countries including India in trouble. Like Eurocommunism and Euro-dollar, petro-dollar has become a fact of life. Perhaps in the future petro-communism will also emerge.

Pandit, Vijaylakshmi

877. Hutheesing, Krishna Nehru. Nehru and Makame Pandit. *Ladies Home Journal* (Philadelphia), 3 January 1955.

Panchayati Raj and Community Development

878. *Jawaharlal Nehru on Community Development, Panchayati Raj and Cooperation*, Delhi, 1965.

Pant, G.B.

879. Pant, G.B. Personification of our hopes. *NAG*; 155-56.

Parliament

880. Gangadeb, P. As the Leader of the Lok Sabha, *NP*; 191-93,

881. Mukherjee, Pranab. Nehru and the Rajya Sabha. *NP*; 194-200.

882. Mukerji, Hiren. Nehru and Parliament. *Nehru Legacy*. New Delhi, 1966; 25-34.

Planning, so dear to Nehru's heart, was a more serious business than being lyrical about the picture of an industrially transformed India travelling with dignified steps towards socialism. Jawaharlal knew it very well himself; no one could put it so beautifully as when he said that his generation of Indians had been sentenced to hard labour and that to take one's ease was sin. His goal was "to take the vision a notch higher every time". Between enunciation and implementation of policies, however, there would always be a wide divergence which he could not eliminate. Even so, new dimensions would flash before the mind's eye when he spoke in Parliament on the plans. "In the final analysis", he said in 1956, "any effort is an act of faith", and then—as with a flash, he would add: "I have faith in the capacity of our people".

883. Nanda, B.R. Nehru's role in shaping the Parliament. *NP*; 155-58.

884. Rajah, Gobind. Jawaharlal Nehru's speeches in the Constituent Assembly. *Socialist India*, 8 November 1975; 5-6, 45.

Jawaharlal Nehru was eloquent often times. . He described the proceedings as "the high adventure of giving shape in the printed and written word to the national dream and aspiration". He described the resolution as a "declaration", a "firm resolve", a "pledge" and as an "undertaking".

Again and again, he reminded the members that they should "always keep in the passions that lie in the hearts of the masses of the Indian people and try to fulfil them." His concern was for the "400 million that comprise India". He urged the members to "rise above the party and think of the nation". He wanted them to think of the "people, not of any party or group but the people as a whole".

885. Ranga, N.G. Democratic thinker and a charming parliamentarian. *NP*; 130-40.

886. Rohatgi, Sushila. Jawaharlal Nehru as a parliamentarian. *NP*; 204-9.

887. Shakdhar, S.L. Nehru and presiding officers. *NP*; 159-70.

888. Shrivastava, L.P.S. Nehru and the Constitution making. *NP*; 141-52.

889. Venkataraman, R. Nehru and representative bodies in India. *NP*; 21-25.

Partition

890. Kidwai, M.H. Nehru and Partition. *Times of India*, 31 December 1985; 8.

According to Maulana Azad, when he explained the whole situation (the Congress-League coalition talks) to Gandhiji, he agreed with him and said he would advise Jawaharlal, and did not press the matter as he should have done (*India Wins Freedom*, p. 145).

Patel, Vallabhbhai

891. Gandhi, Rajmohan. Nehru, Patel and Indira. *Nagpur Times*, 20 October 1983; 4.

892. Gandhi, Rajmohan. Rajaji, Gandhiji, Nehru and Patel. *Illustrated Weekly of India*, 22 July 1984; 32-35.

893. Narayan, Jayaprakash. Nehru, Patel and Socialism. *The States* (New Delhi), 15 August 1972; 63-66.

Nehru never shared the Congress Socialist platform and never lent his support to any important resolutions or amendments to resolutions that we moved in the Congress Working Committee or the All-India Congress Committee.

894. Patel, Vallabhbhai. On Nehru. *NAG*; xviii-xxix.

Patil, S.K.

895. Mathai, M.O. S.K. Patil. *MDN*; 219-221.

Nehru kept Patil at a distance. Rajaji, who was Home Minister after Sardar Patel, suggested to Nehru that Patil might be taken into the cabinet. Nehru was not enthusiastic. However, he worte to B.G. Kher, the Chief Minister, and to Morarji and Patil by not publishing the photostat of the letter. Nehru dropped the idea.

After Patil's strong support for the Government of India's decision to exclude Bombay City from Maharashtra under the states reorganisation scheme, Pandit Govind Ballabh Pant thought that it was no longer appropriate to keep Patil out of the government. Pant pleaded with Nehru. It was only then that Patil could enter the government.

Peace and Security

896. Haksar, P.N. National declaration on Nehru's vision of peace and security in nuclear age. *Secular Democracy*, November 1986; 3.

We observe with great satisfaction that more recently Nehru's vision has also found articulation in the seminal initiatives taken by Mikhail Gorbachev, General Secretary of the Communist Party of the Soviet Union, on the all-important questions of nuclear disarmament and peace in the Asia-Pacific regions. The crucial issue of peace and freedom from the threat of nuclear warfare has, in our times, acquired a new urgency with the ominous prospect of the militarisation of outer space. Similarly, since the centre of gravity of the world has shifted from Europe to the Asia-Pacific region over the past half a century, the question of a just peace in this region concerns not only those who reside there but the world as a whole.

The recent pronouncements by Mikhail Gorbachev regarding the issues under consideration, therefore, deserve to be seriously considered by governments and the people. These pronouncements combine realism with idealism in finely balanced proportions. They take into consideration the interests of all countries, big or small, which have a stake in the region. They take a dialectical instead of a mechanical view of the world system. And most important of all, for India and the Third World, they seek to provide the basis of a world community in which the creative capacities of all people—and only those of a privileged few—will find full scope for expression.

Today, we are not far from a new century which offers the prospects of hope and fulfilment for mankind. The wisdom of centuries and the new vistas of science and technology hold out the promise of a new era of moral and material creativity for common men and women throughout the world. We, therefore, appeal to governments and the people to reflect upon the means whereby we can establish durable peace and harness man's productive capacities for bringing into existence a just world.

897. Haksar, P.N. *Nehru's vision of Peace and Security in Nuclear Age*. New Delhi, *Patriot*, 1987; 296.

898. Jayaramu, P.S. Nehru's approach to Security. *India's national security and foreign policy.* New Delhi, 1987; 11-15.

899. Khan, Rasheeduddin. Nehru's vision of peace and security, *Mainstream*, Republic Day 1987; 35-39.

Nehru's thinking and understanding is imprinted on the many resolutions on international affairs adopted by the Indian National Congress on world affairs and on foreign policy matters.

900. Menon, K.P.S. Jawaharlal Nehru: Apostle of Peace. *Amrita Bazar Patrika*, 14 November 1978; 4.

Jawaharlal Nehru, Apostle of Peace. A high-sounding title? Perhaps, but wholly appropriate. If Nehru were alive, however, he might not have liked it. He disliked all honorifics. He did not even like to be called Pandit, though to millions of people who admired him he was Panditji—a term which was as dear to their hearts as Gandhiji itself.

901. Menon, P. Gopinath. Jawaharlal Nehru and collective security in Asia. *Soviet Review*, 25 May 1974; 41-43.

In his first address over the All India Radio, head of the interim government on September 7, 1946, Nehru declared that India would pursue the policy of non-alignment and would strive for the establishment of friendly relations with all countries, especially in Asia. He also stressed that India stood for the complete liberation of the colonies and dependencies and stated that she was totally opposed to the racialist doctrine, no matter where and in what form it might be applied.

Jawaharlal Nehru advocated that in our era relations between states should be guided by the policy of peaceful co-existence. This policy of peaceful co-existence was first enunciated by

V.I. Lenin in the very first years of the existence of the Soviet state. Jawaharlal Nehru, on whose initiative the first Asian Relations Conference was convened soon after he took over the charge of the interim government, was an ardent advocate of co-operation and peace in Asia.

902. Narain, Iqbal. India's quest for security and the philosophical postulate of the political system: An analysis in the context of Nehru's approach. *SON*; 61-77.

903. Nehru, Jawaharlal. Problems of peace. *New Wave*, 20 December 1987; 2.

904. Rifaquat Ali, S. Nehru : Man of Peace. *Mainstream*, 29 May 1971; 27, 38.

905. Singh, J.N. Apostle of Peace. *National Herald*, 14 November 1980; 15.

906. Thapar, Romesh. Fight for national independence and international peace. *Nehru and the Modern World*. New Delhi, UNESCO, 1967; 23-32.

907. War and peace. *NFC*; 29-44.

Philosopher

908. Abdullah, Sheikh Mohammad. Symbol of peace and progress. *NAG*; 61-63.

909. Acharekar, M.R. *Apostle of Peace*. Bombay, 1956.

910. *Indian Journal of Political Science* (Jaipur), July-September 1971; 261-73.

911. Moore, Arthur. Indian hamlet. *NAG*; 22-23.

912. Nambiar, K.K.G. Nehru as a philosopher. *Illustrated Weekly of India*, 12 November 1978; 20-21.

Jawaharlal Nehru was not a philosopher in the classic sense. There is hardly any evidence to suggest that he gave any formal treatment to aspects of philosophy like metaphysics, epistemology and so on. Further the major pre-occupation of philosophers has been to attempt to answer questions regarding life and existence and the problems of the universe. On this score, too, Nehru's record is not in any way remarkable. He was, of course, attracted towards the Advaita (non-dualism). But the concept of God did not attract him.

913. Rao, Binod. Nehru the Philosopher-Politician. *Free Press Journal*, 13 November 1979; 4.

How much one misses today this living philosophy that must "answer the problems of the day". None, including Nehru's daughter, would appear to have taken a leaf out of his books, although he wrote so many, and a huge variegated bunch of letters particularly to her.

Putting his teachings in reverse gear, the politicians have allowed their philosophies (or lack of them) to be polluted by the day's problems that resolve crazily around their personal ambitions and make them lose their sense of proportion. The way they needlessly (and so unabashedly) evoke the dead in order to justify the wrong doings of the living must disturb and upset his ashes where they lie integrated in India's soil.

For them, they could not care less. For us it is an ominous and fearful portent.

Poetic Tribute

914. Jagmohan. To Nehru, *Patriot*, 27 May 1983.

It is not for you, I weep;
It is not for you, I grieve;
Your tired limbs had one day to sleep;
Your aged efforts had one day to cease,
One day, we knew, cruel Gods would smile
And leave us alone in this ancient shrine,
Broken, shattered by the hands of Time,
The mortal remains
Of your matchless frame,
Are now mingled
In the dust and haze
Of our vast, unending fields,
And in the frowns and smiles
Of our eternal streams;
Still working
For your cherished dreams,

In numerous shapes and forms,
But in the struggling days ahead,
We may not forget your gentle touch,
Your love, your grace,
And your liberal faiths,
In the roaring, senseless strifes
Of our little, selfish tribes;
The fragrance of your flowers,
The flashing light from your towers,
May linger and then die;
While the countless children of your soil,
Who have days and nights to toil,
Lie buried
Beneath heaps of ignorance;
Silent, hungry, and diseased,
For them, these pities;
For them, these fears;
For them, I owe
My frozen tears.

Police Force

915. Khan, Abdul Majid. Police Force. *Jawaharlal Nehru and His Ideas*. New Delhi, 1951; 48.

Policies

916. Attar Chand. Lip Service. *Indian Post*, 3 August 1987.

917. Chopra, V.D. Increasing relevance of Nehru's policies. *Patriot*, 28 May 1979; 4.

Nehru watched the great events that gave shape to India, from the Indus Valley Civilization to the advent of Aryans and successive migrations and invasions of this country by a multitude of races and tribes with all their strength and weaknesses and merging their identity in this land of generosity and catholicism.

918. Dutt, C.P. Nehru policy only panacea. *Hindustan Times*, 27 May 1981.

Political Parties

919. Gandhi, Rajmohan. Charan Singh on Nehru. *Indian Express*, 15 November 1977; 6.

It is true that Nehru did not put agriculture and small-scale industry on an important enough pedestal. In retrospect this was probably a mistake. Was it, however, rooted in a personal or ideological bias in Nehru?

Or was it rather an honest error of judgement, of the sort that anyone confronted with the range of needs that pressed the government during Nehru's time might have made? Moreover, can it be said that the sums of money spent on defence, dams and steel mills were wholly or obviously a waste?

920. Mehta, Krishna. Nehru and the opposition. *NP*; 201-3.

921. Vajpayee, Atal Behari. Realisation of Nehru's dreams. *National Herald*, 14 November 1977.

Politics

922. Bhambahri, C.P. Nehru and the Indian political system. *SON*; 333-46.

923. Das, M.N. Political philosophy of Jawaharlal Nehru. *London*, 1961.

924. Jain, Girilal. Transvaluation of Nehru. *Times of India*, 14 November 1986; 6.

Nehru did precisely that of course, according to his own lights. His deep commitment to the cause of peace was, for instance, his (and a more practical) version of Gandhiji's non-violence. Similarly, he spared little effort to eliminate untouchability from the Indian social scene and to help uplift weaker sections of society, especially the scheduled castes and scheduled tribes, and to protect the Muslims whom the Hindus then tended to hold responsible for the country's partition.

925. Karuna Karan, K.P. Nehru: A meeting ground for different political forces. *Gandhi Marg* (New Delhi) (98), May 1987; 73-87.

926. Nehru, Jawaharlal. Civics and politics. *REW*; 135-36.

927. Rana, A.P. Nehru and international political modernization—A view from the seventies. *India Quarterly*, January-March 1979.

Population

928. Gujral, M.L. Population. *EFING*; 74-92.

Poverty

929. Nehru, Jawaharlal. Fight against poverty and unemployment. *India, independence and social revolution.* New Delhi, 1984; 68-85.

930. We forget Nehru at our peril. *National Herald*, 14 November 1976; 5.

President

931. Durga Das. President and Prime Minister. *India*, London, 1969; 334-39.

The Constitution has defined the powers of the President of the Republic as Head of State and in relation to the Prime Minister. But the written word is not enough to ensure harmony in thought and deed between the two. Mutual sympathy and understanding and a sense of comradeship are required. Between President Rajendra Prasad and Prime Minister Nehru, who had shared the sufferings and the glory of fighting for freedom under Gandhi, one sensed constant friction. Fortunately, this was not permitted to erupt into the open. The President, for his part, was not sure whether he could successfully make a public issue of their differences. As for Nehru, his concern for the proprieties of public conduct inclined him to a similar course.

932. Handa, R.L. Relations with Prime Minister. *Rajendra Prasad.* New Delhi, Sterling, 1978; 39-61.

Rajendra Prasad had gone, succeeded by Radhakrishnan whom Nehru so much liked. But somehow the relationship between the President and the Prime Minister was once again pushed into a state of flux, forced to strike a new agitation. Those days Nehru was known to have been nostalgic. Rajendra Prasad with whom he often differed, Nehru recollected, was so mild as to be always responsive and accommodating. Now he was up against a bit of assertiveness. In the face of it the Prime Minister felt helpless on more than one occasion. Whatever the constitutional provisions and howsoever they might have been interpreted by experts in the past, Radhakrishnan knew well what he should do and none could stop him from doing it. His broadcast talk to the nation on the morrow of the Indian debacle was one instance.

933. Nehru, Jawaharlal. Position of the Union President. *New Wave*, 19 July 1987; 2.

The President has always acted as a constitutional head. The President functions in many places, and if there is anything in the nature of a formal occasion, the Government is responsible for it. Others naturally depend on his own judgement. So far as this particular speech was concerned, we did not know anything about it till it was delivered.

Prime Minister

934. Durga Das. Nehru, man and prime minister. *India*, London, 1969; 376-85.

We live too close to the epoch straddled by Nehru's charismatic personality to assess him as a man or as the undisputed leader of the world's largest democracy. People still speak of him with a feeling not far short of idolatry; many still utter his name like a mantra. But few saw beyond the trappings of greatness and power to his frailties.

Radhakrishnan, who laid down the office of President in 1967, was closely associated with Nehru for seventeen years or more. His last homage to Nehru was a panegyric. Yet, to those very near him, Radhakrishnan once confided that Jawaharlal was a "poor judge of men" and often extended his confidence and protection to unworthy persons. He had in mind Pratap Singh Kairon and Dharma Teja. Kairon was the "strong man" and Chief Minister of Punjab who had to quit when a Commission of Inquiry pronounced him guilty of some of the numerous charges of corruption and maladministration levelled against him. Dr. Teja caught Nehru's fancy as a "dynamic figure" and was able to wheedle out of the Government a loan of Rs. 200 million to finance a shipping company he floated. It was not long before the company was in difficulties and Teja and his wife fled from the country to avoid arrest.

935. Gour, H.S. Politician and Prime Minister. *NAG*; 43-44.

936. Karanjia, R.K. Prime Minister of tomorrow. *Blitz*, 26 May 1984; 13-15, 19.

937. Martin, Gavin C. *India's first Prime Minister*. Bombay, 1969.

938. Rao, Arniya and B.R. *Six Thousand Days—Jawaharlal Nehru : Prime Minister*. New Delhi, 1987; 552 pp. Book Review by K.R. Ravindra in *Financial Express*, 9, 1987; 5.

Nehru's aversion to socialism was self-evident. During the first seven years of his office, he seemed to be skilfully skirting round socialism every time he went anywhere near it. Having rejected the report of the Economic Programme Committee of the Congress, he had moved the Industrial Policy Resolution which postponed nationalisation by ten years. Addressing Chambers of Commerce and Industry in 1949, he declared that he was not harboured of these 'isms'. He said, "my approach is, and I should like to say that the country's approach should be rather a pragmatic approach in considering the problem and I want to forget the 'ism' attached to it."

939. Sinha, Kamaleshwar. There lived such a man. *Tribune* (Sunday), 22 May 1988; IV.

940. Thakurdas, Purshotamdas. India's first citizen. *NAG*; 24-26.

941. Tyson, Geoffrey. *Nehru: the year of power*. London, 1966.

942. Wood, Glynn L. Nehru, authority, intimacy and vocation in a revolutionary. *SON*; 3-22.

Prison Life

943. Diwakar, R.R. Peep into Nehru's prison life. *Amrita Bazar Patrika*, 30 May 1982; 6.

A peep into Jawaharlal's prison-life is sure to reveal to us certain important aspects of his personality which are not normally known and published. He spent ten years in jail. His was a kind of hide and seek with prison life from 1920 to 1945, that is for about twenty-five years in the prime of his life.

As early as 1920-21, Jawaharlal and Motilal, son and father were converted to the Gandhian way of thinking and action so far as the fight for India's Independence was concerned. They began practising sleeping on a mattress in the floor as a preliminary discipline for going to jail. When both the Nehrus were hauled up for the first time before a court in Allahabad early in December 1921 for promoting non-violent non-cooperations against the British Government, they refused to recognise the British courts and offered no defence. They were sentenced to six months and some fine. Jawaharlal writes, "We were intensely occupied with our own struggle. We felt we were right and also effective; that was a great combination." This was but the first experience of jail-life for both and their reactions were elevating in spite of the many inconveniences and discomforts which necessarily go with jail-life.

944. Nehru, Jawaharlal. Prison-land. *REW*; 88-107.

945. Nehru, Jawaharlal. Window in Prison. *REW*; 80-87.

946. Randhir, G.S. When Nehru was in Nabha jail. *National Herald*, 30 December 1983; 6.

Giving his impression about the proceedings in Nabha court, Pt. Nehru writes as follows in his autobiography, "Right through our trial there has been a number of remarkable incidents which gave us some insight into the realities of Indian State administration or rather British administration of an Indian state. The whole procedure was farcical; because of this I suppose no newspaperman or outsider was allowed in court. The police did what they pleased, and often ignored the judge or magistrate and actually disobeyed his directions. The poor magistrate meekly put up with this, but we saw no reason why we should do so. On several occasions, I had to stand up and insist on the police behaving and obeying the magistrate."

947. Santhanam, K. Nabha episode. *National Herald*, 14 November 1980; 11.

When the Gaya Congress refused to accept the policy of council-entry and, as a result, the Swaraj Party was formed and there was a serious split among Congress leaders and workers, Jawaharlal Nehru was in jail. He was released a few months afterwards and, though, he supported the attitude of the no-changers, he was unhappy about the split which put him in opposition to his father and Chittaranjan Das. He wanted to find a *via media* and, in this, he was supported by Maulana Mohamad Ali. As a Congress resolution can be altered only by another session, a special session was held at Delhi in September 1923 where after much discussion, it was decided that the changers should not obstruct or oppose Swarajists in their council-entry programme and the latter should support the former in their constructive programme.

Public Administration

948. *Jawaharlal Nehru and public administration.* Delhi, IIPA, 1975, 120 pp.

949. Sahay, Vishnu. Nehru as first Prime Minister and his impact on public administration. In *Jawaharlal Nehru and public administration.* New Delhi, IIPA, 1975; 9-22.

Politically, the model was that of the British Parliamentary system. One might have expected that the great change from rule by a colonial power to rule by Indians themselves would bring in drastic, radical changes in the administrative system. At the very least, some sort of spoils system could reasonably have been expected. Was the revolutionary work after Freedom to be left to the bureaucratic legacy of colonial rule? Would new cadres not be needed? There would have been no lack of candidates with honourable records in the freedom struggle who could have provided material for these cadres and the leadership for building them up.

None of these changes came about. Even the Constitution in its administrative and political aspects was based on the Government of India Act of 1935. There was no radical change in the administrative set-up. Potential members of cadres turned to elections and to local politics.

How did this come about? I lay no claim to inside knowledge or special insight but will offer some explanations. On this, opinion will vary and there will undoubtedly be other valid explanations also. In my opinion, the continuation of the old structure was basically due to the circumstances of the transfer of power. It was a peaceful transfer under the legal cover of an Act of the British power. The whole atmosphere was one of legality. There were none of the violent impulses of a revolution in any sense of the term. In these conditions, the *status quo* had its own momentum, self-contradictory as the phrase may sound. But when you get into power with a ready-made machine at hand, and you are constitutionally disinclined to violent methods, you inevitably continue with the existing structure and habit strengthens it. The personality of the leaders had also a great deal to do with the acceptance of the existing machinery. Sardar Patel who was directly in charge of the Home Ministry, to which belonged the subject Administration in its narrower sense, was content with the structure of the machine. He is on record as saying that the machine was good enough. Only adequate masters were needed to utilise it properly. Panditji himself was no doctrinaire opponent of the system he inherited. If the truth must be told, there was a good deal of Harrow and Cambridge in him and in spite of his close association with popular movements and his exposure to socialism in action in Europe in the thirties, I believe that as far as methods as distinct from objectives were concerned, he was a liberal in the old sense of the term. If that were not so, when he took up reorganisation of the Secretariat in 1951 after the Sardar's death, when he was on his own in such matters, he would not have entrusted the matter to Shri Gapalaswami Iyengar. Shri Gopalaswami was a former civil servant and was no fiery innovator panting for radical reorientation. I forget the scheme he produced but from what I remember, it was largely concerned with a logical grouping of the subjects the Government had to deal with into appropriate departments and ministries and with setting up overlord ministers. The latter proposal was new and died a natural death. Who was to be an overlord and who was to be his subordinate? It was to be an innovation but not an earth-shaking one. A professor in an Institute of Public Administration could well have fathered it. The Secretariat and agency systems continued as before. The Rules of Business were respected almost *in toto*, the only change being in the substitution of Minister for Executive Councillor, and Prime Minister for the Governor-General. The states were advised to adopt similar rules. The Prime Minister was a radical but he did not wish to experiment with revolutionary and untried systems of administration.

Apart from the personalities of the leaders who mattered and the inherent strength of a working system in a non-revolutionary situation, I think the personality of the officials who directly worked under the Prime Minister had also something to do with the durability of the old machine. I remember a story current at the time. It is no doubt apocryphal. It is about Sir G.S. Bajpai, a senior official who had attained great distinction under the Raj and was alleged to have carried on anti-national propaganda in U.S.A. as Agent of the Government of India, In 1947, he came back to Delhi and was employed as Secretary-General in the Ministry of External Affairs which was in the P.M.'s direct charge. Stout party workers, so the story runs, questioned Panditji why he employed in a key position an official who had been a pillar of the British rule.

950. Shukla, V.C. Nehru's contributions towards the Improvements in administration. *Jawaharlal Nehru and public administration.* New Delhi, IIPA, 1975; 1-8.

In the period of transition, i.e., between the time he assumed office in the interim government till 15th August 1947 under his leadership the interim government had to face gigantic tasks like partition settlements, refugee problems, communal holocaust, border problems and transfer of paramountcy, powers, etc. It goes to the credit of Panditji and his colleagues that many of these apparently insurmountable and intricate problems were handled smoothly and with great tact, capacity and efficiency. It was no mean tribute to their genius that with little knowledge of the working and intricacies of administrative systems and procedures they performed their administrative functions in a superb manner belying the fears and apprehensions of many sceptics in India and abroad.

The outstanding problems faced by Panditji was the administrative framework and the services left over from the British regime. Because of his cherismatic personality and national stature he had no problem in winning over the loyalty of the administrative personnel and without breaking the structure and personnel of the administration, especially when he knew that the British had left an administration, genius helped by Sardar Patel and a band of devoted civil servants that these problems could be met headlong and surmounted reasonably successfully within the administrative framework inherited by the national government.

Circumstances might not have been propitious in undertaking radical changes in the administrative system and personnel, but this should not lead us to lose sight of the fact that Panditji was fully concerned with this problem and in his own way tried to introduce and influence administrative changes which he had visualised even before coming to power. The cornerstone of his views and ideas of administration was human approach to administrative problems. He wanted to bring administration as near to the common man as possible and was very much concerned with the administration at the grass-root levels. That is why he laid great emphasis on administration of Community Development Programme and Panchayati Raj. He wanted to strengthen these institutions and to endow them with real powers. He was of the view that the officials' role vis-a-vis these institutions should be confined to that of advisors. He thought that the Panchas and Sarpanchas should be given greatest latitude to the extent of committing mistakes because he thought that was the way they were going to learn and administer and take care of their immediate and day-to-day problems. A major reason for ineffectiveness of these institutions is the officials' mistrust of the elected functionaries to allow them to function independently of the tutelage of the officials. Panditji strongly felt that greater trust should be put in their ability to function and learn by committing mistakes. He rightly said, "The mistakes of panchayats will not endanger the security of the country."

In one of his Presidential speeches in this very Institute he laid great emphasis on the fact that a great part of the administration in this country at the lower levels was being carried on by these non-official elements. He remarked, "I should like this Institute to devote its attention to the study of the administrative problems lower down than the official scale, and more especially to the question of the non-servicemen coming into the picture and taking part in administration at the lower levels."

951. Sinha, P.N. Nehru's contribution to administration. *Searchlight* (Patna), 14 November 1982; II.

Jawaharlal Nehru had his university education in science. That gave him a certain measure of exactitude and precision. Unfortunately, during his time and later he had been a target of onslaught by rightists, leftists and centrists. He was, according to his detractors, supposed to have had baloney ideas.

Far from it, in Nehru we find a queer blend of thought and action of level of excellence covering the total vista of national and international polity and socio-economic milieu. This requires an in-depth study of Nehru's positive contribution to the art and science of public administration.

The interaction between the fundamental and empirical aspects of Nehru's concepts and concretization of his political and administrative ideology would be fascinating subject for students of political science and public administration.

It is true that Nehru had Sardar Patel, Dr. Rajendra Prasad, Maulana Azad and a host of other leaders of erudition and practical wisdom to assist him. Yet one shudders to think of the sheer magnitude of the problems which beset Nehru when he took over the reins of power in 1946, which was a coalition cabinet of the Indian National Congress and Muslim League. The latter's objective was to obstruct whatever useful measures the Congress took or to wreck the government from within.

After partition in 1947 the massive problem of uprooting the population and the influx of nearly 10 million refugees was a challenge to the ingenuity of the tallest administrators. Added to this was the depressed financial condition, lack of essential commodities, lack of housing facilities and communal riots culminating in the murder of Mahatma Gandhi.

Two hundred years of British musrule in India had taken the sap out of the body fabric of the country. Britishers gave India a parting kick. Nehru took up the challenge with unflinching devotion and courage. Once the storm settled, he addressed himself to the task of national reconstruction.

India had cast in its lot for democracy. The cornerstone of his ideas of administration was to inject a human approach to administrative problems. He wanted to bring administration to the door-step of the common man. That was the reason he gave a lot of importance to 'community development and panchayati raj'.

Quit India Movement

952. Patil, V.P. *Gandhi, Nehru and the Quit India Movement*. Delhi, 1984; 96 pp. Book Review by Gobinder Singh. *Tribune*, 24 August 1984.

There is abundance of political and academic consensus on the issue that the Quit India movement was the most patriotic exercise in Indian nationalism and that the parties like the C.P.I and the Muslim League, which did not support it, sabotaged a national cause.

Ironically, however, most of the nationalists do not know that even within the Indian National Congress, which launched this movement, there was no unanimity on its utility. So much so, even a staunch nationalist of the stature of Jawaharlal Nehru had many differences with Gandhi on this issue and had disapproved of any mass action during the war on many strategic grounds. It may appear blasphemous today but it is the dominating hypothesis which the author has tried to test in the work under review. He has attempted to explore the underlying logic of the dichotomous perceptions of Gandhi and Nehru of a concrete political situation prevailing in the early forties.

Rajagopalachari, C.

953. Rajagopalachari, C. On Nehru. *NAG*; xxvii-xxix.

Rajendra Prasad

954. Rajendra Prasad. On Nehru. *NAG*; xxx-xxxi.

Religion

955. Ayyub, Abu Sayeed. Jawaharlal Nehru on religion. *Quest* (Bombay), (43) October-December 1964.

956. Beg, M.H. Nehru vision of religious freedom. *Patriot*, 5 May 1987; 4.

It is true that Nehru was not obsessed with investigation of traditional religions or with expositions of hidden beauties in their texts. In fact, one could perhaps detect in his thinking a strain of agnosticism or of doubt about even the existence of God just as Gautam Buddha had this doubt.

Nehru does not seem concerned with changing concepts of the godhead or the supernatural as Bishop Robinson was in his books *Honest to God* and *Truth is Two-eyed*. He apparently accepted the essence of Gandhi who applied his own rules for interpreting the *Gita* as a quest of truth and non-violence.

Nehru's attachment to scientific methods of induction and deduction would, presumably, prevent him from accepting the inspiratorial method of acquisition of knowledge of truth described in Fritz Capra's Tao of Physics, experiencing the dance of Shiva lying on a beach, which seems an attractive work of fiction or mythology whose scientific value and reliability can be doubted.

957. Nehru, Jawaharlal. Politics and religion. *New Wave*, 21 June 1987; 2.

958. Nehru, Jawaharlal. Crisis of the spirit. *New Wave*, 1 February 1987; 2.

What is culture? I look it up in "the dictionary and I find a variety of definitions. One great writer has called it "the acquainting ourselves with the best that has been known and said in the world."

Another definition says that it is "the training, development or strengthening of the powers, mental or physical or the condition thus produced; improvement or refinement of mind, morals, or tastes, enlightenment of civilization."

Culture, in this sense, is something basic and international. Then there are the national aspects of culture and there can be no doubt that many nations have each developed a certain genius and individuality.

959. Religion. *QON*; 179-88.

960. Some Nehru values. *National Herald*, 14 November 1983; 4.

Roy, B.C.

961. Mathai, M.O. Dr. Bidhan Chandra Roy 1882-1962. *MDN*; 221-23.

Dr. Roy had been the Chief Minister of West Bengal from 1948 till his death during which period he was the undisputed leader of the state. The relationship between Nehru and Roy was marked by affection for each other. They called each other by their first names. In talking to Nehru, Dr. Roy never minced words. He was one of the very few who could do so.

Roy, M.N.

962. Mathai, M.O. M.N. Roy, 1893-1954. *MDN*; 223-24.

963. Nehru, Jawaharlal. M.N. Roy. *REW*; 110-12.

964. Roy, M.N. *Jawaharlal Nehru.* Delhi, Radical Democratic Party, 1945, 61 pp.

In a press interview, soon after his release from detention, Jawaharlal Nehru is reported to have said: "I do not like M.N. Roy's politics; but there are some good ideas in the People's Plan of Economic Development." That is a typical Nehru pronouncement—emphatic but thoughtless. It would not be unkind to characterize such sweeping summary judgments as dogmatic and nonsensical.

After he has spoken, it can be reasonably assumed that Nehru has read the People's Plan. Having read it, he should have noticed that the economic reconstruction of India outlined therein is postulated on the establishment of a democratic State. The politics very concretely formulated in contrast to the undefined ideal of national independence which Nehru has been chasing all his political life. Does he dislike that programme?

Rural Growth

965. Mishra, Jyoti. Nehru and rural development. *Indian Nation,* 24 May 1987; 2.

Real portrait of an integrated Indian our non-substitutable leader Jawaharlal Nehru encountered formidable obstacles on his way to national solidarity. Different communities, languages and culture were privileged by him to make India a great country.

Sampurnanand

966. Mathai, M.O. Dr. Sampurnanand and basic thinking. *MDN*; 68-77.

Dr. Sampurnanand was a typical example of Plato's conception of the scholar in politics. Nehru once told me that Sampurnanand was a person whose intellect was so razor-sharp that a slight tilt could make him mad. I have heard several junior colleagues of Dr. Sampurnanand, such as Lal Bahadur and Dr. B.V. Keskar, speak in great veneration of Dr. Sampurnanand. He succeeded Pandit Govind Ballabh Pant as the Chief Cabinet. But the "Brahmin by achievement" did not have the infinite patience and capacity to suffer fools which the "Brahmin by birth" possessed in abundance. Apart from all aspects of India's hoary past, including astrology, Dr. Sampurnanand had an abiding interest in books on scientific fiction. He always kept a few of these books by his side in the Chief Minister's office.

Science

967. Baldev Singh. Nehru and Science. *Mainstream*, 28 December 1985; 35-37.

Nehru ascribes his interests in science to his days in Cambridge as student for a science degree and later his realisation, as a mature politician, that economic salvation of India's millions lay in development of science and its application to resolve the problems of ignorance, hunger, poverty and unemployment. Nehru attached great importance to the Indian Science Congress as representing Indian science and made use of the opportunity provided by its annual general sessions to make public the importance he attached personally to science and its applications and the commitment and support of his Government for their advancement. He also used the occasions to win popular backing for science and scientists and impress upon the people their role in social, cultural and economic transformation of the country.

968. Bhabha, Homi J. Jawaharlal Nehru and science. *FON*; 28-35.

969. Chalapathi Rau, M. Science and secularism. *Jawaharlal Nehru*. New Delhi, 1962; 10-14.

970. Ghosh, J.C. Impact of science on industry. *NAG*; 369-77.

971. Jagjit Singh. Nehru and science: Blurring of a grand vision. *Hindustan Times*, 14 November 1982; 9.

The scientist in Nehru did somehow give him a premonition of the shape of things to come—the coming emasculation of the planning process largely due to the diversion of resources from nation-building to national defence, the slow diffusion of scientific temper among the masses, and the future growth of chalta hai mentality among the masses and the consequential adulteration of the national effort to regenerate a backward economy and the like. These forebodings so frustrated him during the last year or so of his life that he was continually repeating to himself the famous lines of Robert Frost:

The woods are lovely, dark and deep
But I have promises to keep
And miles to go before I sleep.

972. Maitra, Ramtanu. Undying spirit of Jawaharlal Nehru. *New Wave*, 29 May 1983; 8-9.

973. Mathai, M.O. Scientifictri. *MDN*; 91-99.

Sir Shanti Swarup Bhatnagar, Prof. P.C. Mahalanobis and Dr. Homi J. Bhabha were the scientists who played a prominent part in the fulfilment of Nehru's cherished desire to rapidly develop science and technology as instruments of economic development and social change in a tradition-bound society. Nehru was anxious to sweep the cobwebs of superstition and obscurantism. He laid great stress on developing the scientific temper in the country.

Nehru did not come into direct touch with the work of Sir C.V. Raman, Dr. M.N Saha, the Indian Council for Medical Research and the Indian Council for Agricultural Research. Dr. Saha was perpetually at logger-heads with Dr. Bhatnagar and Dr. Bhabha. He was on the verge of retiring from active scientific work. Progressively he grew cantankerous and strayed into politics for which he always had a penchant, while Sir C.V. Raman observed his lofty aloofness. The one Nehru personally liked most in the scientific community was Sir K.S. Krishnan who was soft-spoken, dignified and retiring.

974. Mishra, R.K. Nehru tribute: For a scientific renaissance. *Patriot*, 27 May 1980; 2.

Jawaharlal Nehru was conscious of the power of the forces of stagnation and backwardness which reside in the minds of men and women who may otherwise be very sincere to the core. Aware that it is more difficult to fight the crippling influence of "honest", but backward looking friends, colleagues and co-workers, Nehru waged an unremitting battle in the realm of ideas. Gandhi liberated politics from the narrow confines of the drawing rooms of the upper classes or the intelligentsia. Nehru mobilised these masses in the battle of science and reason against obscurantism, dogmatism and sectarianism of all varieties. If the unassailable hegemony of the power of reason over what he described as politics of magic could not be established in our public life during Nehru's life time, the reason must be found in the paucity of men and women who could comprehend the depth of the hold of irrationality on the minds of men and women. The awareness of the crucial significance of fighting a relentless battle of *status quo* became somewhat dull during the post-Nehru period.

975. Morehouse, Ward. Nehru and science: The vision of new India. *SON*; 286-309.

976. Muslehuddin, M. Nehru: Man of science. *Mainstream*, 29 May 1971; 27, 38.

977. Nayak, R.K. Nehru and the scientific outlook. *National Herald*, 14 November 1985; 7.

Nehru as a maker of a modern India had unique quality of scientific enquiry and possessed scientific vision of things. He was such a great visionary that he comprehended the unity, continuity of the past, present and future in order to realise harmony between science and spirituality. He stressed also to inculcate and develop among people the basic values of secularism, socialism and democracy. Nehru had a vision not only of scientist and of laboratories but also the broader horizons and its socio-economic relevance to India's progress and prosperity. Nehru was engrossed in Indian politics but he always had a great aptitude and mind for the development of science in India.

978. Nehru, Jawaharlal. Science and humility. *Naw Wave*, 1 March 1987; 2.

The scientist is supposed to be an objective seeker after truth. Science has grown because in large measures the great scientists have sought truth in that way. But I suppose no man today, not even a scientist, can live in a world of his own, in some kind of ivory tower, off from what is happening.

979. Nehru, Einstein saw world differently. *Times of India*, 14 November 1983.

980. Nehru on science, ethics and practical politician. *New Wave*, 13 November 1983; 8-9.

981. Nehru's approach to science, technology still relevant. *National Herald*, 17 November 1976.

Nehru had only encouraged development of indigenous know-how in sophisticated fields such as atomic energy and space research, but also started a major effort to harness science for the farmers in the villages. The idea of setting up agricultural universities and research centres came from Nehru. The infra-structure of agricultural technology was also created due to his encouragement.

982. Ranganathan, A. Vision of Nehru's scientific humanism. *Yojana*, 1-15 January 1986; 20-22.

Nehru's philosophy, whether we view it now as a confluence of the streams of Gandhian ethics, Indian sensibility and Western liberalism, as a transition of and in cultural theory of trusteeship, as a continuation of the tradition of Raja Ram Mohun Roy's scientific humanism, or as a part of the process of the fusion of disparate materials into an artistic re-creation, matters less than the vision which inspires it. This vision pervades Nehru's writings with three recurring themes. They are major themes, and of relevance to us today. First, a humanistic reassessment of the goals of economics, to highlight the equality of life.

983. Sondhi, Sunil. Science, technology and foreign policy: Nehru years. *Mainstream*, 18 April 1987; 11-14.

Although Jawaharlal Nehru is known more for his passion for world peace, his attitude towards national security was more than merely pacifist. Being himself an ardent advocate of modern technology, he could not have been ignorant of its military potential. In fact, he showed remarkable realism in his views on military uses of technology. Barely four months after independence Nehru remarked at an industries conference in New Delhi, "Many things contributed to the winning of the last war, but I think the chief reasons were the amazing capacity of American industry and scientific research. It is this which won the war, not so much the soldiers and others."

984. Subramaniam, C. Nehru and the temper of science. *Economic Times*, 15 November 1981; 5.

Along with Mahatma Gandhi, Nehru dominated the Congress organisation. While it was Gandhiji's philosophy which ultimately prevailed in the Congress Working Committee, Nehru's thinking had great influence on even Gandhiji's ultimate decision. Even during the freedom fight, Nehru made the Indian nation conscious of the fact that even after attainment of freedom we will have to live in an interdependent world.

Secularism

985. Anthony, Frank. Nehru and secular democracy. *NP*, 86-92.

986. Ayyub, Abu Sayeed. Secularism. *In Socialism, democracy and secularism: A symposium in memory of Jawaharlal Nehru* : New Delhi, 1965; 48-71 and Secularism and Jawaharlal Nehru, *Quest* (47), October-December 1965.

987. Azeem, Anwer. Dreamer's vision of secularism. *Patriot*, 30 November 1985; 4.

What happens to Gandhian perception and Nehru's dream ?

Mahatma went to Noakhali, Calcutta, Patna, and then tired and exhausted but still fighting, fell to an assassin's bullets. So did Indira. How much more blood do these Deorases and Thackerays need to turn the blooming garden of our nation into a wasteland of cacti ? How can we stop the degeneration ?

Nehru suggests : "If some aspect of the truth has been petrified by dogma in a past age, it ceases to grow and develop and adapt itself to the changing needs of humanity . . .It is with the temper and approach of science, allied to philosophy, and with reverence for all that lies beyond, that we must face life . . ." Are we inclined ?

988. Beg, M.H. Nehru and India's secular identity. *Patriot*, 29 April 1987; 4.

The means adopted by Nehru for achieving what is no less than a cultural revolution, were our dynamic values and potentialities for healthy change and growth gathered from all sources. His method was different from that of either Mao of China or Lenin of the USSR. Nevertheless, his objectives were similar.

989. Beg, M.H. Nehruite Secularism—educational purpose. *Patriot*, 19 May 1987; 4.

Jawaharlal Nehru's secularism was far more clear-cut with sharper edges which could cut out what has been called "flabbiness" of our notions of secularism. The question before us, however, is : Can we cut this approach out altogether so long as it appears to be good and effective for the mass of our people, or, indeed, for the majority of people throughout the world ?

990. India owes secular image to Nehru. *National Herald*, 14 November 1976.

991. Jagmohan. Jawaharlal Nehru : The dreams of India he realised. *National Herald*, 27 May 1977: 5.

Having known intimately and at bitter cost the evils of communalist politics Nehru, right from the pre-Independence days, counselled the nation to be secular and modern. His secularism was partly anti-acclesiastical for he could not put up with mumbo-jumbo doctrines, rituals of organised religion and fanaticism. But his secularism was more of tolerance, co-existence of religions and understanding of the fellowman. Nehru was a missionary of secularism since he was a self-proclaimed "pagan". He knew fully well that communalism would dissipate the nation's energies, while secularism would contribute much to nation-building. Fighting against orthodoxy, and vested interests behind the seemingly religious orders, Nehru made it possible for secularism to be the third pillar of our national polity.

And, the fourth pillar Non-alignment, was the philosophy which Nehru gifted to the world of power politics, secret diplomacy, military pacts and nuclear arms race. In the long history of mankind, no such thing had ever existed before. It is to the resounding credit of Nehru and his two close friends, President Tito and the late President Nasser of Egypt that they created a new powerful force of the Non-aligned Movement, out of which emerged such wonderful concepts of co-existence, mutual respect, tolerance of different systems of governance, respect of territorial integrity and non-use of force.

It was 40 years ago, even before India attained Independence that Nehru outlined his concept of Non-alignment. And today, it is a dynamic force that is now being respected by the super powers. The Helsinki document is a tribute to the vision of Nehru. With each passing year, the Non-aligned Movement has gathered momentum and ensured peace and mutual co-operation. Now the sheet-anchor of India's foreign policy, Non-alignment as further refined and developed by Mrs. Indira Gandhi, has preserved the country intact and enabled its counsel heard everywhere.

It has become so much a part of Indian polity that when the Janata Party took over the reins of the Government in New Delhi, they had to accept the wisdom of Nehru and continue the policy of Non-alignment indulged during the election campaign was subsequently given up.

The greatness of Nehru was that he not only turned his dreams into realities, but he made it possible for these realities to withstand the rigours of time and the shifts and changes of politics, both national and international. He turned his dreams into the very foundations of our national life. It was because he so very much understood the ethos and the collective subconscious of this nation that he was able to formulate the ideal set-up and get it accepted by generations to preserve and cherish the heritage that Nehru left for us. Only in this way it will be possible for us to love him even as much we loved him abundantly during his lifetime.

992. Joshi, P.C. Gandhi-Nehru Tradition and Indian secularism. *Mainstream*, 14 November 1987; 5-8, 35-38.

It is not surprising that nothing constructive has emerged from the several rounds of border talks during the 1980s and China still does not appear to have made clear the basis or principles on which a settlement may be possible. A closer reading of the facts would only reveal Nehru's perceptiveness and vision in dealing with the issues involved. It is still the most rational basis for an approach to the problem. Any realistic approach to the resolution of the Sino-Indian border territorial problem must take into account an objective assessment of the merits of the case, the established international principles in resolving such issues and China's reluctance to conform to them only in relation to India and China's incentives if any in settling the problem, it is not necessary to remain captive to history, of the principles involved, the facts and veracity of respective claims is vital to the success of any fresh initiatives, whether at official or political levels.

993. Kohli, Manorama. Secularism in India and Nehru. *SON*, 255-65.

994. Mukerjee, Hiren. For a secular democracy. *Gentle Colossus*, Calcutta, 1964; 113-39.

995. Mushtaq Ahmed. Secular India of Nehru's Conception. *National Herald*, 27 May 1972; 5.

Nehru's friendly relationship to Czechoslovakia was by no means new. Indologist Vincene Lesny had invited Nehru to come to visit Prague some years before, and Nehru had been unable to take advantage of the invitation. But this time Jawaharlal Nehru's interest was not so much in his personal friends as in the political problems that had begun to pile up in this country, particularly since Hitler's annexation of Austria (Anschluss), forming a threat of international conflict.

996. Nehru and secular identity. *Mainstream*, 2 May 1987; 31-32.

As we dwell upon the vision which sustained the people of India in their struggle for freedom and in their endeavour, in the decades since 1947, to fashion for themselves a society, wherein their material and cultural creativity would flourish in an environment free of exploitation and irrational strife, the crystallisation of a national identity and the generation of secular order stands out in bold relief.

Perhaps the vision, which contemplated the transformation of a classical civilisation of antiquity into a modern industrial state, socialistic in structure, democratic in form and secular in ethos, was expressed most clearly of all by Jawaharlal Nehru.

997. Nunil Hasan, S. Jawaharlal Nehru and secularism. *New Wave*, 12 December 1982; 6, 12.

998. Rehman, Ubaldur. Nehru was an angel of secularism. *Northern India Patrika* (Allahabad), 28 May 1987; 4.

Jawaharlal regarded modern dams as the temples of our times. What he meant was that in this global race for material joys and progress, India cannot afford to live on spiritualism alone. That is why he laid so much stress on rapid industrialisation of the country. In fact it was because of the efforts in this direction made by him that a sound and solid base was laid and we are enjoying the fruits of that early pioneering efforts of Panditji.

Panditji had conquered hate. How many of us can afford to do that? He had the greatest love even for his critics. That is why he was always successful in winning over most of them. There might have been a few hard-boiled critics. But even they conceded that there were many facets of Jawaharlal's personality which had no comparison.

999. Sarin, L.N. Secularism. *Jawaharlal Nehru.* Delhi, 1968; 64-69.

1000. Seminar on secularism eulogizes Nehru, Tagore. *Statesman*, 15 April 1987; 6.

"The basic meaning of secularism is the separation of the State from religion, even though religion has played and continues to play an important role in the life of the Indian people; secularism cannot be divorced from the seminal issues of equitable social and economic development and the fostering of a scientific outlook and liberal values in the community."

These were the two main conclusions reached at the end of a four-day seminar on Jawaharlal Nehru and India's Quest for a Secular Identity held in New Delhi in April 1987. The seminar was organized by the Indian Institute of Advanced Study, in collaboration with the Indian Council of Social Science Research, the Indian Council of Historical Research, the Indian Council of Philosophical Research and the Nehru Memorial Museum and Library.

1001. Singh, Gurmukh Nihal. India—a secular state. *NAG*; 36-68.

1002. Sinha, V.K., ed. *Secularism in India*. Bombay, 1968.

1003. Smith, D.E. *India as a State*. Princeton, 1963.

1004. Syed, M. Hafiz. Spiritual basis of Nehru's secular government. *NAG*; 131-35.

1005. Zakaria, Rafiq. Nehru—the prophet of secularism. *Pree Press Journal* (Bombay), 27 December 1985; 10.

Pandit Nehru in power was not the same as he was in opposition; perhaps he could not be. He himself has admitted: "Some years earlier I would not have been so hesitant. There was a definiteness about my thinking and objectives then which has faded away since. The events of the past few years in India, China, Europe and all over the world have been confusing, upsetting and distressing and the future has become vague and shadowy and has lost that clearness of outline which it once possessed in my mind".

Sikhism

1006. Gill, Tejwant S. Sikhs in Nehru's writings. *Tribune*, 15 July 1984.

The event convinced Nehru of the need to bring into the national fold the religious morcha launched by the Sikhs under the hegemony of the Akalis. It was at his suggestion that a publicity-cell was set up at Amritsar for this purpose. He recommended the names of A.T. Gidwani and K.M. Pannikar for conducting the affairs of the publicity-cell. Their reports bears testimony to the fact that the basic hindrance in the way of the Sikhs' espousal of the national cause under the leadership of the Congress Party was the strain that prevailed between the Hindus and the Sikhs.

Nehru's perception of the communal strain revealed to him the negative feature of the Sikh-Hindu relationship. He realized that the Sikhs were obdurate and had no generous word or gesture for people of the other community. This perception of the obduracy of the Sikhs was fair enough but the historical reasons for the Sikhs adopting such an attitude were not articulated anywhere in his writings. Rather than dialectical and historical, this perception was positivistic and empirical for that matter.

1007. Harbans Singh. *Nehru Family and the Sikhs.* Delhi, 1984, 160 pp.

Sinha, S.N.

1008. Mathai, M.O. Satya Narain Sinha. *MDN*; 256-59.

Satya Narain Sinha was a member of the Central Legislative Assembly before Independence. He became a member of the Constituent Assembly in 1946 and continued to be a Member of Parliament until he was appointed Governor of Madhya Pradesh around 1970. Since 1946 he had been chief whip of the Congress in Parliament. On 15 August, 1947, as chief whip, he was appointed as Minister of State for Parliamentary Affairs. He was an unconcealed partisan supporter of Sardar Vallabhbhai Patel.

Rafi Ahmed Kidwai was a sworn opponent of Satya Narain Sinha. Once Rafi got hold of some information about certain financial dealings of Satya Narain Sinha and reported it to the Prime Minister. Sinha had to do a great deal of explaining before he was let off the hook.

I once told Rafi, while Sardar Patel was alive, that his apprehension that Sinha was dangerous to Nehru was misplaced. I added that "I would rather suspect you than Satya Narain". He asked me why ? I said, "Imitation is the best form of flattery. See how every new sherwani of Nehru is duplicated by Satya Narain; see how he is imitating Nehru by always having a rose bud in buttonhole."

Social Changes and Justice

1009. Dutt, V.P. Jawaharlal Nehru and social changes in India. *Socialist India*, 13 November 1976; 9-12, 25-28, 40.

Jawaharlal Nehru's was a fascinatingly complex and many-splendoured personality. He was an intellectual, a practising political, a statesman of vision, a keen student of history, an outstanding world leader, a thinker, head of the Government of a vast and abysmally poor country, an administrator at the top of a bureaucracy known for inertia and wooden-headedness, a sensitive human being who has at the same time to function daily with innumerable and diverse kinds of human beings, an engineer of the human mind, a moulder of opinion and yet subject to the pressures of limited minds around him, and a symbol of the hopes and urges of millions of Indians who also influenced him and moulded him and his outlook in a myriad ways.

1010. Mehta, Asoka. Nehru: Social justice and national development. *Nehru and the Modern World.* New Delhi, UNESCO, 1967; 33-38.

1011. Myrdal, Alva. Social justice and national development. *Nehru and the Modern World.* New Delhi, UNESCO, 1967; 39-52.

1012. Nehru, Jawaharlal. *India's Independence and Social Revolution.* New Delhi, Vikas, 1984, 162 pp.

Socialism

1013. Appadorai, A. Mr. Nehru's concept of socialism. *Hindustan Times*, 14 November 1968.

1014. Attar Chand. Nehru and socialism. *Newstime*, 4 August 1987.

1015. B. Singh. Nehru's philosophy of socialism. *AICC Economic Review*, 27 May 1965.

1016. Bhambhri, C.P. Nehru and socialist movement in India, 1920-1947. *Indian Journal of Political Science*, April-June 1969; 130-48.

1017. Bhambhri, C.P. Nehru and the socialist movement in India, 1920-47. *SON*; 96-116.

1018. Chakravarti, P.R. Jawaharlal Nehru: A Republican and a socialist. *Socialist India*, 3 April 1976; 8.

After his visit to the Soviet Union in 1927 Jawaharlal Nehru, in his tribute to the Soviet leader Lenin, said: "By an amazing power of will he hypnotized a nation and filled a disunited and demoralized people with energy and determination and the strength to endure and suffer for a cause." He found something allied to his own innate urge for self-expression and the promise to help the people, yoked to foreign domination.

1019. Chalapathi Rau, M. Planning development and socialism. *Jawaharlal Nehru*. New Delhi, 1962; 6-9.

1020. Chopra, V.D. Nehru and socialism. *Patriot* (Annual), 1984; 33-35.

Jawaharlal Nehru led the restructuring of the economy along the lines of planned development, and started a policy of industrialisation, which became a decisive factor in modernizing India. It was at his initiative that the country embarked on the path of building and strengthening the public sector. This is how he helped India breathe life again. He laid the foundations of new India by abolishing colonialism, the legacy of feudalism and age-old backwardness. That explains how his name is inseparably linked with the struggle for the liberation of India from colonial enslavement, for its rebirth and development as a sovereign State.

For almost 17 years when he led the country towards a new social order, Jawaharlal Nehru often self-critically reviewed his original ideas and tried to move forward. The direction of his political and social searches was in tune with a changing and developing society.

1021. Dalip Singh. Jawaharlal Nehru—Father of Indian Socialism. *Socialist India*, 13 November 1976; 17-21.

If Mahatma Gandhi earned the unique distinction of being "Father of the Nation" for liberating India from British yoke, Jawaharlal Nehru can legitimately be called "Father of Indian Socialism". Political institutions grow out of the demands and genius of the people. Since the times of Plato, an endless search is going on in the world for evolving an ideal political system which may serve as a panacea for solving all the problems of men.

1022. Das, Dharnidhar. Parliamentary democracy and socialism. *Mainstream*, (Annual Number) 1966; 76-78.

From the socialist stand-point democracy is bound up with the law-governed process of social development, of which the ultimate outcome is socialist democratic mass foundation. Historically democracy was the forerunner of socialism, and socialism provided democracy the soil to strike roots in the social basis to become society's way of life. Both socialism and democracy have to be conceived together. For socialism democracy is an objective necessity and for democracy to have practical meaning in life, there is no system except socialism.

1023. Das, M.N. *Content of democratic socialism of Jawaharlal Nehru.* Bombay, 1965.

1024. Dikshit, Uma Shankar. Perfect democrat and an ardent socialist. *NP*; 125-129.

1025. Dutt, R.C. Nehru's contribution to socialism. *National Herald*, 14 November 1980; 5.

1026. Dutt, R.C. *Retreat of Socialism—Two decades without Nehru,* 1964-84. New Delhi, Abhinav, 1984, 236 pp.

R.C. Dutt's Retreat of Socialism is a remarkable book. It is contemporary history. It is the Economic History of India since Independence. It is remarkable because it is totally unbiased, in spite of the author's own leanings and predilections, which seep through the pages. He has not bestowed fulsome praise on anyone nor has he indulged in malicious criticism. He has praised where praise is due and criticised where criticism is called for. He has put everyone and everything in his or in its proper place as should be done in every book on history. He is able to do this because of the detached but not disinterested view that he has taken of maintaining a very high degree of intellectual integrity, a commodity which is fast becoming very rare.

1027. Dutt, R.C. *Socialism of Jawaharlal Nehru.* New Delhi, Abhinav, 1982. Book Review by B.R. Nanda. *Times of India*, 19 December 1982.

In the spate of books and articles on Jawaharlal Nehru, a recurrent theme has been his commitment to socialism. He has been judged by his critics according to their own preconceived notions. The conservatives would have us believe that he was a dangerous radical whose socialist predilections prevented India from staging the industrial miracle of Japan and West Germany. His left-wing critics lament his failure to understand the nuances of Nehru's thought as well as the political and social milieu in which he had to act. This richly documented and well-arranged volume by R.C. Dutt, a former senior civil servant, seeks to provide the historical context in which we can analyse Nehru's approach to socialism.

1028. Ganesh Prasad. Nehru : Step by step towards socialism. *Mainstream*, 12 November 1966; 11-21.

Nehru was no convert to socialism; he never became a full-fledged socialist or a member of a socialist organisation. All his life he remained an active member of the Indian National Congress. He was a colonial patriot with bourgeois upbringing and with humainst-liberal-scientific training. But, curiously enough, it was his ardent patriotism that made his advance towards acceptance of some principles of socialism. His ideological progress reflects the predicaments of the colonial patriot of the period following the First World War. Let us analyse how that nationalism advanced "painfully, step by step", towards socialism.

1029. Ghose, Sankar. Nehru, planning and socialism. *Socialist India*, 13 November 1976; 14-16.

1030. Ghosh, Ajoy. Pandit Nehru's Socialism—A Hox. *New Age*, 2 January 1955.

1031. Jagmohan. Jawaharlal Nehru and his socialism. *Mainsıream*, 24 May 1986; 28-31.

1032. Joshi, P.C. Nehru and socialism in India. *Socialism in India*, Ed. by B.R. Nanda. New Delhi, 1982.

1033. Joshi, Navin Chandra. Nehru's Socialist India. *Western Times* (Ahmedabad), 11 January 1983; 2.

1034. Joshi, Navin Chandra. socialism Nehru wanted for India. *Patriot*, 14 November 1986; 4.

1035. Joshi, Shashi. Nehru—Champion of socialist ideology. *Patriot*, 22 April 1988; 4.

1936. Karanjia, R.K. Indian road to socialism. *Mind of Mr. Nehru*. London, 1960; 37-44.

1037. Kidwai, Anser. Nehru's ideals and march to socialism. *National Herald*, 17 November 1983; 5.

The nation has been amidst Nehru's birthday celebrations and, as such, a stock-taking of the strides made by the country in fulfilling the promises made to the people in terms of Nehru's ideals and aspirations should be timely. The occasion becomes all the more poignant in the wake of the constant threats to our democratic goals which Nehru and other leaders of the freedom movement had set before themselves on the dawn of Independence.

1038. Malaviya, H.D. (*ed.*) *Jawaharlal Nehru Congressman's Primer for Socialism.* New Delhi, 1965, 199 pp.

1039. Mature socialism. *National Herald*, 15 November 1970.

1040. Mehta, Dinkar. Nehru's socialist dream. *Economic Times*, 15 November 1984; 4.

To ask and answer the question whether Nehru was a failure or a success would be very crude. Essentially, he worked during a period of rapid transition and he himself was more a victim than a master of the forces which began to sharpen during the transition. If it is possible to remember his inspiring call for socialism in the midst of the tragic inadequacy of economic policy efforts, such memory would be useful as an impetus to bringing about social transformation.

1041. Mukerjee, Hiren. Towards socialism. *Gentle Colossus*, Calcutta, 1964; 150-78.

1042. Namboodiripad, E.M.S. Nehru as a socialist. *NCV*; 141-44.

1043. Nayak, R.K. Socialist path. *National Herald*, 14 November 1981; 15.

1044. Nehru, Jawaharlal. Socialist pattern. *New Wave*, 8 February 1987; 2.

The problems of unemployment and of raising the level of our people are not solved by broad decisions or slogans. I say this without any disrespect to those who wield striking words, because I myself have been a wielder of words all my life, drafting resolutions, getting them passed and so on. But a time comes when you have to forget words and deal with hard actualities.

1045. Nehru, Jawaharlal. *Socialist pattern.* Avadi, 1955.

1046. Nehru and socialism. *National Herald*, 14 November 1972; 5.

1047. Nehru's concept of socialism. *Patriot*, 14 November 1976.

Nehru was a nation builder who not only sought to give economic and social substance to the idea of Indian nationhood on the basis of modern and scientific thought but all his life worked for it. His interest in and even passion for planning grew out of this approach. Throughout his life until his death in May 1964, economic planning as a powerful instrument of advance and social transformation not only remained undiminished but acquired increasing depth, insight and understanding from his experience of the formulation and implementation of the three Plans in the country.

1048. Nehru's influence on socialist movement. *Patriot*, 14 November 1976.

CPI General Secretary C. Rajeswara Rao, in an interview to *Patriot*, said that Jawaharlal Nehru was a great democrat and respected the Opposition both inside and outside Parliament. Even when the right-wing Opposition in the early sixties tried to side-track the national issues facing the country, he could not be provoked or distracted from his chosen path.

1049. Patel, Rajni. Nehru and socialism *Swarajya*, 23 July 1978; 5-8.

1050. Raghunatha Reddy, K.V. Nehru's democratic socialism. *FON*; 36-43.

1051. Raj, K.N. Socialism. *Socialism, democracy and secularism: A symposium in memory of Jawaharlal Nehru.* New Delhi, 1965; 14-31.

1052. Rajiv, V.B. Nehru and Indian socialism. *Patriot*, 14 November 1976. *Socialist India*, 27 November 1976; 32-33.

Nehru attended the Congress of the Oppressed Nationalities at Brussels in 1927 as the representative of the Indian National Congress. In the month of November, the same year, he, with his father, wife and sister, visited Moscow for the 10th anniversary celebrations of the Soviet Union great changes taking place under the powerful influence of Marxism. But he did not agree with everything that was happening there though it excited him.

1053. Ray, Sankar. Need for ideological scrutiny. *Mainstream*, 24 June 1967; 31-32.

1054. Rothermund, Dietmar. Nehru and early year of socialism in India. *Socialist India*, 15 August 1970; 15-18.

The connection of Jawaharlal Nehru with the socialist movement in India cannot be described in institutional or ideological terms because Nehru's political loyalties and doctrines were always highly personal. He was the enthusiastic agitator and the detached mentor, who influenced the generation of Indian patriots and gave their thought a socialist tinge.

This process may be analysed by looking at three aspects of Nehru's socialism. The first aspect is the element of Vedanta philosophy in Indian socialism, the message of Vivekananda, which influenced Nehru in his interpretation of the Brahminical ideal of service and in his skilful use of Socialism as an instrument of diagnosis and therapy. The second aspect is Nehru's role as a radical mediator who conjures up a new vision of the political development in the important decade of 1927-37. The third aspect is seen in the evolution of the economic programme of the Indian National Congress in those years of intensive political agitation for national freedom.

1055. Roy, Ranajit. Socialism for the rich. *Business Standard* (Calcutta), 19 March 1983; 4.

1056. Sarin, L.N. Socialist pattern. *Jawaharlal Nehru*, Delhi, 1968; 34-42.

1057. Socialism. *QON*; 140-45 and *NFC*; 24-28.

1058. *Socialism, democracy and secularism: A symposium in memory of Jawaharlal Nehru.* New Delhi, National Book Trust, 1965, 71 pp.

1059. Yajee, Sheel Bhadra. Nehru: The greatest socialist. *Socialist India*, 8 November 1975; 37.

Nehru openly declared at Behrampur (Orissa) that the Congress as a political party had to accept Socialism as its creed. He always stressed that the people of India had accepted Socialism as their goal not only because it seemed to them right and beneficial but because there was no alternative solution to their economic problems.

1060. Yajee, Sheel Bhadra. Nehru—the Harbinger of Socialism. *Pioneer*, 27 December 1983.

Pandit Nehru openly declared at Behrampur (Orissa) that the Indian National Congress as a political party had to accept socialism as its creed because socialism had got a background and achievements. The present modern India which is fast developing on the basis of socialism, secularism and planning are all due to the role and great efforts of Pandit Jawaharlal Nehru, and so he is the harbinger of socialism in the country.

Sri Prakash

1061. Mathai, M.O. Sri Prakash, 1890-1971. *MDN*; 252-56.

Son of the renowned Sanskrit scholar and philosopher of Banaras, Dr. Bhagwan Das, Sri Prakash was a personal friend and contemporary of Nehru at Cambridge. The friendship between the two was abiding and life-long, cemented by common endeavour and suffering in the cause of India's freedom. They called each other by first names. Nehru called him "Prakash" and the latter called Nehru "Jawaharlal".

States and Union Territories

1062. Abbas, K.A. Nehru on Punjab. *Blitz*, 26 May 1984; 32.

I thought I asked him what he thought of the situation in the Punjab.

"For many years I wandered about India and millions of faces passed before my eyes. I saw a thousand faces of this country of mine and all the rich diversity, and yet always with a unifying impress of India upon them. I sought to understand what lay behind these millions of eyes that stared at me, what hopes and desires ? What untold sorrows and misery unexpressed ? Glimpses came to me that illuminated my vision and made me realise the immensity of the problems of the hundreds of millions of our people."

1063. Banerjee, A.K. Nehru : Firm believer in fair play. *Daily* (Bombay), 4 June 1983; 15.

Pure as crystal, is how Gandhi described Nehru when he designated him as his heir after bypassing Vallabhbhai Patel. When

Nehru took over as Prime Minister in 1947, he had one of the best cabinets in the world to work with. The clash between the two contenders for succession was prevented from reaching a critical stage, first, only by the tragic circumstance of Gandhi's death, and second by Vallabhbhai's own.

1064. Durga Das. Linguistic states. *India*. London, 1969; 326-27.

Linguistic states ? Have they strengthened national unity or weakened it ? These and many not perhaps have arisen but for the fact that Rajagopalachari's Ministry in Madras after the first general election was not a happy family. His differences with T. Prakasam, popularly known as Andhra Kesari (Lion of Andhra), accentuated the clash between the Tamils and the Telugu-speaking Andhras. The Andhras now revived their demand that the Madras State, as formed by the British, be carved into two separate states. Tamil and Telugu leader, Potti Sriramulu, undertook a fast unto death. Nehru told his Cabinet colleagues he would not be intimidated by these tactics. But when the fasting leader died and the tragedy was followed by widespread riots and destruction, Nehru yielded.

1065. Indian States. *NFC*; 67-71.

1066. *Jawaharlal Nehru : Letters to Chief Ministers*. New Delhi, Project of the Jawaharlal Nehru Memorial Fund, 1985; 547 pp.

Pandit Jawaharlal Nehru, political commentator, man of letters and independent India's first Prime Minister, was one of modern India's most versatile figures.

Again, even if Nehru had not written such outstanding works as *An Autobiography*, *Glimpses of World History* and *The Discovery of India*, his letters to the Chief Ministers would bring back the personality as we knew him.

Further more, Prime Minister Rajiv Gandhi rightly remarks that "these letters reveal a great mind and a large heart at work".

1067. Jawaharlal Nehru's letters to Chief Ministers, 1952. *Mainstream*, Republic Day 1987; 6-9.

Jawaharlal Nehru, when he was Prime Minister of India, used to regularly write a fortnightly letter to the Chief Ministers of the States. These fortnightly communications were in the nature of Nehru's survey of the prevailing national and international scene.

In a sense, they amounted to a remarkable correspondence course for continuing political education imparted by him to his colleagues so necessary for a unified understanding of the fast changing reality that confronted and still confronts those at the helm of affairs of this great country.

1068. King, Shamim Ahmed. Nehru in Assam. *National Herald*, 27 May 1983; 5.

In December 1945, Jawaharlal Nehru was in Assam. He made an effective whirlwind electioneering tour and raised a large amount for the Assam Election Fund. My father had accompanied him throughout the tour.

A Dandi March satyagrahi, the late Lila Barooah was in the front seat of a car, with an enormous money-bag, spreading his tentacles, as it were, for the election fund that Nehru was raising. In the sung back seat only Nehru chain-smoking and reading proofs of his manuscript '*The Discovery of India*', and now and then merrily gossiping just to enliven or to break the monotony.

1069. Mathur, P.S. Thousand names of Nehru. *Telegraph* (Calcutta), 14 November 1982; 4.

1070. Mir Qasim, Syed. Nehru and Kashmir. *Mainstream*, 26 May 1973; 11-12.

As a valiant fighter for the rights and privileges of the State people, Panditji addressed a number of public meetings under the auspices of the J&K National Conference during the pre-Independence period. He made intimate and lasting contacts with the rank and file of the organisation and also guided their activities and programmes on various crucial occasions. Giving personal impressions of the mass movement in the State he observed: "I sensed that Kashmir was astir and the masses were on the move. That had been a common experience to me in many parts of India during the past twenty years. But it was an experience on that scale in an Indian State. There could be no doubt of widespread awakening among the people of a growing feeling of self-reliance and strength. In this respect, in some ways, Kashmir seemed to be advanced."

1071. Nayar, Kuldip. Nehru: Those were the days. *Tribune*, 26 May 1983; 4.

Assam was very much before the public eye during Nehru's days also. But he did not blame the Opposition as Mrs. Gandhi is doing day in and day out. He wrote to the Chief Ministers after the language riots in the State: "The language issue was dominant and, yet, surely, it was not merely because of language that these passions were roused. There were economic causes, more especially the Bengalis got the lion's share of employment in their own State. There was the fear of Bengalis which led so many to leave their identity. When fear grips people, it is difficult to reason". This analysis goes to the root of the problem and Nehru did solve it at that time. Mrs. Gandhi has only complicated it.

1072. Nehru, Jawaharlal. Andaman prisoners. *REW*; 108-9.

1073. Nehru, Jawaharlal. Indian states. *REW*; 133-34.

1074. Parthasarthi, G. ed. *Jawaharlal Nehru : Letters to Chief Ministers 1947-64. Vol. 1*; New Delhi, 1985; 547 pp. Book Review by Nikhil Sinha. *Indian and Foreign Review*, 15 November 1986; 29-30.

The letters provide evidence of Nehru's acute political acumen, at times bordering on prescience. The letters leading upto Mahatma Gandhi's assassination constantly warn of the threat of communal forces. In fact these early letters are in many ways indicators of the shape of things to come and provide the motivations and reasoning which brought them about. The re-organisation of States on lingual lines can be seen to have its well-springs in his letter of November 15, 1947, in which discussing the troubles in some areas Nehru writes: "...... To some extent these developments indicate a move for closer cultural ties between men of the same stock and language, living in different provinces, and I have no doubt eventually some readjustment will be necessary."

1075. Satinder Singh. Harking back to Nehru. *Tribune*, 12 November 1980; 4.

1076. Schlesinger, Arthur M. Nehru and Goa. *A thousand days.* London, 1965; 457-59.

Tagore, Rabindra Nath

1077. Dasgupta, R.K. Nehru admired Tagore's interpretation of ancient indian Wisdom. *National Herald*, 7 May 1967.

Prof. Dasgupta said: "In this search for a complete life Nehru discovered in Tagore an inspiring exponent of the ideal. If we have so far given little attention to this relationship between the two it is due to our preoccupation with Nehru's political life alone which is influenced mostly by Gandhi and a consequent neglect of his achievement as a humanist and an intellectual. Moreover, the circumstances of Nehru's political life did not permit a close and continuous contact with the poet."

1078. Tagore, Rabindranath. Majestic Character. *NCV*; 165-66.

Technology

1079. Gujral, M.L. Choice of Technology. *EFNIG*; 203-18.

1080. Science and Technology. *QON*; 123-28.

Teja, Jayanti Dharma

1081. Mathai, M.O. Jayanti Dharma Teja and shipping, *MDN*; 170-75.

Prime Minister Nehru was impressed by Teja as a man who could get things done. He was taken in by Teja's grandiose scheme of shipping development in India. Teja was able to quote facts and figures about shipping and its importance to the economy which appealed to Nehru. Teja also enlisted the support of Mrs. Vijaya Lakshmi Pandit's son-in-law who is the senior executive of the multi-national pharmaceutical firm in India, Ciba-Geigy of India Ltd. In fact this firm acquired financial interest in Jayanti Shipping Company floated in India by Teja under the Indian Companies Act.

Tilak, B.G.

1082. Nehru, Jawaharlal. Tilak. *Indian spokesman*, Ed. by C.D. Narasimhaiah, Madras, 1960; 273-77.

Travels

1083. Abid Hasan. Travelling with Nehru. *Hindustan Times*, 1 December 1985, 4.

It was perhaps March 1950. Pandit Nehru was proceeding to Babina for a Buddhist function at Sanchi. It was a unique journey later Prime Ministers could hardly hope to repeat. Imagine India's Prime Minister travelling close to 14 hours seated in a non-airconditioned coach on a passenger train hauled by an old steam engine on a single-track, broad-gauge route. And to cap it all, a man like Nehru having to wait over six hours for his morning tea. The tea was finally served just one station before the destination. Yet, Nehru neither flared up nor reprimanded anyone, revealing that his impatience and anger were in the cause of state business and never on personal counts.

Tribal Development

1084. Mehta, K.L. Nehru and tribal development. *Socialist India*, 27 November 1976; 28-29.

Essentially, Nehru's approach was to win over the tribal people through persuasion and example and to see that only minimum force was used against miscreants.

In his book, *A Philosophy for NEFA*, Verrier Elwin said that we in NEFA, were trying to apply Nehru's humane and scientific ideals to concrete situations. It redounds to the credit of the great-man that in the Foreword which he wrote for Elwin's book, he said that he had learnt much from Elwin for he was both an expert on tribal administration and also a friend of the tribal folks. He wrote, "It would, therefore, be more correct to say that I have learnt from him rather than that I have influenced him in any way."

1085. Mehta, K.L. Pandit Nehru and tribals. *Akashvani* (New Delhi), 16 August 1983; 4-6.

Panditji (Jawaharlal Nehru) told me that his first contact with the tribal people were with Gonds, the Santhals and the Bhils and it was only later that he came in touch with the people of NEFA. He added, "My liking for them grew and with it came respect. I had no sensation of superiority over them. My ideas were not clear at all, but I felt that we should avoid two extreme courses : one was to treat them as anthropological specimen for study and the other was to allow them to be engulfed by the masses of Indian humanity".

Unemployment

1086. Nehru, Jawaharlal. Fight against poverty and unemployment. *India's Independence and Social Revolution*, New Delhi, 1984; 68-85.

Will and Testament

1087. Nehru, Jawaharlal. Will and Testament. *Mainstream*, 24 May 1986; 36.

I have received so much love and affection from the Indian people that nothing that I can do can repay even a small fraction of all classes of the Indian people has come to me in such abundant measure that I have been overwhelmed by it. I can only express the hope that in the remaining years I may live, I shall not be unworthy of my people and their affection.

Wit and Wisdom

1088. Haksar, Urmila. Breakfast with Nehru. *Mainstream*, 5 December 1987; 11.

1089. Jayaswal, Anwar P. Nine minutes with Nehru. *Indian Nation*, 14 November 1986; 4.

It was in mid-fifties. Teen Murti Bhawan, the official residence of the Prime Minister on a bright winter morning. We had arrived as per appointment. Graciously fixed through the good offices of Mrs. Lakshmi N. Menon, Dupty Minister, Foreign Affairs, Government of India.

We were fifteen post-graduate students of Political Science Department of Patna University. With us was Dr. M.V. Pylee as our team leader. We were ushered in Teen Murti Bhavan. It was bedecked with blooming winter flowers.

Soon, Pandit Nehru was stopping down the stairs. Flamboyantly buttoning up his brown Achken and sporting a spotless white Gandhi cap. Coming close to us he enquires how many of us had come from Patna. Someone said fifteen only. Why only fifteen, was the next quick question. Because the Varsity funds only for fifteen, answered a colleague, Kamla Prasad, presently a Secretary to the Govt. of Bihar. The Prime Minister also enquired of Parliament and the other places we had been to in the capital.

1090. Zakaria, Rafiq. Moments with Nehru. *National Herald*, 14 November 1983; 5.

Women

1091. Bhagat, Dhiren. Was Jawaharlal actually in love with this beautiful woman? Edwina Mountbatten. *Illustrated Weekly of India* (Bombay), 16 October 1983; 66-71.

Did Nehru really have it off with Edwina? Certainly the rumour began pretty soon after the Mountbattens landed in India as Viceroy and Vicereine on March 22, 1945. But then India has always been strong on rumours. Evidence of the 'affair' is difficult to find; the publication of the Edwina-Nehru letters will go a long way towards clearing the matter but it is certain that the correspondence will ever be published, despite Mountbatten's stated intention. Hough claims Mountbatten told Marie Seton that it was his intention that the letters 'will ultimately be published' p. 82.

1092. Dubashi, Jay. Nehru-Edwina affair. *Organizer* (New Delhi), 21 April 1985; 2.

1093. Mathai, M.O. Shradha Mata. *MDN*; 1-8.

Shradha Mata has lost all credibility when she made the absurd and astounding assertion, "Nehru asked me many times to be Vice-President, but I always refused. I was not going to sit in Parliament". I do not think that Nehru suffered from temporary insanity at any time to implore a young female like Shradha Mata repeatedly to be gracious enough to become Vice-President. Any further attempt on my part at contradicting her is redundant. Nevertheless, I shall make some observations to set the record straight.

I notice that Shradha Mata often refers to herself in the third person especially when referring to Nehru and herself. The only other persons of comparable importance in history who resorted to this practice are Charles de Caulle and Kautilya !

1094. Men and women. *QON*; 237-57.

1095. Mukherjee, R. Nehru pulled up for ignoring women. *Telegraph* (Calcutta), 20 May 1986.

Towards the end of May, Gandhi taxed Nehru on the latter's explanation of why there were no women in the Working Committee of the Congress. Gandhi said that if Nehru had shown the slightest inclination to include a woman, one of the old guard would happily stand down.

1096. Nehru, Jawaharlal. Message to the Prayag Mahila Vidyapitha. *REW*; 143-48.

1097. Sharma, Jai Vir Pratap. Nehru and the emancipation of women. *Third Concept* (New Delhi), March 1988; 55, 57.

The Indian women always found in Jawaharlal Nehru a champion of their emancipation. We often find in his writings and speeches a French writer's view that "if you want to judge the culture and civilization of a people, you can find that out by the status and condition of the woman of the country". He actually wanted this test to be applied to the state of affairs in India.

Nehru believed that economic condition of women must be improved. Otherwise women could have no freedom. Addressing the students of Mahila Vidyapith at Allahabad in 1934, he said, "Freedom depends on economic condition even more than political and so if a woman not economically free and self-earning she will have to depend on her husband or someone else, and dependents are never free."

1098. Women and Children, *QON*; 198-202.

World Wars

1099. Nehru, Jawaharlal. India and the War. *Nation* (New York), 1 February 1941.

Youth

1100. Cong. (I) usurps Nehru Yuvak Kendras. *Statesman* (New Delhi), 3 August 1987; 1.

Steps are being taken to remove the old cadre of Youth Co-ordinators in four more States—West Bengal, Bihar, Orissa and Assam. It is learnt that another four States would be taken over by the Nehru Yuvak Kendras Sangathan after three months. The "coup" is being completed in a phased manner.

1101. Desai, V.H. Today's Youth and Nehru. *Deccan Chronicle*, 19 November 1987.

Nehru was a dreamer. He enthused the country's youth with a fire to act. Unfortunately today it has lost its power to dream and build life's pattern on the solid foundations of lasting dreams of justice and progress. Yet, Nehru was the darling of the then youth.

Hence the youth of today should come forward prospective and thus clear the way of all evils and march boldly forward towards a world designed by our Constitution.

We need not idolise Nehru. We have to understand him frankly and intelligently. He represented the mighty forces of our Enduring Culture of Peace and his bold ventures into the realm of international understanding must call us to be up and doing.

He was essentially a thinker for whom in his own words, "Working for a great cause is a pleasure and an inspiration." In short, he was a 'pilgrim' of the New World. And, that was Jawaharlal Nehru the architect of Modern India.

1102. Nehru Yuvak Kendra at work. *Kurukshetra* (New Delhi), November-December 1986.

Situated at the capital of Rajasthan, in the semi-arid region is the *Nehru Yuvak Kendra*, ranking as a fore-runner in the mobilisation of rural youth for durable human resource development for more than a decade. The Kendra's jurisdiction extends to over 3000 villages spread over 20 Panchayat Samitis in Jaipur district. The Kendra has 111 Navyug Mandals and eight Mahila Samitis affiliated to it, of which nearly half are actually engaged in Youth development These clubs are nurtured through guidance, motivation and assistance.

The programme mix of the Nehru Yuvak Kendra reveals a wide assortment of economic, social and educational programmes for rural areas. The vocational training programmes, which occupy a pride of place encompass electric fitting, animal husbandry, repair of pumpsets, soap-making, tailoring.

1103. Vazeeruddin, M. Nehru and Youth. *Tribune*, 10 November 1985; IV.

It is a measure of the love Jawaharlal Nehru had for Children's Day. But what did India's first Prime Minister think of, and expect from, the young man is at the helm of national affairs and trying to promote the youth of the land.

Index